Conversations with Edward Albee

Literary Conversations Series

Peggy Whitman Prenshaw
General Editor

Conversations
with Edward Albee

Edited by
Philip C. Kolin

University Press of Mississippi
Jackson and London

Copyright © 1988 by the University Press of Mississippi
Manufactured in the United States of America

92 91 90 89   4 3 2 1
The paper in this book meets the guidelines for permanence and durability of the
Committee on Production Guidelines for Book Longevity of the Council on Library
Resources.

Library of Congress Cataloging-in-Publication Data

Albee, Edward, 1928-
  Conversations with Edward Albee / edited by Philip C. Kolin.
     p.   cm. — (Literary conversations series)
  Bibliography: p.
  Includes index.
  ISBN 0-87805-341-7 (alk. paper).   ISBN 0-87805-342-5 (pbk. : alk. paper)
     1. Albee, Edward, 1928-   —Interviews.   2. Dramatists,
American—20th century—Interviews.   I. Kolin, Philip C.
II. Title.   III. Series.
PS3551.L25Z473   1988
812'.54—dc19   87-21481
                                                                     CIP

Books by Edward Albee

*The Zoo Story, The Death of Bessie Smith, The Sandbox: Three Plays
    Introduced by the Author.* New York: Coward-McCann, 1960.
The American Dream. New York: The Dramatists Play Service, 1961.
FAM AND YAM. New York: The Dramatists Play Service, 1961.
Who's Afraid of Virginia Woolf? New York: Atheneum, 1962.
The Ballad of the Sad Café. New York: Atheneum, 1963.
Tiny Alice. New York: Atheneum, 1965.
Malcolm New York: Atheneum, 1966.
A Delicate Balance. New York: Atheneum, 1966.
Everything in the Garden. New York: Atheneum, 1968.
Box and Quotations from Chairman Mao Tse-tung, Two Inter-Related Plays.
    New York: Atheneum, 1969.
All Over. New York: Atheneum, 1971.
Seascape. New York: Atheneum, 1975.
Two Plays: Counting the Ways and Listening. New York: Atheneum, 1977.
The Lady from Dubuque. New York: Atheneum, 1980.
The Wounding: An Essay on Education. Charleston, WV: Mountain State
    Press, 1981.
The Man Who Had Three Arms. New York: Atheneum, 1987.

Contents

Introduction

When British theatre critic and columnist Michael Smith confessed to
Edward Albee "I get the impression that you don't really like being
interviewed," Albee responded with characteristic candor and verve:

> It's not that I mind being interviewed. I think it's really a waste of time.
> Critics would do better to write essays upon the plays and not upon the
> writers. I get a little disturbed by the concentration upon the writer rather
> than what he writes. All the matters we've been trying to talk about—
> what a writer thinks about his own craft—are very private, and it's best
> that most writers don't think about them consciously. And there is the
> awful jeopardy that the interviewer is in by having to phrase questions
> that will make communicable sense both to the interviewee and to the
> audience if the questions are answered. It's a mess. Interviews are a
> mess.[1]

Despite this distrustful view of the interview (and his satiric use of
the form in *FAM AND YAM),* Albee has been no stranger to the
interviewer's tape recorder or pen. He has granted more than one
hundred and twenty-five interviews to television reporters, to critics
of various political persuasions and temperaments, to
correspondents at home and abroad, on college campuses where
he is a frequent lecturer, at his retreat at Montauk, at his townhouse
in Manhattan, and at his warehouse apartment in the Tribeca
section of lower Manhattan.[2] For nearly three decades Albee has
been interviewed before, during, and after productions of his plays.
Unlike Himself in *The Man Who Had Three Arms*, who ceased to
be interviewed when his third arm disappeared, Albee has been
questioned with spirited interest after hit and disappointment alike.

Unquestionably, Edward Albee reigned over the American theatre
in the 1960s and the 1970s. Acknowledging Albee's significance,
Tennessee Williams proclaimed: "I have a great feeling for Edward
Albee. I've never seen any play of his that I didn't think was

absolutely thrilling. He is truly a major playwright, America's major
playwright."[3] And Dorothy Gordon engaged in contemporary
bardology when she said that reviewers thought of Albee as "the
great new Shakespeare of the American theatre." By transporting
European absurdism to our native soil, Albee ushered in a new era
in the American theatre in 1959-60. As C. W. E. Bigsby astutely
observed: "If Edward Albee had not existed he would most certainly
have been invented."[4] Indeed in 1959 American theater was in
desperate need of a change, and Albee the angry young man
supplied it. If Albee was right for the times, the times were right for
Albee. As he told Terrence McNally, "There was just a handful of
us. Lanford Wilson hadn't even begun yet. I don't think. People
were sort of waiting for this new generation of American theater, so
it was an ideal time for us to come along." The new rebels—Albee,
Gelber, Kopit, Richardson—attacked the psychological realism of an
earlier decade and in its place established the avant-garde.

In the last thirty years or so, Albee has written over twenty plays,
a number of screenplays, five adaptations, and he shows no signs of
diminishing his contributions to the American stage. In almost a
prophetic strain, he told Digby Diehl in 1963 that he was "the most
eclectic playwright who *ever* wrote," a pronouncement fulfilled in
the succeeding decades. Never wishing to repeat himself, Albee has
written an impressively varied group of plays, adaptations, and
librettos. Perhaps best known for his commercial successes—*The
American Dream, Who's Afraid of Virginia Woolf?*, and *A Delicate
Balance*, the last two winning him Pulitzers—Albee must also be
acclaimed for his experimental plays that may have brought him few
critical honors but which did earn him the epithet he claimed for
himself in the Diehl interview.

But, as the interviews in this collection show, Albee has other
major accomplishments in addition to writing plays. His close friend,
onetime roommate, and collaborator William Flanagan characterized
Albee as "a sort of complete man of the theatre." Albee has
directed his own and others' work with precision and grace. He has
been a producer, having founded Albarwild with Richard Barr and
Clinton Wilder and promoted such playwrights as Terrence McNally,
Sam Shepard, Baraka, and Howard Sackler. Judging from the
comments of actress Irene Worth, Albee may also be a furtive actor

(Rich interview). A patron of the arts—dramatic and plastic, Albee established the Edward F. Albee Foundation and presides over a colony of artists at his Montauk home. Albee is also an art collector and curator whose tastes are as eclectic as his own plays. A "cultural hero" (Zindel and Yerby interview), Albee—like Mencken—continues to be both scourge and sage on the American cultural scene. Finally, Albee has been a cultural ambassador for the U. S. State Department, a visiting professor, and remains an ardent animal lover.

These numerous roles suggest that Albee may adopt different poses with his interviewers, too. His conversations reveal many different sides of the playwright from the public Albee with his "barbed, elegant, poised press style" (Flanagan interview) to the vituperative Albee (Flatley interview) to the suave and guardedly amiable Albee (Adam interview). Albee answers questions carefully but does not always pull his punches. "I don't behave myself. I strike back," he has said. As the undaunted British theatre critic Irving Wardle observed, Albee "is not a man to take liberties with."

Interviewers have often been struck by Albee's physical appearance, and their descriptions provide amusing vignettes of the playwright over the years. From the 1960s through the 1980s interviewers have praised Albee for his youthful good looks, his vigor, and his self-confidence. However, he has been alternately characterized as cold and tough as well as charming and cordial. The paradoxes behind these descriptions of the man rival the critical contradictions that have persistently greeted Albee's plays. An admiring Lillian Ross saw the early Albee as a "handsome, lean, dark-haired young man with a crew cut and considerable charm." Emphasizing Albee's muscularity, Jerry Tallmer observed that the playwright with "sobersided Ivy League costuming" is an "urbanite with the loping stride of a plowboy."[5] More than one interviewer has drawn parallels between the handsome playwright and the Young Man in *The American Dream*. Yet numerous interviewers have maintained that Albee looks nothing like the angry young man the critics painted him to be. As Edward Kosner cautions, the "slight, polite young" Albee "with close-cropped dark hair, a firm handshake and an affinity for crew-neck sweaters, is anything but the enraged voice that flays the audience" in the early plays. Two

Sienna College undergraduates, who interviewed Albee in the fall of
1965, remarked that he "is a quiet, intense person, a darkly good-
looking man who could pass for twenty-five instead of his real age
of thirty-seven, and who talks very like George in *Who's Afraid of
Virginia Woolf?:* a low, cultivated, almost brooding speech with a
flair for sudden wit or a mildly cynical comment."[6] By 1965–1966,
Albee had donned, in the words of William Flanagan, "a
neo-Edwardian haircut . . . . "

The Albee of the early 1970s continued to be "impeccably
dressed, cordial, and just a bit elusive."[7] When she revisited him in
1974, some thirteen years after the *New Yorker* interview included
in this collection, Lillian Ross exclaimed, "We were happy to find
that Mr. Albee, who we hadn't seen for a few years, still looked
youthful (he's forty-six) and trim." She did, however, direct her
readers' attention to a provocative addition to the Albee visage—
"He now has . . . a black mustache."[8] The mustachioed Albee has
aroused much controversy among interviewers obsessed by the
tonsorial. Uncharitable about Albee's looks, David Richards
quipped: "His hair, not quite shoulder-length and his droopy
gunslinger's mustache combine to give him the look of a slightly
perverse denizen of Marlboro country." Others have described the
mustache as "hangdog" and of "riverboat gambler" vintage. Could
the mustache be an Albeean symbol? Regardless of the mustache's
meaning, Albee's perpetual youth continues to win him
compliments, sometimes of dubious distinction as the following one
from Marilyn Preston:

> It's easy to understand why Albee is *still* angry, still intense, still looks
> like a young man. Not simply young for 51. But 31.
> It's almost absurd for him to look so boyish, so benign. A writer's
> anguish should show on his face. For someone so distinguished, who
> writes so well and speaks so sincerely about human pain and suffering
> and existential kvetchiness, Albee's face is remarkably clean and
> unblemished. With freckles, he could do cereal commercials.[9]

Turning from the man to the playwright-social critic, perhaps the
most frequent question fired at Albee asks him to explain how he
writes. Although Albee has warned that we cannot "investigate the
creative process too carefully; it will evaporate" (Flanagan interview),

his answers over the years have been predictably consistent and agree with many contemporary theories of composition. Writing is "an act of discovery" for Albee in which, as he explains to Paul Zindel and Loree Yerby, he "does not know what a thing is about until after finishing it." To Adrienne Clarkson of CBC Albee reveals that "I don't get ideas for plays. I discover that I have been thinking about a play; that somewhere in the unconscious the idea has been formulating. And when it pops up into the conscious mind, a certain amount of the work has already been done." Albee often declares that he will keep a play (sometimes two or three) in his head for two years or more. The actual composing process, therefore, is often much longer than the few months he spends writing. Albee tests his characters in situations outside the play; and he asserts that situation, character, and style coalesce without his having to divide them into separate creative compartments. Over the years Albee's style—the prized hallmarks of which are wit and precision—has not changed; and he resents the designation "late style" since his canon is still in the making (Anderson and Ingersoll interview).

Usually, Albee says he makes two drafts, but he does not revise the second draft, nor does he allow others to do so, defending his decisions with this characteristic self-assurance: "I am not the same person who wrote it" (Clarkson interview). Once finished with a play, Albee, like G. B. Shaw, is eager to observe the production, a phase he has labeled "a pleasant agony" (Ross interview). Many times Albee the director has assumed control: "I made a decision around 1974 that I'd direct all my own plays from there on. I wanted to set the record straight on my own stuff."[10]

Equally popular with interviewers are questions asking Albee about the writers who have influenced him. Coming from a theatrical family and having seen many plays during his boyhood and his Greenwich Village years, Albee easily identifies numerous playwrights whose work he absorbed. To Bob Woggon (and to others) Albee jokes that someone once drew up a list of twenty-five authors who had influenced him, five of whom he had never read. More seriously, though, Albee mentions many of the same names over the years—Genet, Ionesco, Beckett, Brecht, Pinter, Williams, and O'Neill. The last two playwrights—Albee's forebears in the

American theatre—often receive extended comment. As he claimed in the Anderson and Ingersoll interview, "I think I probably became a playwright as much as anything to refute that whole argument of O'Neill, expressed most forcefully in *The Iceman Cometh*." While Albee agrees with O'Neill that people need deceptions, he emphasizes that they must admit the existence of such illusions in their lives. In the McNally interview, Albee acknowledges Williams's special influence; as a young man, Albee recalls, "I remember being enormously moved by one of Tennessee Williams' plays, *Suddenly Last Summer*. That was an extraordinary theatrical experience for me." In a 1980 interview, when asked if *Who's Afraid of Virginia Woolf?* was written in response to the O'Neill play, Albee more specifically commented on his indebtedness to *Iceman* and *Suddenly Last Summer*: "It wouldn't surprise me that it was influenced by O'Neill—in the same way that I'm sure *The Zoo Story* was affected by, again, *The Iceman Cometh* and also by Tennessee's *Suddenly Last Summer*. How else would I have dared write a speech that long? Jerry's. Yeah, how else? Except without those two examples, I am sure of it. I wasn't consciously carrying them in my mind when I wrote it. I came to that conclusion quite a while after."[11]

A widely read and discerning critic, Albee has called attention to other major figures who have influenced his work—Thornton Wilder, Artaud, Susan Sontag, and Chekhov. Providing negative influences are Clifford Odets whose agitprop plays Albee detests because they never transcend propaganda and Neil Simon whose comedies Albee brands as pornographic, without redeeming social value. Finally, the most pervasive influence on Albee is music. Every chance he has Albee compares the construction of his plays to musical structure acknowledging (to Diehl) that a dramatist can "notate" a play just as a composer does a musical score. In conversation with Kathy Sullivan, Albee pinpoints specific ways in which musical forms might be discerned in his plays.

Albee has consistently and enthusiastically spoken about the nature of art and his role as an artist. An outspoken defender of the arts, Albee explains to Peter Adam why they are unique and significant. In many interviews (the Wager interview is a notable one), he laments that since the arts are vulnerably linked to politics,

governments may control, distort, or suppress them and thus
endanger human freedom. As he observes, "art is determined by
the type of government we elect." Albee's own view of art is best
termed combative. A foe of escapist entertainment entrenched on
Broadway, Albee professes to Patricia De La Fuente that "Art is not
pacification. It's disturbance." He believes that the theatre must
disturb in order to reform society. Often sounding like the
Savonarola of off-Broadway, Albee declaims that art should shock a
lazy, complacent audience back to life: "I don't think you should
frighten them, I think you should terrify them" (De La Fuente
interview). He amusingly recalls how people walked out of a
production of *The Zoo Story* because they were shocked. And
speaking of *The American Dream* Albee once bristled: "Is the play
offensive? I certainly hope so. It is my intention to offend—as well
as to amuse and to entertain."[12] Over the years Albee's view of
himself as raileur may have mellowed as his plays moved from being
frontal assaults on destructive social customs to becoming more
subtle scrutinies of the dangers of what he has termed "individual
self-censorship."[13] However, while Albee's dramatic techniques have
evolved, his intentions as an artist have remained constant—to rouse
people from their lethargy, to expose them to the invigorating
dangers of communication and commitment, and to force them to
ask probing questions.

A major voice in the contemporary theatre, Albee talks
knowledgeably and frankly about every phase of mounting a play,
the many personalities involved in the process, and the playwright's
prerogatives that he jealously guards. From his insider's perspective,
Albee supplies interviewers with memorable details about the
American (and world) theatre of the last thirty years. He sets the
record straight about the costs, casting of *Who's Afraid of Virginia
Woolf?* (it was never intended for an all male cast), and screen
version of that play, explains how he came to work with David
Merrick on *Breakfast at Tiffany's* and offers candid opinions about
the productions of his plays he has witnessed. Albee reminisces
about colleagues whose achievements he admires profoundly—
William Flanagan the musician, Alan Schneider the director, Bill
Ritman the set designer, Clinton Wilder and Richard Barr the
producers. Although Albee has a dubious opinion of most

producers (often calling them "export/import people"), he respects
Wilder and Barr because they believe that the "theatre belongs to
the playwright" (Clarkson interview). Albee also lavishes praise on
Katharine Hepburn (whom he admits was very close to his idea of
Agnes in *A Delicate Balance*) and the indomitable Tallulah
Bankhead. Albee comments on a few of the theatre critics he
respects (Elliot Norton, Harold Krenen, and Harold Clurman) and
some of the many he loathes (John Simon, Martin Gottfried). He
recalls the playwrights whose careers he helped to launch, one of
whom (Terrence McNally) conducts a highly rewarding and
revealing interview. Last of all, Albee accentuates the differences
between the ways plays are done in America and the ways they are
subsidized, staged, acted, received, and respected in western
Europe, Russia, and South America. Albee's Baedeker is our
playbill.

A common thread running throughout Albee's views on the
theatre is his belief in the sanctity of the script, the play as logos, so
to speak. Albee frequently emphasizes (and relishes doing so) the
control he has as playwright over a production of his work—in the
casting, the staging, the directing, and the acting. For Albee, unlike
Tennessee Williams, the text is never dependent on performance. It
is a little ironic for the veteran director Albee (whose directorial skills
have been frequently praised as "definitive") to take such a dim
view of performance. But as he tells Peter Adam: "I find that with a
good play—anybody's good play—seeing it on stage is merely a
proof of what exists on the page and not an improvement on it, not
a completion of it, merely a proof of it. A bad play could be
improved by production, a first-rate play can only be proved, not
improved, by production." Albee's justification for holding such
views is, as he points out to Diehl: "No performance is as good as
the performance the author saw when he wrote" the play. And,
directors, beware! "A director needs exert very little creativity the
better the play" (Flanagan interview). Albee is wary about letting
anyone tamper with his script; he quips to Patricia De La Fuente
that "if an actor comes up with something I think is better than I
intended, I'll incorporate it and pretend it was my idea." Albee
quickly points out, too, in conversation with Jeanne Wolf, that he
never writes for a specific audience or actor for that matter. While

Albee can be hard on actors, he can also be uniquely helpful to them, as the following testimony makes clear: "I've learned to talk to actors in their language, I think. I don't let them get away with nonsense, but I let them have their heads . . . until I have to give them their heads on a platter. And I probably can help them with their character's subtext more than an ordinary director. I'm the one who created the subtext in the first place."[14]

The author of *Virginia Woolf* has a well-deserved reputation for his lively wit. Humor—as a subject for conversation and as a technique—surfaces often in his interviews, although Albee distinguishes between mindless humor and serious comedy. David Richards observed that Albee is "judged to be dour and hermetic, and yet his work is, as he himself puts it, 'funnier than it's not.' " Characterizing his particular brand of comedy, Albee stated in a 1971 interview: "I'm not a joke writer. I prefer wit and humor to jokes. I couldn't possibly write a Neil Simon play and if we are to judge by *Gingerbread Lady*, he is incapable of a play that attempts to be serious."[15] As Albee tells Patricia De La Fuente, "any writer without a sense of humor is suspect." The Albee canon contains broad satires with farcical action as well as serious, dark, problem comedies. Frequently admitting that his plays do contain comic elements, Albee has called *Tiny Alice* a "little comedy" and *Lady from Dubuque* a comedy as well (Woggon interview). To Otis Guernsey, Jr. Albee confided that *"Virginia Woolf* was a comedy in the sense that everybody ended up with what they wanted (I'm being just slightly ironic)."[16] No irony was involved in Albee's blunt refusal, though, to classify *Seascape* a comedy. Unquestionably, much of Albee's work illustrates his belief that "pain and laughter are very close" (Anderson and Ingersoll interview).

In his interviews Albee frequently employs his characteristic wry, many times subtle humor. Ready targets of Albee's witty ire are the critics. He informs Guy Flatley that "a majority of the critics are qualified to cover brush fires in New Jersey"; and for Diehl he stigmatizes their approval as "the palsied nod of the Seven Men." Other favorite Albee targets are Hollywood, television, and the Great White Way. Of the capital of filmdom Albee conceded: "I have an interesting arrangement with Hollywood. They commission me to write screen-plays. They pay me handsomely and then they don't film them. It's invisible work."[17] Skeptical about a film version of *Who's Afraid of Virginia Woolf?* Albee jokes with Flanagan that he thought the movie might star Doris Day and Rock Hudson; and in conversation with Adrienne Clarkson he is relieved to find that they did not make the play into a "swimming flick with Esther Williams." Albee has little faith in television as well. He doubts that it can present serious drama and he fears that it has turned the brains of the youth of America into "Cream of Wheat." Albee's attacks on Broadway's commercialism and escapism are too numerous to single out one vituperative comment; they all sting.

Albee occasionally uses humor for a bit of self-mockery. Asked about beginning his career off-Broadway, Albee jokes: "I started way off-Broadway in West Berlin" (Clarkson interview). When McNally observes that people believe *The Zoo Story* was his first play, Albee, unwilling to discuss his early, unpublished attempts, responds, "Let's perpetuate that." In his interview with Irving Wardle, Albee humorously refers to *Seascape* as "the fish play." Among my favorite slices of Albee's self-deprecatory humor is his description— to McNally—of what happened when he revised *Breakfast at Tiffany's*: "I did indeed take the show over and managed, in only two weeks, to turn something which would have been a six-month mediocrity into an instant disaster." The remark is vintage Albee.

This collection includes twenty-seven interviews, a generous share of the many Albee has granted. As with other books in the Literary Conversations Series, the interviews in this volume are organized chronologically by the date the interview was given or, where that is unlisted, by the date of publication. These interviews are presented unedited, but for the sake of consistency all play titles have been italicized. Since the interviews remain otherwise unchanged, readers will find some inevitable repetition. Given the fact that Albee has been asked the same questions in different parts of the country (and the world) at different times, it is useful to see such repetition reflecting the importance of the question and the consistency and sometimes amplification of Albee's answers.

These interviews come from a variety of sources—international newspapers (*London Times, New York Times, Washington Post*), local publications (*Connecticut Magazine*), campus newspapers (*Choate News;* University of Houston *Cougar*), televised interviews

("The Dorothy Gordon Youth Forum" on NBC; "The Private World of Edward Albee" on CBC; "Conversation with Jeanne Wolf" on Miami's WPBT TV), scholarly publications (the interview from *Edward Albee: Planned Wilderness*), trade journals in the arts (*ARTnews, Playbill*), and little magazines (*Wagner Literary Magazine, Transatlantic Review*).

The interviews come from foreign (British, Canadian) and American sources. Among them is a self-interview that appeared in the *Baltimore Sun*. Four of the interviews were previously unpublished (those with Dorothy Gordon; Anderson and Ingersoll; Jeanne Wolf; and Kathy Sullivan). Of special merit, too, are the interviews conducted by Albee's associates in the arts—William Flanagan and Terrence McNally. It is interesting to note as well that an early Albee interview was conducted by two young individuals destined to be famous playwrights themselves—Paul Zindel and Loree Yerby.

The interviews that I have included focus on Albee's diverse accomplishments and interests, scaling the high points of his life in the theatre and also documenting some of the low ones. They reveal Albee setting the record straight, giving his views on contemporary culture, and conversing about a life in and for the arts. For the most part, I tried to include interviews that have not been easily accessible, especially televised interviews. Unfortunately, a few of the interviews I wanted to include were unavailable; lost to me were the interviews done by Dick Cavett for WNET and by Barbara Walters for ABC. I regret that I could not include Howard Schneider's "Albee: Hard Act for Himself to Follow," from the *Los Angeles Times* (March 23, 1975), where Albee recounts with terrifying detail an apocalyptic dream he had. In addition to this interview, I recommend the one done with Richard Barr, George Grizzard, Uta Hagen, and Alan Schneider on *Who's Afraid of Virginia Woolf?*, included in *Broadway Song & Story: Playwrights/Lyricists/Composers Discuss Their Hits*, edited by Otis L. Guernsey, Jr. and moderated by Terrence McNally (New York: Dodd, Mead & Company, 1985). Although the playwright is absent, many significant things are said about him by those who helped to make *Virginia Woolf* one of the major achievements of the twentieth century.

My thanks go to the many interviewers and/or copyright holders who granted me permission to include their work; to Scott Nations who helped me to retype some of the interviews and to transcribe one of them; to Lea Carol Owen whose earlier thesis and later article on Albee's interviews were a pleasure to read; and to Edward Albee and his secretary Carl Capotorto for their gracious cooperation. Finally, I express my love to my wife Janeen for her help in proofreading this book and in assisting me prepare the index; and to my son Eric and my daughter Kristin for patiently listening to conversations about Edward Albee conversations.

PCK
Dec. 1986

Notes

1. "Edward Albee in Conversation with Michael Smith," *Plays & Players* (March 1964), 14. Statements from the interviews included in this volume are not footnoted but are documented parenthetically in this introduction.

2. Lea Carol Owen includes 75 interviews in her "An Annotated Bibliography of Albee Interviews with an Index to Names, Concepts, and Places," in *Critical Essays on Edward Albee*, eds. Philip C. Kolin and J. Madison Davis (Boston: G. K. Hall, 1986), pp. 200-218.

3. Quoted from John Gruen, *Close-Up* (New York: Viking, 1968), p. 92. Reprinted in *Conversations with Tennessee Williams*, ed. Albert J. Devlin (Jackson: University Press of Mississippi, 1986), p. 120.

4. *A Critical Introduction to Twentieth-Century American Drama*. Vol. 2 *Tennessee Williams, Arthur Miller, Edward Albee* (New York: Cambridge University Press, 1984), p. 249.

5. "Edward Albee, Playwright," *New York Post*, 4 November 1962, 10.

6. Michael Narducci and Walter Chura, "Edward Albee," in *The Playwrights Speak*, ed. Walter Wager (New York: Delacorte Press, 1967), p. 25.

7. Carol Kramer, *Chicago Tribune*, 28 October 1973, sec. 6:13.

8. Lillian Ross, "Theatre," *New Yorker*, 3 June 1974, 29.

9. "At 51, Edward Albee still lives up to his own expectations," *Chicago Tribune*, "Tempo," 26 March 1979, sec. 2:1.

10. Dan Sullivan, "Edward Albee: Playwright with More Than One Act," *Los Angeles Times*, "Calendar," 15 October 1978, 6.

11. Matthew C. Roudané, "An Interview with Edward Albee," *Southern Humanities Review*, 16 (Winter 1983), 38.

12. Quoted in "Towards a Theatre of Cruelty," *Times Literary Supplement*, 27 February 1964, 166.

13. "A World where Governments Fear the World," in "Playwrights on the Podium," *Dramatists Guild Quarterly*, 22 (Winter 1986), 9-11, here 10.

14. Sullivan, 6.

15. William Glover, "Albee: A peep within," *Houston Post*, "Spotlight," 25 April 1971, 21.

16. "Edward Albee Confronts Broadway," *Diplomat* (1966), 62.

17. Mel Gussow, "Albee Prepares Play In 'Woolf' Mold," *New York Times*, 23 May 1978, sec. C1; C4.

Chronology

1928   Born 12 March in Washington, D.C. and adopted two weeks later by Frances Cotter Albee and Reed Albee of Larchmont, New York, Edward Franklin Albee III is christened in honor of his adoptive grandfather Edward Franklin Albee II, owner of a series of vaudeville theatres in the Keith-Albee circuit.

1938-39   EA attends and is later expelled from Rye Country Day School in Westchester County, New York.

1940-43   At the age of 12, EA writes his first play, a three-act farce entitled *Aliqueen*. EA attends Lawrenceville School, Lawrenceville, New Jersey, and Valley Forge Military Academy, Wayne, Pennsylvania, but is dismissed from both.

1944-46   EA goes to the Choate School in Wallingford, Connecticut. He publishes six short stories, thirteen poems, and two essays (one on Chaucer, the other on Richard Strauss) in the *Choate Literary Magazine*. His first published play, *Schism*, also appears in the *Choate Literary Magazine* in May 1946. Two of his poems see publication in *Kaleidoscope*, a Texas literary magazine: "Eighteen" (September 1945) and "Chopin" (September 1946). After graduating from Choate in the spring of 1946, EA matriculates at Trinity College, Hartford, Connecticut. Active in amateur theatricals at Trinity, EA plays Emperor Franz Joseph in Maxwell Anderson's *Masque of Kings*.

1947   After being dismissed from Trinity after three semesters for failing to attend math classes and chapel, EA takes

his first job—a writer of continuity material for music
programs for station WNYC in New York City.

1948-49   EA is briefly engaged to a debutante named Delphine.
He leaves home and holds a series of odd jobs in New
York City, including being a copy boy for the advertising
firm of Warwick and Legler, a record sales clerk at
Bloomingdale's, a sales clerk at G. Schirmer's, and a
counterman at the luncheonette of the Manhattan
Towers Hotel. EA receives a trust fund from his maternal
grandmother ($250.00 a month) and shares a series of
cold-water flats in Greenwich Village with composer
William Flanagan, with whom he rooms for nine years.
EA recalls living in a walk-up on Mulberry Street, a loft
on Seventh Avenue, and a flat on Henry Street. In 1949
he writes a three-act play "The City of People," an
unpublished and unperformed script about a young
man's conflict with his father and his struggle to find
love. EA spends a few months in 1949 at Columbia
University.

1950-54   EA writes another play, "Ye Watchers and Ye Lonely
Ones," also never performed or published, about a
painful encounter. In 1952, EA travels to Italy and
spends five months in Florence. In the summer of 1952
he meets Thornton Wilder, at the McDowell Colony in
Petersborough, New Hampshire, and is advised to give
up writing poetry and turn to drama.

1955-58   EA works for Western Union for two and a half years
and continues to write plays and operas, all unpublished.
As a present to himself on his thirtieth birthday EA writes
The Zoo Story.

1959   EA sees the world premier of *The Zoo Story (Die
Zoogeschichte)* on 28 September at the Schiller Theater
Werkstatt in Berlin and is highly praised in the German

press, especially by the noted theatre critic for *Die Welt*,
Friedrich Luft. EA receives the Berlin Festival Award.

1960   On 14 January *The Zoo Story*, the first EA play
              performed in America, is part of a double bill with
              Samuel Beckett's *Krapp's Last Tape* at the Provincetown
              Playhouse in Greenwich Village; *Zoo Story* runs for 582
              performances. On 21 April, EA's *Death of Bessie Smith*
              has its world premiere at the Scholosspark Theater in
              Berlin. On 15 May, EA's *The Sandbox*, originally
              commissioned for but never staged at the Festival of Two
              Worlds, Spoleto, Italy, is performed at the Jazz Gallery
              in New York City. EA wins an Obie Award on 22 May
              and on 25 May the Vernon Rice Award for the *Zoo
              Story*. *FAM AND YAM*, billed as an imaginary interview
              between a new playwright (Albee?) and an established
              one (William Inge?), opens on 27 August at the White
              Barn Theatre in Westport, Connecticut, before going to
              off-Broadway in October.

1961   On 24 January the *American Dream* begins 360
              performances at the York Theatre. *Bartley*, an
              adaptation of Herman Melville's story for which EA
              collaborated with James Hinton on the libretto and for
              which Flanagan wrote the music, premieres with the
              American Dream but closes in early February. *The
              Sandbox* is televised with Sudie Bond in the role of
              Grandma. In June EA receives the Lola D'Annunzio
              Award for original playwrighting. In the fall of 1961,
              Albee receives a Fulbright Professorship to Würzburg
              University, Germany.

1962   On 25 February EA's "Which Theatre Is the Absurd
              One," his spirited attack on Broadway, appears in the
              New York Times. In the spring EA buys a Cape Cod
              home (with guest house) on Montauk, Long Island, his
              artist's retreat. The first full-length EA play to appear on
              Broadway, *Who's Afraid of Virginia Woolf?*, opens on a

rainy Saturday night, 13 October, at the Billy Rose
Theatre; directed by Alan Schneider, produced by
Richard Barr, and starring Uta Hagen, Arthur Hill,
George Grizzard (and later Ben Piazza), and Melinda
Dillon. *Virginia Woolf* runs for 664 performances.

1963   With Richard Barr and Clinton Wilder EA establishes
Albarwild, the New York Playwrights Unit Workshop at
the Cherry Lane Theatre, off-Broadway, to assist young
writers, including Terrence McNally, Sam Shepard,
Lanford Wilson, John Guare, Baraka, and others. In the
spring EA wins a Tony, New York Drama Critics' Circle
Award, and Outer Circle Award for *Who's Afraid of
Virginia Woolf?* EA is denied the Pulitzer Prize for the
play even though he is recommended for it. The Pulitzer
Trustees object to the language and subject matter of
Virginia Woolf; one member, J.D. Maxwell, vilifies
Virginia Woolf as a "filthy" play. Jurors John Mason
Brown and John Gassner resign on 6 May from the
Pulitzer committee in protest. *Newsweek* for 30
September contains EA's letter "Albee on Censorship."
On 3 October *Virginia Woolf* is banned in
Johannesburg, in part because Albee objects to
segregation. On 30 October *The Ballad of the Sad Café*,
EA's adaptation of Carson McCullers's novella, opens for
123 performances at the Martin Beck Theatre in New
York. In October and November EA (with John
Steinbeck) travels to Russia and other Iron Curtain
countries as a U.S. Cultural Exchange Visitor.

1964   In February *Who's Afraid of Virginia Woolf?* premieres in
London. EA receives the *Evening Standard* Award for
Virginia Woolf. *Tiny Alice*, starring Sir John Gielgud and
Irene Worth, opens on 29 December at the Billy Rose
Theatre and runs for 167 performances.

1965   EA is elected to the Council of the Dramatists Guild in
New York. He wins a Tony and the New York Drama

Critics' Circle Award for *Tiny Alice* and receives the
Margot Jones Award for encouraging new playwrights.
EA writes the introduction to *Three Plays by Noel
Coward* (New York: Dell Publishing Co.), and reviews
Sam Shepard's *Icarus's Mother* for the *Village Voice*
(November 25).

1966   *Malcolm*, EA's second adaptation (from the James
            Purdy novel), opens at the Shubert Theatre on 11
            January but closes after only 7 performances. In June
            EA purchases a 19th century carriage house (formerly
            belonging to Maurice Evans) in Greenwich Village and
            publishes a brief article "Creativity and Commitment" in
            Saturday Review (June 24). In July Warner Brothers
            releases the Oscar-winning film *Who's Afraid of Virginia
            Woolf?* (running time: 130 minutes), screenplay by
            Ernest Lehman, directed by Mike Nichols, and starring
            Elizabeth Taylor, Richard Burton, George Segal, and
            Sandy Dennis. The film is the third biggest moneymaker
            of the year and carries this warning: "No one under 18
            will be admitted unless accompanied by his parent." EA
            claims that Lehman added only 25 words of his own to
            the original play. On 22 September, *A Delicate Balance*,
            starring Jessica Tandy and Hugh Cronyn, opens at the
            Martin Beck Theatre in New York for a successful run of
            132 performances (four months) before going on tour. In
            December EA is elected to the National Institute of Arts
            and Letters. EA's third adaptation *Breakfast at Tiffany's*,
            for which David Merrick asked EA's help in rewriting the
            script, closes on December after four preview
            performances.

1967   On 2 May EA wins his first Pulitzer Prize for *A Delicate
            Balance*; the Committee may have had pangs of guilt
            over not awarding it to *Who's Afraid of Virginia Woolf?*
            In June EA receives a D. Litt. from Emerson College in
            Boston. EA's fourth adaptation *Everything in the
            Garden*, from Giles Cooper's play, opens 29 November

and runs for 84 performances at the Plymouth Theatre
in New York.

1968-70   On 6 March 1968 *Box* and *Quotations from Chairman
          Mao Tse-tung* premiere at the Studio Arena Theatre in
          Buffalo; in September of that year these companion
          pieces open at the Billy Rose Theatre for 12
          performances. A story in the *New York Times* for 24
          April 1969 announces Albee is to adapt the novel *The
          Tenant* for the screen, but this never materializes. On 31
          August 1969 William Flanagan dies at the age of 46.
          On 27 September 1969 William Ball's American
          Conservatory Theatre troupe begins a popular revival of
          Tiny Alice at the American National Theatre and
          Academy. EA's article "Decade of Engagement" is
          published in the *Saturday Review* (24 January 1970).

1971-72   On 27 March 1971 *All Over*, directed by John Gielgud
          and starring Jessica Tandy and Colleen Dewhurst, opens
          at the Martin Beck Theatre and runs for 40
          performances. In 1971 EA establishes the William
          Flanagan Center for Creative Persons in Montauk, Long
          Island. In early 1972 EA is given the Alumni Seal Prize
          at Choate and delivers the speech "Building
          Responsibility," published in the *Choate Alumni Bulletin*
          (Winter 1972-1973). On 31 January 1972 *All Over* is
          produced by the Royal Shakespeare Company in
          London at the Aldwych Theatre.

1973-74   In March 1973 EA testifies about federal funding of the
          arts before the Congressional Committee on Education
          and Labor. On 10 December 1973, the film version of
          A Delicate Balance, directed by EA himself, is released
          as a part of the "American Film Theatre Series," starring
          Katharine Hepburn, Paul Scofield, Lee Remick, Kate
          Reid, and Joseph Cotton. The film is classified PG. In
          1974 EA becomes a member of the Board of Directors
          for the Montauk Writers Colony. In spring 1974 EA

receives a Litt. D. from Trinity College, Hartford, Connecticut.

1975   EA with other artists signs letters protesting imprisonment of Vladimir Bukovsky (*New York Times* [15 January]: 42). *Seascape*, directed by EA, opens on 26 January at the Shubert Theatre in New York and runs for 65 performances. Deborah Kerr and Barry Nelson play the human couple; Frank Langella and Maureen Anderman the saurian mates. EA's poem "Peaceable Kingdom, France (La Vieille Eglise-Gard)" is published in *The New Yorker* (29 December).

1976   In April *Who's Afraid of Virginia Woolf?* begins a three-month Broadway revival, directed by EA and starring Colleen Dewhurst and Ben Gazzara. On 28 April the Hartford Stage Company production of *All Over* airs on public television's "Theatre in America" series. *Seascape* earns EA his second Pulitzer Prize on 6 May. On 29 May EA delivers the commencement speech and is awarded an honorary doctorate by Southampton College of Long Island University. EA moves to a former cheese warehouse (14 Harrison Street) near the World Trade Center and the Hudson River in the Tribeca section of lower Manhattan. *Listening*, a radio play commissioned by National Public Radio's Earplay, airs on the BBC in April, with EA and John Tydeman directing, and on the U.S. public radio stations in the fall. *Counting the Ways*, a companion piece to *Listening*, makes its world premiere in London at the National Theatre on 7 December.

1977-79   The American premiere of *Counting the Ways*, joined by *Listening*, takes place at the Hartford Stage on 28 January 1977, with EA directing both plays on this side of the Atlantic. In 1978 EA establishes the Edward F. Albee Foundation for which he serves as president. In October 1978 EA directs a troupe presenting eight of his

one-act plays ("Albee Directs Albee") on a 35-week tour
of colleges in the U.S. and in Canada. In February 1979
Counting the Ways and *Listening*, again directed by EA,
are presented off Broadway by Columbia University
Theatre Arts productions.

1980-81   On 31 January 1980 EA's *Lady from Dubuque*
(originally entitled *The Substitute Speaker*, starring Irene
Worth, Tony Musante, and Frances Conroy, opens at
the Morosco Theatre for a run of only 12 performances.
In May EA wins a Gold Medal in Drama from the
American Academy and Institute of Arts and Letters. EA
writes a lengthy critical introduction to *Louise Nevelson:
Atmosphere and Environments* (New York: C.N. Potter,
1980); sculptor Nevelson, according to EA, is one of the
most sensitive critics of *Tiny Alice*. In November 1980
EA is one of six artists appointed to share the directorate
of the Vivian Beaumont Theater in Lincoln Center. EA's
fifth adaptation *Lolita*, from Vladimir Nabokov's novel,
opens on 19 March 1981 at the Brooks Atkinson
Theatre for an 11-day run starring Donald Sutherland
and Ian Richardson. EA's *The Wounding: An Essay on
Education* is published in 1981 by Mountain State Press.
EA and other artists sign letter demanding the release of
Czech playwright Vaclav Havel (*New York Times* [July
10]: A:22). Volumes 1 and 2 of *Edward Albee: The
Plays* are published in 1981 by Atheneum.

1982-83   Volumes 3 and 4 of *Edward Albee: The Plays* are
published by Atheneum. *The Man Who Had Three
Arms*, commissioned by the Miami Arts Festival, opens
in June 1982 at the Coconut Grove Playhouse. On 4
October 1982, *Man* is staged at the Goodman Theatre
in Chicago. As a resident playwright at the Atlantic
Center for the Arts (in New Smyrna Beach, Florida) in
November 1982 EA devises a theatre exercise, *Scenes
From a Non-Marriage*, for the six playwrights he chose
to work with, arranges the scenes, writes a prologue and

epilogue, and directs the workshop production. On 5 April 1983 *Man* makes its New York debut at the Lyceum Theatre, directed by EA and starring Robert Drivas, but closes on 17 April after 16 performances. EA strongly denies any autobiographical elements in *Man*. On 10 May 1983 EA's one-act play *Finding the Sun*, commissioned by the University of Northern Colorado, premieres in Greeley with EA directing. In 1983 EA chairs the committee for the Brandeis University Creative Arts Awards. EA is appointed Regents' Professor of Drama at the University of California at Irvine during the spring of 1983.

1984-86 On 3 May 1984 Alan Schneider dies in London. *Walking* (another one-act play), commissioned by the University of California at Irvine, has its world premiere at Irvine on 22 May 1984; it is performed with EA's *Finding the Sun*. EA once again is Regents' Professor of Drama at University of California at Irvine in the spring of 1984. In February 1985 Nagel Jackson's *Faustus in Hell* opens in New York; EA is one of seven authors asked to provide an updated dramatic version of one of the seven deadly sins. EA pens the humorous play-within-a-play on Envy. EA participates in the Budapest Cultural Forum on 24 October 1985 and delivers a speech "A World Where Governments Fear the World," subsequently published in the *Dramatists Guild Quarterly* (Winter 1986).

1987   EA is presented with the Grand Master Award at Birmingham-Southern College's Seventh Annual Writers' Conference on 21 March in Birmingham, Alabama. On 29 April EA, together with sculptor Donald Judd and poet Adrienne Rich, is honored for his lifelong achievements in the arts at the 31st Annual Brandeis University Arts Awards. EA's *Marriage Play* has its world premiere at Vienna's English Theatre in May.

Conversations with Edward Albee

Albee

Lillian Ross/1961

From *The New Yorker*, 25 March 1961, 30–32. © Lillian Ross.
Reprinted by permission of Lillian Ross.

We had a talk last week with Edward Albee, the thirty-three-year-old playwright whose three one-act plays now on the boards Off-Broadway have established him as the critics' current man-of-promise. *The Zoo Story* opened at the Provincetown Playhouse on January 14, 1960, and has been produced in London and in Berlin, among other places; *The American Dream* and *The Death of Bessie Smith*, which opened January 24, 1961, and March 1, 1961, respectively, are both at the York Playhouse. We found Mr. Albee at home, in a ground-floor, six-room apartment in a ninety-year-old, yellow-stucco-front house on West Twelfth Street—an apartment packed to the gills with modern paintings, a stereophonic record player, fresh white pompons, books on the drama, a roommate named William Flanagan (who composed the music for *Bessie Smith* and another Albee one-acter, called *The Sandbox*), and three orphaned cats rescued by Albee: Cunegonde, three and a half; Vanessa, two and a half; and a still nameless thirteen-week-old semi-Siamese kitten. Albee, who is a handsome, lean, dark-haired young man with a crew haircut and considerable charm, and who was wearing a gray tweed sports jacket, gray flannel slacks, a button-down-collar white shirt, and a black wool tie, directed us to avoid a collapsing modern sofa and to sit in a non-collapsing modern chair, out of which he shooed his cats with a few firm, authoritative, affectionate, non-sticky words.

"I get them from the Greenwich Village Humane League," Albee told us. "The League people go out and look for abandoned cats on the street, and save them from the awful things that happen to homeless kittens in New York, like being tossed into bonfires by mean kids. That sort of thing can happen in the Village, I'm sorry to say. Although I wouldn't live anywhere but in New York. I like to be in the center of things. There are ten thousand things you can do in half an hour in New York if you feel like it. I've lived in a lot of places—a fifteen-dollar-a-month cold-water flat on the lower East Side, a great big loft right in the middle of the garment district, for seventy a month, and a couple of other places around the Village. All the good places in the Village, all the lovely nineteenth-century houses, are being torn down now and six-story tenements are being put up instead. Do you want to see something amazing in my back yard? A real one-story little cottage, with somebody living in it." He showed us the amazing view through a rear window. "Will probably be torn down soon. But I'll try to stay in the Village. It's one of the few areas where you can be in the center of things and still feel removed."

Albee lit a cigarette and sat down carefully on the sofa, and we asked him to give us an autobiographical outline. "Born in Washington, D.C., on March 12, 1928, and came to New York when I was two weeks old," he said. "I have no idea who my natural parents were, although I'm sure my father wasn't a President, or anything like that. I was adopted by my father, Reed A. Albee, who worked for his father Edward Franklin Albee, who started a chain of theatres with B.F. Keith and then sold out to R.K.O. My father is retired now. My mother is a remarkable woman. An excellent horsewoman and saddle-horse judge. I was riding from the time I was able to walk. My parents had a stable of horses in Larchmont or Scarsdale or Rye, or one of those places. I don't ride any more. Just sort of lost interest in it. My parents gave me a good home and a good education, none of which I appreciated. I attended Rye Country Day School until I was eleven, and then Lawrenceville, where I got thrown out after a year and a half for refusing to go to classes. It was probably that I was too young to be away from home, but instead of going home I was sent to Valley Forge Military Academy—Valley Forge Concentration Camp—where parents send their children for one of three reasons: discipline, or preparation for West Point, or in hope that they'll get an education. You march practically all the time and wear a grayish-blue uniform like West Point's, with the hat with the patent-leather brim. I had the usual routine of discipline, institutional food, and dreary living quarters. When I finally left, after a year, I decided not to get thrown out of another school. I went to Choate next, and it was marvellous, but by then I was a few years older. I appreciated Choate after the aridity of a military school. I was very happy there. I went on to Trinity College, in Hartford, for a year and a half. I didn't have enough interest to stick it out for four years. I wouldn't go to chapel, and I wouldn't go to one of the math courses. It was probably a basic discontent with myself that hadn't taken a specific form yet. After a year and a half, the college suggested that I not come back, which was fine with me."

Albee gave a quick laugh and, inhaling with all the abandon of the carefree pre-filter age, continued, through the smoke, "I got my first job at Station WNYC, where I spent a year and a half writing continuity for the music programs. After that, I had an awful lot of jobs: forty-dollar-a-week office boy for Warwick & Legler, the ad agency; salesman in the record department of Bloomingdale's; salesman in the book department of Schirmer's; luncheonette counterman at the Manhattan Towers Hotel. Then, starting in 1955, I was a Western Union messenger for three years, all over the city. I liked it. It wasn't a job that tired you out with mental work. I liked walking, and I met all sorts of interesting people. In 1949, I had come into a very small income, from a trust fund set up by my maternal grandmother, that was not quite enough to spoil me. In 1952, I went to Florence for four or five months and tried to write a novel. The novel was awful. I had written a lot of poetry, and had even managed to get one poem published, when I was seventeen, in a Texas magazine called *Kaleidoscope*. It had something to do with turning eighteen. Then, in the spring of 1958, when I hit thirty, a kind of explosion took place in my life. I'd been drifting, and I got fed up with myself. I decided to write a play. I was getting a little bit of money from the trust fund—thirty-five hundred dollars a year—and I quit work.

"I wrote *The Zoo Story* on a wobbly table in the kitchen of the apartment I was living in at the time—at 238 West Fourth Street. I did a draft, made pencil revisions, and typed a second script, and that's the way I've been doing my plays since. I finished *The Zoo Story* in three weeks and showed it to a few uptown producers, who said it was nice but they wanted a full-length play. Then Bill Flanagan sent a copy of the play to David Diamond, the American

composer, who was living in Florence, and Diamond sent it to a
Swiss actor, Pinkas Braun, in Zurich, who later did all the German
translations of my plays. Braun made a tape recording of the play in
English and sent it to Mrs. Stefani Hunzinger, in Frankfurt, who is
head of the drama department of S. Fischer, one of the biggest
publishing houses in Germany. From there it went on to a producer
named Barlog, in Berlin, and that's where I had my first audience—
on September 18, 1959. *The Death of Bessie Smith* was produced
in Berlin about a year ago, before it was put on here. Aside from
the interest that German audiences take in the contemporary foreign
theatre, they seem to find some application to their own lives in my
plays."

We asked how things were going financially.

"Strange," he said. "My income is growing. In 1959, I made
about a thousand dollars on my work. In 1960, it was ten thousand
dollars. In 1961, I've made five thousand dollars in two months.
The New York income is a small part of it. It means I don't have to
take an outside job, and I like that. Although my tastes are
inexpensive, I like to sit in good seats at the theatre, so I can see
what's going on. I don't think about clothes. I don't own a suit. I
have a couple of sports jackets, and what I like to wear is sweater,
slacks, and sneakers."

"Any plans?" we asked. "Any special thoughts on your last
birthday?" "I'm not looking forward to getting older, but I'm not
horrified by it, either," he said. "I've got about two—maybe three—
years' work planned out, considering how lazy I am about what I
want to be doing. I'm behind, but I'd rather be behind than be
completely caught up. I have three plays in mind and I'm trying to
finish two others—*Who's Afraid of Virginia Woolf?* and an
adaptation of Carson McCullers' *The Ballad of the Sad Café*. I'm
doing the second because it's sort of a challenge. I've never seen an
adaptation of anything that was any good. I'm curious to find out if
it's possible to do one without running into what usually happens—
the lessening and coarsening of the material. The other play is about
a two-in-the-morning drunken party of two faculty members and
their wives. These will both be what they refer to as full-length plays,
'they' being people who think the theatre has got to start at
eight-forty and end at eleven-ten."

"Any special influences in your writing?" we asked.

Albee gave us a cool laugh. "There are anywhere between five hundred and a thousand good plays, and I'd have to go back to the Greeks and work my way right up," he replied. "It's been an assimilative process. Of my contemporaries, after Brecht, I admire Beckett, Jean Genêt, Tennessee Williams, and Harold Pinter. In fiction, I have a special preference for Salinger and Updike. I feel happy and comfortable in what I'm doing. I've become freer and less free. One develops obligations to oneself, having had one's productions reasonably well received. I more or less play it by ear. Unless you're a man like Bernard Shaw, who knew what he was doing at all times, you get yourself in trouble trying to talk about the way you write. It makes for self-consciousness. I'd like to preserve an innocence, so that what I do can surprise me. I've been forced lately to articulate what's been happening to me, and that makes you self-conscious about trying to remain unself-conscious. I go to more parties than I used to. I find I start talking and other people shut up. And that's terrible. I've met more people this past year than I ever met in the past thirty. It's interesting and valuable to meet accomplished people. It's instructive. You can always learn from your elders and betters. When I sit down to work, four or five hours at a time are all I can manage. Then I have to go out to the San Remo and have a couple of beers with friends. Summers, I go off to the beach at Riis Park by subway and bus. I stayed with all the plays throughout casting and rehearsals. It's a pleasant agony."

Social Critics, Like Prophets, Are Often Honored from Afar

Edward Kosner/1961

From *New York Post*, 31 March 1961, 38. © by the *New York Post*. Reprinted by permission.

There are no crossed American flags sprouting from the walls of the playwright Edward Albee's living room, no gilt-encrusted furniture to assail the eye, no Mommy and Daddy exchanging inanities in desperate, strident tones.

There is, instead, a peaceful, often sun-drenched calm enhanced by modern paintings, tall, graceful plants, three quiet cats and Albee himself, lolling in a comfortable chair. It is as far from the world of *The American Dream*—the bitingly comic commentary on middle-class vapidity that cemented Albee's reputation as possibly America's foremost young playwright—as his taste and talent, both of which are considerable, can take him. It is clearly where he wants to be.

And Albee, a slight, polite young man (he's 33 but looks 25) with close-cropped dark hair, a firm handshake and an affinity for crew-neck sweaters, is anything but the enraged voice that flays the audience in *The American Dream* and his other short plays, *The Death of Bessie Smith* and *The Zoo Story*. He is quite pleased with that, too.

In fact, for an artist whose work reflects a keen dissatisfaction with the values of his society, Albee seems remarkably uncommitted. His smile reflects satisfaction with himself that occasionally shades into smugness. He likes his apartment on West 12th St. near the North River because "it is in the city, but yet apart from the city." He is pleased that the critics have lavished their choice adjectives on his plays, but he basks in an inner glow. "They're not the greatest plays ever written, but they're good plays," he says with certitude.

"Angry? No, I'm not angry," he told a visitor the other day. "John Osborne rather exhausted the angry pose for everyone else." A wry

8

smile crinkled the tiny lines around his eyes. "I think [author] Jimmy Baldwin has the right idea. You meet Jimmy at a party and you find him to be a quiet guy with good manners and a nice sense of humor. He doesn't *come on* angry. The anger comes out in his writing. I write angry plays, but I don't come on angry."

Albee, a quiet man with good manners and a nice sense of humor, talks about his angry plays in a subdued voice nearly devoid of emotion. It is more than faintly reminiscent of the voice of the handsome (but far more muscular) young man who is the heart's desire of Mommy and Daddy, the lost parents of *The American Dream*—the young man who is that beautiful shell, the American dream.

Although Albee, like the young man in his play, is an orphan adopted by rich parents (the Albee theater family), he disclaims any autobiographical inferences.

The American Dream, he says, speaking of the play and its inspiration, "is the substitution of artificial values for real values, the acceptance of appearance for content, the slow drift of accommodation. People try so hard to escape being touched by unpleasantness that they wind up being unable to feel anything or to communicate anything."

When Albee wants to communicate something, he leans forward in his chair, takes a deep drag on his filter-tip cigaret, and speaks earnestly, although the level of his voice never rises.

He talks about his adolescence with reluctance ("I was in revolt and revolting") and rejects with a smile the suggestion that the outfit he feels "most comfortable" in—gray flannel slacks, blue oxford shirt open at the throat, shaggy sweater and crepe-soled shoes—reflects an unconscious attempt to recapture a youth not quite beyond recall.

It was an adolescence spent at three prep schools, Lawrenceville, Valley Forge Military Academy and Choate ("I didn't write *The Catcher in the Rye* or *End as a Man*; I lived them") followed by a year and a half at Trinity College, where he defied enough rules to be "excused" from further attendance.

Then came a string of odd jobs—writing continuity for WNYC ("I had to make sure the announcer said the symphony was in F minor, not just F"), copy boy at an advertising agency ("I filled the water pitchers for the executives"), short order cook, and Western Union messenger ("I did that for 2½ years and liked it fine. I love to walk"). All the while, he was writing poetry, which went unpublished.

In the spring of 1958, he wrote *The Zoo Story* and when, after complex transatlantic negotiations, the play was successfully produced in Berlin that summer, he realized he had found his medium and gave up poetry.

The Zoo Story has just given its 500th off-Broadway performance and is being seen—and hailed—all over Western Europe. *The Death of Bessie Smith* and *The American Dream* followed, and are now being presented as a double bill at the York Playhouse on the East Side.

For the future, Albee is at work on a longer play called *Who's Afraid of Virginia Woolf?* and an adaptation of Carson McCullers' story *The Ballad of the Sad Café*.

"I think I'm doing my part by writing plays," he says.

Interview with Edward Albee

Paul Zindel and Loree Yerby/1962

From *Wagner Literary Magazine*, no. 3 (1962), 1-10. Reprinted by permission of Wagner College.

Zindel: Mr. Albee . . .

Albee: Mr. Albee (all be).

Zindel: Mr. Albee? Oh, good—how injuring!

Albee: I don't care.

Zindel: Mr. Albee, you're known to be very dissatisfied with the state of the American Theater. Why is this?

Albee: Yes! I'm dissatisfied with the state of the American theater because I don't think it's particularly healthy, and I think it is the responsibility of the person working in a craft to be concerned with the health of that craft. Everyone knows, pretty much, and has read a good deal about the usual, economic problems which beset the commercial theater; everyone usually believes it, that it is just an economic problem that is destroying the commercial theater in the United States. Why call it the United States? Let's just call it *New York*, because that's where theater exists in the United States despite the efforts that are made outside of New York City.

But actually, there is a greater problem than just the rising costs and timid producers and greedy theater owners and megalomaniac actors in the New York commercial theater. The problem is somewhat greater than that—and cowardly playwrights, I should add. The problem is basically the one that there is in the New York theater, and has been for years, the desire on the part of almost everyone concerned with the commercial theater, to bring it down to the easiest level of acceptance by a rather lazy audience. Now that's the commercial theater.

Off-Broadway the problems are a little different, but the basic problem is one, it seems to me, of the direction the theater should take and the courage of the people working in the theater. In Europe, there's been a movement away from the sagging post-Ibsenite-Chekhov theatrical idea which has been running along for seventy-five to eighty years now—and running steadily downhill—and to mix another metaphor in with this, running just plain down like a wristwatch which has stopped. I could go on, but I'd rather not.

Yerby: This is on the same subject: During the conference, we had Mr. _____, a producer of Off-Broadway shows, and Mrs. _____, from Actors Studio—and both of them presented an entirely different viewpoint of the relationship between the actor, director, and playwright. Can you tell the main difference between these two outlooks?

Albee: Well, I can tell you the main difference between these two outlooks. You've described the main difference between these two outlooks, actually—it's the main difference between these two people. Mrs. _____, from all of her sincerity and all of her wide experience in the theater, is dedicated to the proposition of the status-quo and accommodation to things as they are. Mr. _____, on the other hand, is entirely opposed to this. Mrs. _____, assumes that the theater is a collaborative effort and that's marvelous. Everybody knows the theater *has* to be a collaborative effort because you can't work in it alone. Mr. _____, feels that the playwright is the most important thing in the theater. Mrs. _____, feels that, since in the commercial theater in New York the playwright is relatively unimportant, that's the way things should be since that's the way things are.

Zindel: Is Off-Broadway better than Broadway as far as artistic sincerity is concerned?

Albee: Sincerity doesn't mean anything. A person can be sincere and be more destructive than a person who is insincere. Sincerity means nothing! What do you really mean?

Yerby: What is the playwright's responsibility?

Albee: A playwright's responsibility is . . . Golly! That's something that usually people other than playwrights should talk about. It seems to me that a playwright has a responsibility in his society not to aid it, or comfort it, but to comment and criticize it. A playwright has the responsibility of artistic integrity.

Yerby: During the conference you mentioned several times the relationship between music and words, notes and words, and music and playwrighting. Would you say something about this connection? Could one allow a play to be without content and just have sound and music?

Albee: Well, of course, concentration on form for the sake of form is usually inhibiting and quite often destructive, but there is a definite relationship it seems to me; not necessarily a conscious one, but certainly a relationship between musical structure and dramatic structure. They are quite similar.

Plays are constructed rather the way music is, and also, there is usually, in a well-written play there is a kind of internal music that also relates to music as it goes along—rather the total form of a piece of music—in the same way that plays have their own kind of poetry, which doesn't necessarily use verse form, but is surely as much poetry as anybody else writes.

Yerby: Do you find music in, say *Death of a Salesman*—Arthur Miller type of social realism?

Albee: I don't think that *Death of a Salesman* is a piece of social realism, and yes, I very definitely do find a strong internal music—internal rhythm—work there . . . yes, a kind of music, too; on the surface it might not seem so, but he's rather careful with the rhythms.

Yerby: Do you play a musical instrument or do you compose yourself?

Albee: I wanted to be a composer when I was around twelve, and I have absolutely no aptitude for it—but I've been rather closely involved with music for many years.

Zindel: You were busy writing your first play about that time, weren't you? *Aliqueen?*

Albee: Well, yes, I was. My only three act play, oddly enough, so far. It was a great deal shorter than any of the one act plays I've written recently.

Zindel: You have said that it is virtually an evil to accommodate yourself to the theater. In the past, the theater was used to a full length, three act play—and now there is the appearance of a number of successful one act plays, including your own. Would you have preferred your one act plays to have run separately? Is there a condition of the audience required to have a short play successfully appear as a complete evening?

Albee: Now, you have asked a number of questions and made a number of statements there. I don't know, but I'll try to handle them whether it be backwards or in order—somehow I don't know.

Of course the theater in the past was not used to three act plays. It was used to one act plays in the Greek theater, four and five act plays in the Elizabethan theater, and five act plays in the French theater, so—I know what you mean, though: a *three act play*—the supposed full-length play. There has to be an audience conditioning because audiences tend to be lazy. Ideally an audience should be able to get its intellectual and emotional gratification within any time length; it should be able to get it in a play whether it's twenty minutes long or twelve hours long, ideally—but audiences don't. I suppose you can't change everything all at once, and if you're going to write short plays, you'll have to have two of them together in an evening. Ideally, just one—yes, I think.

Yerby: You mentioned a few days ago that drama is always about twenty years behind the other art forms, such as poetry and the novel. Why is this?

Albee: I don't know exactly. I suspect it's true. Maybe it's because it relies so much on—on what? On the necessary evil of collaborative association with other people—and also audiences expect easier things from the theater than they do from the novel or the poem; and the more the audience is catered to, the further behind the times the theater falls. The circle is, of course, vicious.

Zindel: Profanity is used far less frequently in the drama than in the novel. Would you say that?

Albee: No!

Zindel: No? I thought . . .

Albee: Well, profanity is a large term. I find that most of the plays put on profane the theater.

Zindel: You had mentioned once in a discussion about profanity in the drama that you could justify the use of extremes as far as character development goes—or character consistency. Would you comment on that?

Albee: Yes, I find the use of the basically meaningless Anglo-Saxon terms that seem to offend the post office minor, minor matters at best. I find the kind of dreadful obscenity that inflicts so many of our supposed comedies in the New York theater—that are really just elaborate dirty jokes put on stage—I find these things a great deal more offensive than the use of specific words which, while theater dialogue shouldn't be just factual reporting, it seems to me—that the use of these words that really don't have any meaning that relates to much of anything—they're just *expletives*. You could actually just say expletive—I mean, the word *expletive* means a great deal more than these words mean. They seem to me to be useful exclamation points in writing dialogue. I find nothing offensive about them at all, unless they're used for their own sake—to titillate. Naturally, that's not a very good idea.

I'm not trying to suggest that you can make good theater by having four letter words in it. Not that at all.

Zindel: We were wondering about how long it takes you to write a play, and, more particularly—not to make the question *too* complex—do you create the characters first or the plot, or is it a combination of both? Perhaps you might use *The Death of Bessie Smith* as an example?

Albee: I might. You've only asked two questions there—at once. The actual writing time in the three plays I've written is usually about three weeks. The semi-conscious thinking time is usually about three months—but I would imagine that there's a good deal more assimilation that goes before that. Now, what was the second part of the question?

Zindel: Do you create characters first, or the plot?

Albee: The plot. No! I don't know what *plot* means actually. Characters, the situation they're in, and the style in which the play is written have got to come together. You can't really separate one from the other in your mind when you're working, it seems to me. I don't know what comes first. The necessity to write about certain people in a certain situation in a certain way—they develop as the work progresses, and their relatedness develops as the work progresses.

Yerby: The history of *The Zoo Story*—or the history of its production—has been quite unusual. It was produced in Germany first, wasn't it?

Albee: It was done in Berlin, and then six months later it was done Off-Broadway.

Zindel: We understand that *The Death of Bessie Smith* is going to be made into a movie. Now, are you going to do the scenario?

Albee: I will be! Certainly.

Zindel: Fine. And this will require possibly an expansion of your play as it exists.

Albee: I certainly hope so, because *The Death of Bessie Smith* has never completely satisfied me as a stage piece in the shape that it's written.

Zindel: That's what we were wondering about. Just what aspects of it do you think you'll expand?

Albee: I don't know exactly. I hope to make it into a better piece. I feel that I've left things out that . . .

Yerby: Do you feel you've left Bessie Smith out and that she should be included? Or will . . .

Albee: No, not at all. I left Bessie Smith off-stage quite on purpose because I thought it would be cheap and opportunistic to put her on-stage. It was a calculated risk. If I put her on-stage or used recordings of her singing, I could have been accused of opportunism. I preferred to take the chance of being accused of bad dramaturgy.

Zindel: Some critics attacked your play because there was no feeling of Bessie Smith on the stage. As you said this was intentional . . .

Albee: It wasn't intentional that there should be no feeling of Bessie Smith on-stage. But the play wasn't *about* Bessie Smith. In a sense the play is more about what happens and what goes on in the minds of the people that produce situations that result in the death of Bessie Smith. She was more a catalyst than anything else.

Zindel: Critics also use the term "neurotic nurse" in speaking of *The Death of Bessie Smith*. Is she a *neurotic*, or do you have another term for her?

Albee: Well, I think people who prefer a sadistic sex dance to other forms of love-making tend to be a bit neurotic. Yes.

Yerby: We understand that you're writing a longer play—I won't say a three act one—but a longer play, called *Who's Afraid of Virginia Woolf?* Can you tell us anything about it? . . . Will it open uptown on Broadway or will it be Off-Broadway?

Albee: Well, if anybody wants to put the play on after I'm done with it, I'd like to have it put on where it can be produced most effectively as written. I have no idea where that will be. Can't tell.

The play—I think—is going to be three acts, although I don't know at the moment, and I don't care. I'd like to have it maybe all in one act and have it run about two and a half hours, but, although people can accept this in the movies, the audience in the theater isn't trained to sit still for two and a half hours; so I probably will have to put arbitrary interludes. Did you want to know what the play is about? Did you ask that?

Yerby: Yes, although I feel I shouldn't have.

Albee: Well, I always give a very vague answer to that because I never know what a thing is about actually until long after I've finished it. The only thing I can tell you about the action is that it concerns the exorcism of a non-existent child, and that most of the last part of the play is going to be in Latin.

Zindel and Yerby: Oh!

Albee: I think it has something to do with what I thought *The American Dream* had to do with—the substitution of artificial for real values in this society of ours. It's sort of a grotesque comedy.

Zindel: Also on your future schedule you have the dramatization of *The Ballad of the Sad Café*—Carson McCullers.

Albee: Yes, I do.

Zindel: I understand this was a favorite story of yours. Could you give us some idea of how you came to get the privilege of writing the play, and just why isn't Carson McCullers doing it herself?

Albee: She couldn't! She tried, she couldn't. She wanted to turn it into a musical, and I felt there was too much music in the writing to do that. How did I get the privilege of doing it? Because I was having lunch with a Broadway producer one day who said, "Is there anything I can possibly do for you; I'd love to do it." And I said, "Sure. You can get me the rights to *The Ballad of the Sad Café* and commission me to do it!" So he *didn't*. But there was a lady from the agency that I used at that lunch, and she started the wheels rolling.

Yerby: Since you mentioned *agency* and *agents*, perhaps we might be interested in whether an agent is necessary for a playwright, and what is his basic function?

Albee: Their basic function is to be an efficient collection agent, to be a fairly good law firm, to open doors, and—that's really their basic function. They have other things that they do. They try to build the person they get a hold of, first by calling him *a property*; then they try to increase the value and size of their property. These people work on a percentage basis, so naturally they're more concerned with income than art, inevitably, but they try to have both.

Zindel: With your great interest in music and drama it wouldn't be unlikely that you might try a drama in verse. Have you ever thought about this?

Albee: Yes, it would be unlikely. I have thought about it and decided not to. As I said, the theatre has its own kind of poetry. Usually the use of verse form by playwrights these days is terribly inhibiting and produces windy plays about hollow people, and can even go so far as to render rather dramatic Old Testament characters completely invalid and unpoetic.

Yerby: How do you feel about Federal theater? Do you feel there should be either a national theatre or a specific aid to playwrights?

Albee: I'm all in favor of various theater movements receiving money so long as there is absolutely no control. Though money itself can corrupt. It should be probably not quite enough.

Zindel: Now there is one other question we'd like to ask just for your reaction. *The Zoo Story* has captured the interest of a good many people, and there is this question, which is rather complex, that we'd like to ask: Are you Jerry or the dog?

Albee: I've been asked before whether I was Jerry or Peter. I've never been asked before whether I was the dog. It's a refreshing question but I probably won't give a refreshing answer.

Yes, no and maybe—to all three characters. I was not consciously doing an autobiographical work in any sense, but I imagine I was drawing and distorting intentionally many experiences of mine to give dimension and validity to the characters for themselves, and therefore maybe to an audience. The dog! Isn't that interesting? The dog . . . I don't know, but I doubt it. I would have to think a good deal about that.

Yerby: Now that the Writers Conference is just about at a close, we'd like to hear about what you think you've gotten from it, and what you might have given to it?

Albee: Of course, I've never taught before this NYC Writers Conference, nor had I ever been to a writers conference, so I was rather mystified before I came here as to what exactly it would be like. I hoped I'd be able to learn something, because quite often unless you have to talk about what you do, you really don't think terribly consciously about what you believe—or articulate. I don't know what the accomplishment has been in so short a time. The writers conference has been so—not rushed—but so compressed. I don't think ten days is enough for fifteen people to meet with one instructor whether it is for two hours a day—and working by themselves in the afternoon. I don't know what writers conferences are *supposed* to accomplish, but I rather hope that the fifteen playwrights who have gathered here have gotten something by association with each other—from being put into the position of being outspokenly critical of each other's work, and getting hit in the face by criticism back; of being forced to work, to write while they're here—to write quickly and under rather stringent, suppressive circumstances. I hope a sense of practical theater, how it works, has been gotten through—and I hope also that that hasn't been confused with a need to accommodate to the supposedly practical necessities of the theater. I hope that something has been gotten more about what it is to be a playwright and how one works as a playwright.

Ideally, though, it should go on for either a shorter period of time or longer.

Zindel: We might declare that the general agreement among your students here at the conference is that you are, in one word, a *blockbuster* as far as impact and influence on them. Have you felt this success, or do you dismiss it as a natural phenomenon which always occurs when students meet a celebrity of your caliber?

Albee: If they feel this by being exposed to a celebrity of *my* caliber, I wonder what would happen to them if they were exposed to a real celebrity.

Zindel: Would you do it again?

Albee: I might.

Edward Albee Interviewed

Digby Diehl/1963

From "Edward Albee Interviewed," *Transatlantic Review*, 13 (Summer 1963), 57-72. Reprinted in *Behind the Scenes: Theatre & Film Interviews from the Transatlantic Review*, ed. Joseph McCrindle (New York: Holt, Rinehart & Winston, 1971). 223-242. © Digby Diehl. Reprinted by permission of Digby Diehl; all rights reserved.

This interview took place in Edward Albee's brownstone apartment in New York's Greenwich Village shortly after the much acclaimed opening of *Who's Afraid of Virginia Woolf?* It was the first major interview to be granted by Albee, and in many of his remarks there are suggestions of themes from plays which followed. The conversation has been transcribed almost verbatim, in an attempt to remain faithful to the spirit of the discussion.

Interviewer: What is the most current thing you are doing?

Albee: I'm at work on the adaptation of Carson McCullers' novella, *Ballad of the Sad Café*, but at the same time I'm beginning to write a play of my own, called—right now I can't remember what I am going to call it. Yes, *The Substitute Speaker*, which I think is going to be in two acts, and I'm not sure which one I'll finish first.

Interviewer: What can you tell me about *The Substitute Speaker?*

Albee: Very little—I don't want to tell you anything about it, except that I think it's going to be in two acts and I suspect it is going to probably have either six or eight characters and I think it's going to be—I hope it will be—just about unbearable.

Interviewer: What is this unbearable theme?

Albee: That's something you're going to have to find out when you go see it.

Interviewer: Okay, fine. What about the McCullers novella? Why did you choose to do a task that you yourself have said has not been done well in the past? You have not seen yet an adaptation of a novel for the stage that has been done well. Is that correct?

Albee: Exactly for that reason. No. Two reasons really, but one of them is that I am interested in finding out what happens when people do adaptations of novels for the stage. Usually there is a tendency to cheapen—to lessen the work that's adapted, but then again, I can't think of very many good playwrights that have ever done adaptations. They're usually second-rate people who do adaptations. I'm not suggesting here that I'm a first-rate person, but I am interested in finding out if it is possible to do an adaptation of somebody else's work—to move it from the pages of the novel to the life of the stage—without cheapening or lessening the work. And then again, ten years ago—Is it ten? yes, probably eleven years now . . . When I first read *Ballad of the Sad Café*, I said to myself, "If I ever start writing plays I'd like to make this into a play." So you put the two together and maybe you have a fairly decent reason for wanting to do it.

Interviewer: Why this novel from a number of other very good novels?

Albee: When I read it, it seemed to me to belong on the stage.

Interviewer: Just a dramatic event?

Albee: Exactly.

Interviewer: You have been saying some very interesting things about the difference between compassion and pity. *Time* magazine in particular criticized *Who's Afraid of Virginia Woolf?* for being written by a man who has no compassion for his characters. I understand that you feel exactly opposite.

Albee: Yes, indeed. Pity is the sentimentalizing of compassion . . . in a way. Pity is a demeaning emotion for the person being pitied. Compassion is not demeaning. I'm not concerned with pity—I'm concerned with compassion.

Interviewer: Do you feel your audience should be too?

Albee: Indeed yes. One of the troubles with audiences is that they concern themselves with the residue of things. They concern themselves, for example, with pity rather than compassion—they concern themselves with sentimentality rather than with sentiment. Pity is smug—pity is a smug emotion. Compassion is a sharing emotion. Sentimentality is a facile substitute for sentiment.

Interviewer: The real way to empathy with a play is compassion?

Albee: Define empathy.

Interviewer: A feeling of togetherness with—a projection of yourself into what is happening on the stage.

Albee: At the same time, I am not so sure that I like what audiences want as empathy. They don't really want something healthy, they prefer to have a kind of vicarious experience rather than real experience. They don't want to be affected for themselves. They want to have the illusion of being affected by something. They don't want the real thing.

Interviewer: Well, you said that you write to arouse audiences. You want them to be aroused in this way—affected by the real thing?

Albee: That's not the reason I write. I imagine that somewhere along the line I was trapped into saying that I wrote to arouse people. I write for me. For the audience of me. If other people come along for the ride then it's great. After I've written a play and people have talked about it, then I start making up answers for "the intention." And a lot of people are aroused, Off-Broadway at least—Broadway audiences are such placid cows. At almost every performance of *The Zoo Story* and *The American Dream* people used to get up and walk out and yell at the actors saying, "God damn you, how dare you talk this way, how dare you do this, how dare you offend me?" I suppose that's affecting, getting at, an audience—I'd prefer the people stay rather than walk out, only because the people who walk out disturb the people who are staying. But you have two alternatives; you either affect people or you leave them indifferent. And I would loathe to leave an audience indifferent. I don't care whether they like or hate, so long as they're not indifferent.

Interviewer: You've said that you have material in your mind now for something like two years in advance of what you're writing. How do you construct this in your mind? How does it come to you?

Albee: I've material for two years in advance because I'm very lazy; I usually write only one play a year. How does the material come? I don't know. All of a sudden I discover that I have been thinking about a play. This is usually between six months and a year before I actually sit down and start typing it out. The characters are sort of cloudy but clear at the same time; the nature of the play is quite clear but unspecific; what is going to happen is sort of definite but terribly imprecise. And so I think about it on and off for between six months and a year. I may not think about it for two or three weeks but all of a sudden I'll be walking down the street looking in a window or doing whatever I do when I walk down the street and all of a sudden, the idea of the play or something about the play that I discover that I have already started thinking about—something about the play will pop into my mind. It may be something that I have never thought about before, which would suggest—and make me very happy to think about it this way since I'm such a lazy person—that a great deal of the work that I do, I do unconsciously, that a great deal of the play is formed when I am thinking without using the most limited part of my mind which is the conscious part.

Interviewer: When you speak about the form of a play, you have said that the best advice you could give to a young playwright was to study musical composition, and it seems to me that the studied structure of a musical composition is something very different from the workings of the unconscious mind.

Albee: I don't think so at all. The only thing that the unconscious mind can do is make use of the things that the conscious mind has assimilated. Musical composition should be studied by playwrights, I think, because I find play construction and musical composition enormously similar.

Interviewer: Can you give me an example of its use in one of your plays?

Albee: No, but I can carry on an analogy between musical form and play structure all night if you'd like me to. For example, musical notation and play notation can be and should be quite similar. A composer can notate, can take a note and equate that to a word. He can take a note and he can put a dot at the end of it which suggests if it's above the line that it's to be extended more than it should be if it's below the line—it should also be extended more than its value except less or one or the other, above or below— depending upon the number of brush marks he puts on the note. This also suggests how long it should be spoken. He has tempo markings he can put down—for a violinist he has bowing markings—a musician can be terribly precise just by little marks that he puts on a page of music. And a playwright can be exactly that precise since it's an imprecise craft at best, since one must deal with actors and a director, who also pretend to be human beings. So a playwright can notate enormously precisely—Shakespeare for example, never had stage directions; he didn't need them because he was a pretty good playwright. The only good playwright that I know of who has enormously precise stage directions (which is not the same thing as notation)—is Eugene O'Neill. He was a good playwright in spite of those stage directions. The playwright should be able to write a line and notate it in such a way that it's impossible for an actor to say the line incorrectly. It can be just as precise as musical notation. Look at Samuel Beckett, for example.

Interviewer: But this notation is not in the stage direction?

Albee: No. Beginning playwrights always make the mistake of putting their entire play in stage directions and not bothering to write it in. O'Neill's one act play, *Hughie*, which hasn't been done in this country, exists in its stage directions. So much so that when anybody does the play they're going to have to find some way to act the stage directions.

Interviewer: I know you have done a lot of traveling in Europe and South America and so forth; what are the currents over there? Do you think that this is where the real leaders in drama are coming from?

Albee: Well, I suppose that Paris is the center at the moment of twentieth-century theater—it's moved away from Germany. Brecht is dead and he's being misplayed all over New York right now, but he was a unique phenomenon. But I would imagine that the nature of what is going on in the theater is stated pretty much by French playwrights. An Irishman like Beckett, a Rumanian like Ionesco and a Frenchman like Gênet. Ionesco is sort of a sleight of hand artist. He's nowhere as important or interesting as Beckett and Gênet.

Interviewer: What about some of your American contemporaries?

Albee: By contemporaries do you mean people who are writing for the theater at the same time that I am writing for the theater?

Interviewer: Like Gelber, Richardson.

Albee: In other words you are talking about Jack Gelber, Jack Richardson, Arthur Kopit and not people like Arthur Miller and Thornton Wilder and Tennessee Williams?

Interviewer: That's right. How do you place their contribution?

Albee: They're alive and they're writing and they're writing things that are alive and the fact that we have people like Jack Gelber, Jack Richardson, Arthur Kopit, who are writing for the theater now in this country and are writing with their own voice—well, more or less—is an exciting phenomenon. I hope that you're not asking me to tell you what I think about Jack Gelber or Jack Richardson or Arthur Kopit?

Interviewer: No, I am trying to get an idea about your feeling about where the real life of the theater is at this time. What are the currents—what are the cross-currents between Europe and America and so on and so forth.

Albee: This is always in a state of flux. I think we're moving away from a naturalistic base and we're moving away from Ibsen and Chekhov—No, I won't put it that way because they are always good men to learn from—Ibsen and Chekhov—but I think we are moving away from the facile use of their technique which has been a misuse, a misunderstanding, a facile misunderstanding, of the naturalistic tradition of theater. Reality isn't as simple as it used to be and I suspect that the theater, the adventurous, the new, if you will, the new theater in the United States, is going to concern itself with the re-evaluation of the nature of reality and therefore, it's going to move away from the naturalistic tradition.

Interviewer: Your view of reality has been rather harsh. You said that contemporary society represents the substitution of artificial values for real. What do you think caused all this? Where did this come from?

Albee: It came because it's easier.

Interviewer: Sheer laziness?

Albee: Yeah. Moral, intellectual, and emotional laziness. People would rather sleep their way through life than stay awake for it.

Interviewer: Well, you seem to be interested in awakening them. In other ways than your own plays. . . .

Albee: What do you mean by that?

Interviewer: Well, I mean some of the things that you have participated in . . . You've been going to several colleges; you've been helping out in judging writers' contests; you've been teaching in writing schools, theater schools.

Albee: No, that is slightly inaccurate—I don't teach at writing schools. I do like to go to speak at colleges because that is where the new audiences are coming from and I think that people should be corrupted young. I like to participate in judging playwriting contests also so that I can corrupt and make sure that something new and alive will win the contest rather than something that is the imitation of the familiar. I referee a playwriting workshop at The Circle in the Square which is not the same thing as teaching playwriting and anybody that says that he can teach playwriting is either a charlatan, a liar, or a fool. I referee a playwriting workshop in which people come and have a play of theirs performed on a stage for them by acting and directing students at The Circle in the Square and then they're asked to examine the relationship between their intention and what occurred on the stage. They're asked to talk about their dealings with actors and directors. People ask me a lot, "How do you do this?"—"What are the rules, how do you make a play good, how do you do this and how do you do that?" There is only one rule, which is: you can do anything in the world that you like as long as you make it work. There is only one length for a play for example and that is the play's proper length. There are no rules except for the rule of a successful work of art, as it is in all things. And for some obscure reason, people think that playwriting can be taught. Playwriting can't be taught, musical composition can't be taught. The *elements* of musical composition can be taught—harmony, theory, counterpoint—but that's because musical craft is more precise than the theatrical craft. I never dream of teaching playwriting but I like to indulge in a discussion of why and where a thing was successful, where it wasn't and why. And I suppose in the long run, the greatest value of a theater workshop, of the sort that I referee, is to let people find out whether or not they have the playwright's mentality and whether or not they should continue writing for the theater.

Interviewer: You're also interested in a Pan American project—is that right? Encouraging better cultural relations between South American and American writers and musicians and so forth.

Albee: There was a conference in the Bahamas last fall of fifteen United States and fifteen South American writers, composers, poets, anarchists and all the rest, in which views were exchanged and during which it was discovered that the South American members feel that there should be an enormous kinship with United States writers, composers, painters and anarchists. I'm not convinced that there should be since South American writers, etc., are still a good deal more alive to the European tradition than people in the United States are. They are (not intellectually, but in the sense of how they have been able to form any sort of national statement—or national voice) about fifty to seventy-five years behind the United States. However, the assumption on the part of the South Americans is that there is or that there should be an enormous relationship between North and South American writers. Well, naturally we are interested in finding out what's being written by Latin Americans. In the theater for example, Gore Vidal and Paddy Chayefsky and Harold Clurman and I are concerned with reading plays by Latin American playwrights in rough translation. The only time we have at the moment is to read them in rough translation, decide which are the good ones or the better ones, and assign them, either to ourselves or to other people for accurate translation (not adaptation, I dislike the word adaptation). Between the four of us we know the majority of the people involved in the theater (producers, directors and actors) and know about finding outlets for the plays. Some may be done Off-Broadway—those will be the best plays, since the best plays are done Off-Broadway, the second-best on Broadway and the others farmed out to college theaters. I don't know what will come of it—I don't know very much about Latin American writing. But we are interested—this is one of the outgrowths of the conference we had in the Bahamas.

Interviewer: You seem to take very seriously your somewhat new role as a cultural hero or leader in the arts and are doing a lot to encourage this sort of thing. How has this changed your way of life? How has this affected your writing?

Albee: One of the few values that the idiotic "success bit" brings to a man is that he is placed in a better position to try to change the situation that brought him his idiotic recognition in the first place. When you put a play on, there are two alternatives: it is either going to be successful or it is going to be unsuccessful. Ideally, it would be successful with honor. Now any playwright who has any respect for his work and is successful assumes that he has been successful with honor. And since he assumes this, he assumes that he can now corrupt, he can try to move the theater into the image of himself or the people whom he admires. (And the playwright always admires himself beyond all other playwrights. He knows that there are better playwrights than he is but he admires himself.) One of the really good things that happens from being caught up in the talons of the Bitch Goddess is that you can say a sentence and it's going to be believed by people you know, whether it's a stupid sentence or not. And so a playwright can, indeed, corrupt the audience in the direction of the good or at least what he thinks is the good. Ideally, the theater should be made up of only good playwrights. And in spite of the fact that playwrights are a suspicious, envious, anti-social bunch much as all writers are, I can't imagine any playwright as good as he thinks he is. So success is useful not only because a playwright is able to have the security to do what he wants without feeling that he is going to lose anything by it but also he is in a position to influence. Now if you had a theater of successful playwrights, all of whom were insane—and only half of us are— then you would probably have an audience that would eventually be corrupted the wrong way. But I think that playwrights are saner than most people and I think the theater can be corrupted in the right way. The audience can be corrupted in the direction of the truth as the playwright sees it. And if that can't happen, there is no point in having a theater at all.

Interviewer: How about the corruption of the playwright as he reaches success? Did you find that you had to make a great number of compromises when you came on to Broadway with *Virginia Woolf?* Did you feel for instance that you underwent the same experiences that William Gibson relates in the *Seesaw Log?*

Albee: *Who's Afraid of Virginia Woolf?* was produced by the same two men that I worked with as producers all the way along the line Off-Broadway, Richard Barr and Clinton Wilder. These were two men who had both produced on Broadway and they didn't like Broadway very much—they didn't like the compromise and the corruption of Broadway. And so they both decided more or less simultaneously to produce Off-Broadway where plays are allowed to exist on their own terms. So we all got together by great fortune and we started working Off-Broadway and it was their

intention to bring the Off-Broadway standards to Broadway. And for
some reason which can be explained only by them, the first play
they decided to do on Broadway was one of mine—*Who's Afraid of
Virginia Woolf?* But what we did—I say we because I was made one
of the producers on the assumption, on Barr and Wilder's part, that
a playwright should have some say in the matter—was to decide just
to do a play exactly as we would have done it Off-Broadway, which
means that we got the best actors for it and we got the best director
for the play. The result was that the playwright was allowed to make
his own mistakes—I was allowed to make my own mistakes, rather
than have to suffer the mistakes of other people. These men should
be given medals hammered out of solid gold because they don't
know what the term Broadway means (except in the business sense;
they are the shrewdest producers I have ever met). When Richard
Barr worked on Broadway before—before he went Off-Broadway—
he produced *Richard III* in about 1948 on Broadway for $12,000.
(I have to bring money into it because this is the only thing that
people who are concerned with the Broadway theater will
understand and I assume that maybe somebody will read this
interview to the people who produce on Broadway.) Of course
prices have gone up since then. But it was unheard of to produce a
play on Broadway in 1948 for $12,000. Barr and Wilder produced
my play, *Who's Afraid of Virginia Woolf?* for $42,000 which was
unheard of, because most Broadway productions today cost upward
of $100,000. The money bit is important because theater costs have
been priced out of sense and intelligence, and this attrition leads to
high ticket prices; it leads to the theory that a play must please all of
the critics or close because it is so expensive. There was a time, not
before the time I started going to the theater, because I started going
to the theater when I was five years old and the first play that I ever
saw was *Jumbo* at the Hippodrome and that was around 1935. (I
wasn't five, I was seven, because I'm thirty-four, aren't I?) There was
a time when good plays—plays that were not constructed for the
mass market only but plays that were honest with themselves and
also honest to the historical continuum of the theater—there was a
time when those plays could run on Broadway, if they didn't get the
palsied nod of the Seven Men. That's no longer true. As an
example, the play that won the Pulitzer Prize last year or the year

before—the Pulitzer Prize is being given to adaptations and musicals these days—was the adaptation of James Agee's novel *A Death in the Family*. The title was changed to *All the Way Home* because the producers thought they couldn't have "death" in the title and have a successful play, forgetting *Death of a Salesman*. It got mediocre reviews, but Fred Coe and Arthur Cantor kept it going for a whole season and they ended up getting the Pulitzer Prize for it. A play just as good by Hugh Wheeler got the same kind of notices and closed after four performances. The panic set in, in other words. These aren't very good examples because I have to qualify each one. *All the Way Home* was not a good adaptation and it was kept running (which is a good thing because it was interesting and it was better than the run of the mill) for the right reason for the wrong play. And the Hugh Wheeler play was just as interesting but it was closed for the wrong reason.

Interviewer: Let's talk about *Virginia Woolf*.

Albee: I think she's a very nice writer.

Interviewer: No, I mean your play. Why did you move from the sort of surrealism of *The Sandbox* and *The Zoo Story* and *The American Dream?* . . .

Albee: There is no surrealism in *The Zoo Story*.

Interviewer: It's all realism?

Albee: Uh huh.

Interviewer: Okay—of *The American Dream* for example . . .

Albee: You're talking about stylization.

Interviewer: . . . into the surrealism of *Who's Afraid of Virginia Woolf?*

Albee: Is *Who's Afraid of Virginia Woolf?* a surrealist play?

Interviewer: Well, do you have that impression?

Albee: No.

Interviewer: All right, why did you write *Who's Afraid of Virginia Woolf?* in a fashion different from the Theater of the Absurd as we know it? *Who's Afraid of Virginia Woolf?* is not really related to that stream.

Albee: I've written five plays; each of them is in a different style. I consider myself in a way the most eclectic playwright who ever wrote. As a matter of fact, I made a list about a year and a half ago, of the number of playwrights, according to the critics, that I

had been influenced by and it got to be a drag after I had listed
twenty-six. And this list of twenty-six included three playwrights
whom I had not read or seen. So I made a point of reading these
playwrights and I found that I had indeed been influenced by them.
Every play, I think, is written like this: form and content, matter and
manner, substance and style must occur at the same time. They
determine each other. A man's style as a writer is his voice, the
sound he makes—a playwright's voice is the sound that he makes
and the style that he works in doesn't determine that at all. It is
something that one catches by the ear. Take Tennessee Williams for
example, who has written in a number of styles, but all of his plays
sound like Tennessee Williams—thank heavens. That is the
Tennessee Williams style. Something that gets you by the ear. . . .
Something you can hear and say, "Yes, this is Tennessee Williams"
or "yes, this is Beckett." The manner and matter determine each
other and have nothing to do with the style of a playwright. In other
words what most poeple think of as the style has nothing to do with
style at all.

Interviewer: Do you think the critics and the drama theorists
have much to offer in the way of helping a playwright or helping the
theater today?

Albee: Inevitably no, since everything they say is after the fact.
They'd be a great deal more use if they would advise the playwright
before he made his mistakes. But, the pride that some critics take in
coming upon The Error and pinpointing, that is fairly useless.
Ideally, a critic should be able to contribute to a playwright, but
damn few of them do. A man like Harold Clurman does; Walter
Kerr, once you get to know his vaulting prejudices, does; Kenneth
Tynan, once you get to know his insupportable prejudices, does.
Very few critics are the teachers that they should be. After all, most
of them consider their job to be only that of a reporter and most of
them write like reporters. And most of them write like bad reporters.

Interviewer: A sad commentary on the state of criticism.

Albee: As I think Bernard Shaw said when he was a critic—A
critic should be an enormously prejudiced man. Indeed he should.
A critic should know something about the craft he is commenting
on. Ideally, I think he should be a prejudiced practitioner of the craft
he is commenting on. But the majority of critics assume that their

responsibility is to reflect the taste of the people who buy the paper they work for, and therefore their opinion is of no more value than any lay audience's opinion—which is of no value.

Interviewer: Well, I suppose that's true. To shift very radically, getting back to the so-called influences on your writing, do you feel that the background of the Albee family, the whole theater tradition behind them, had much influence on your writing? Do you think you got a lot out of what happened in your youth?

Albee: Do you mean the fact that my grandfather, who died when I was two years old, owned a bunch of vaudeville theaters?

Interviewer: Well, yes.

Albee: I have no way of knowing. It may have been a theater family ending with my grandfather, but I had no connection with the theater at all. But I was exposed to theater young. You know, when other kids would go to movies on Saturday afternoon, I was shipped off to live theater. It may or may not have had an influence, I don't know—I have no way of judging. I wouldn't say that it was a theater family at all. My mother was not a chorine nor was she an actress either. I don't know, I have no way of telling.

Interviewer: You've been quoted as saying that the theater is a collaborative effort at best. What do you mean exactly by this?

Albee: What I meant by it, very simply, is the fact that getting a play from the author's intention onto the stage and back to the audience is crowded with imponderables and difficulties. It is imprecise. Ideally a playwright can get his play from a page onto the stage and back to the audience, rather like playing tennis against a backboard. But this very seldom happens, because you have to deal with human beings. You have to deal with actors and the director. No performance of a play that is halfway decent is ever as good as the performance the author saw when he wrote it. You must accept this as fact. The worse the play, the better the performance, in that sense, because the actors and the director compensate for what the author did not do. The best play in the world will never get its best performance, because the best play in the world has its best performance in the ear and eye of the man who wrote it. But the most disturbing thing is the encouragement that has been given to directors and actors—mostly directors, I suspect—in the United States in the past fifteen years, to consider themselves coauthors of a work. The corruption—you notice I use that word a lot, I must be obsessed with corruption—has gone so far that many playwrights compose their plays on the assumption that the director and the actor will do their work for them. And indeed some directors in the United States want plays to come to them that are not thorough so that they can impose their personality on the work. The playwriting craft is enormously imprecise since it has to be filtered through other people. It seems to me that it is the playwright's responsibility to come as close as he can to the ideal—the ideal is that everything that has gone before, the nature of the characters, the style that the play is written in, the author's intention, is so precise that any sentence that comes in the middle of a play can be spoken only in one way and understood only in one way. This relates back to what I was saying before about music. We've been breeding playwrights in this country for a while against this theory. We have been breeding playwrights who think of themselves only as craftsmen rather than artists, and bad craftsmen at that, who consider themselves small cogs in the wheel. I think they'd do better to remember the fact that damn few actors and damn few directors have their names survive their time, and playwrights do. The craft is not imprecise, the relationship between playwright and audience has become enormously imprecise, and basically because the playwrights have been abdicating their responsibility to their craft.

Interviewer: What happens when there is another voice beyond that of the playwright (and the producer, director and actors) thrown in? For instance, when you are adapting another person's novel and I am speaking specifically, of course, of *Ballad of the Sad Café*.

Albee: My responsibility, of course, in putting Carson McCullers' novel on the stage is to make it seem as if Carson McCullers had written it for the stage. So I must indeed become Carson McCullers. I must think like Carson McCullers. The novella *Ballad of the Sad Café* has two lines of dialogue. That's all in the entire 110 page book. A play must be mostly dialogue. It's my intention (and I hope I succeed in it) to turn all of that narration into dialogue which sounds as though it were written by Carson McCullers. That's my particular function in that particular item. It's involving to do that but it's involving in a different way. I know that any play that I am working on is going right if I become involved in it, and if I am not involved in it, I think it is going badly. If I am moved, then it is moving. If I laugh, then it is funny. If I am indifferent, then it is indifferent. But in doing an adaptation, I have discovered, I must think that things are moving, involving, funny or whatever in Carson McCullers' terms. It is rather an eerie experience. I think that "eerie" is the word that Carson would use.

Interviewer: You think that you're attempting to speak in her voice?

Albee: I am using my judgment and whatever craft I have (and naturally I must be speaking of my own voice). I am using whatever craft I have to make the piece completely Carson McCullers.

Interviewer: You remarked last week—after a rather hectic series of sessions with students from a New Jersey college—that if Shakespeare had been alive today he might have killed himself from having been asked so many questions. What did you mean by this?

Albee: I didn't say that he might have killed himself. I said that he would have killed himself. People tend to be in this country more interested in the person who does the stuff, than in the stuff itself. And we are interested in persons and personalities rather than the work that they do. This has destroyed or helped to damage a lot of first-rate writers in this country. Thank heaven, for example, that Melville wasn't exposed to it. It's a shame that Whitman was. Ernest Hemingway, for example, started to think that he was Ernest Hemingway, in caps, which was a bad thing. What I meant was that if Shakespeare had been exposed to the glaring klieg-lights questioning of how he wrote, and why he wrote, he might very well have killed himself. Either that or moved to the country. The only depressing thing about facing any sort of audience for questions and answers is that most people ask questions like, "Why do you write?" and your only answer is, "I write because I am a writer," and that doesn't satisfy people. They not only ask "Why do you write?" but "Tell us how you write," and the only answer is when I am writing I get up at seven in the morning and go for a swim, come back to the house and have breakfast, smoke a cigarette and go to the bathroom and come out and sit down at the typewriter and write for four or five hours until I get a headache. That is *how* a man writes. The invasion of it, it isn't even privacy, it's the invasion of the nature of the man who is a writer, is one of the most puzzling and unfathomable things to me. Writing is a job in the sense that it is what one does but you can talk until you are blue in the face and say to people over and over again, "I write because I am a writer and I do not wish to examine the reasons why or how because that would lead to an enormous amount of self-consciousness." And people will frown and they will mutter because they are disappointed. They seem to want—a very strange thing—do you have any idea what it is they want?

Interviewer: I think they want to know what makes a creative person.

Albee: The thing that makes a creative person is to be creative and that is all that there is to it. And they must not concern themselves with how or why. I know for example of two playwrights who had never thought about why they wrote and a number of their well-wishing friends said, for a variety of reasons, that they should go into analysis. Well, they went into analysis and they found out why they wrote and in both cases it took them two years before they could get back to writing. They became terribly well-adjusted people but they weren't writers any more. I am suggesting that people write only through social maladjustment. They are not adjusted to society as it is. That is the only reason that people write—the predominant reason that people write. And if you ask them why or how, you are going to tamper with something very rare and very private, you're going to start these writers asking the questions of themselves and when they start asking the questions of themselves they will start thinking of themselves in the third person and they will eventually go quietly and finally insane.

Interviewer: You've criticized the writers of the thirties for being somewhat dated in their sort of "social message" outcry, and you and most of the other contemporary writers don't seem to offer a way out of our contemporary dilemma.

Albee: I never criticized the American playwrights of the thirties for being dated. I don't like most of them, which includes the thirties work of Clifford Odets and all the people who were called Clifford Odets during the thirties, because they were aggressively socially conscious and propaganda took over from art. It may be as simple as this: that in the thirties, with all the crypto-Communists we had in this country, the intellectual Left, the innocent Left is probably the best way to describe it, was enormously popular. The majority of the innocent Left came to its senses after the purge trials of 1935 and 1936 but during that period the whole Popular Front movement of art in the United States substituted propaganda for art. That's why naturally the works by basic political innocents, if nothing else, were bound to date, once political sophistication occurred. But there are larger things involved here, I think. Maybe there were easier answers in the thirties than there are now in the sixties, even indeed than there were in the fifties. I suspect that there were easier answers. We were gullible, naive, and we also did not have at that point potential for destroying ourselves quite so efficiently as we have now. The existentialist and post-existentialist revaluation of the nature of reality and what everything is about in man's position to it came shortly after the Second World War. I don't think that it is an accident that it gained the importance in writers' minds that it has now as a result of the bomb at Hiroshima. We developed the possibility of destroying ourselves totally and completely in a second. The ideals, the totems, the panaceas don't work much anymore and the whole concept of absurdity is a great deal less absurd now than it was before about 1945, for example.

Interviewer: What I meant is that you and other people are writing about the absurdity of modern contemporary life and about the somewhat meaningless so-called dilemmas of our present society and about the artificial values that we have accepted and yet you don't show us any utopian way out. What is the way out?

Albee: I have absolutely no idea if there is a way out or not.

Interviewer: Have you found a way out?

Albee: Me, personally? For me?

Interviewer: Yes.

Albee: I'm getting through it in a way that makes sense for me. I'm not sure that it's the responsibility of a writer to give answers, especially to questions that have no answers. The responsibility of the writer is to be a sort of demonic social critic—to present the world and people in it as he sees it and say, "Do you like it? If you don't like it change it." Too many people go to the theater wanting to be taken out of themselves, to be given an unreal experience. The theater must always be entertaining, but I think that *Oedipus* is entertaining. I don't think that it is the responsibility of the playwright

to present a dilemma and then give its solution, because if he does
that, and he is at all concerned with how things are and how people
are now, almost inevitably he is going to present a slightly less
puissant dilemma. Because you have to do that to be able to give
an answer to it.

Playwright at Work: Edward Albee

Walter Wager/1964

From *Playbill*, 1 no. 5 (May 1964), 11-13. Reprinted from PLAY-
BILL magazine. PLAYBILL® is a registered trademark of Playbill
Incorporated, N.Y.C. All rights reserved. Used by permission.

Edward Albee, a lean taciturn bachelor of 34, is one of today's most
respected and controversial playwrights. A few months ago, he
visited four Iron Curtain countries (with John Steinbeck) at the
request of the U.S. Department of State as part of the cultural
exchange program. His reactions to the theatre in Russia and his
own plans are set forth below in a recent interview with Walter
Wager, Editor of PLAYBILL.

Playbill: How long did you spend on this cultural exchange
mission?

Albee: A month in Russia, and then a week each in Poland,
Hungary and Czechoslovakia. I saw more than 30 different
productions in the Soviet Union alone.

Playbill: Were these Russian plays?

Albee: Mostly, although they do some works by foreign writers. I
had a look at Bill Gibson's *Two For the Seesaw*, and I saw the finest
production of Brecht's *Arturo Ui* of my life in Leningrad. They will
be doing more American plays—*selected ones*.

Playbill: How good were the productions that you saw in the
Soviet Union?

Albee: The general level of production in Moscow and
Leningrad—and in Warsaw—is *very* high. Almost all theatre in
Russia operates on the repertory system, which gives the advantage
of actors working together on a sustained basis. This generates an
integration of performance we don't get on Broadway. Even a
routine or mediocre play gets a good production.

Playbill: Are there many "routine" dramas on the boards?

Albee: Well, I'd say that there is a genuine question as to
whether most of the new plays in the Soviet Union are as good—in
writing and conception—as they might be.

Playbill: To what would you attribute this?

Albee: With no disrespect to my recent hosts—who certainly take the theatre seriously as a government and as a nation—I'd say that I believe the whole concept of "socialist realism" doesn't allow for much experimentation. There is a sad lack of avant-garde plays. These are rarely done.

Playbill: Does this mean your own works are unknown there?

Albee: People employed in the Soviet theatre and students are familiar with Tennessee Williams, Arthur Miller and Gibson, but they have little or no contact with my plays or those of other writers such as Pinter, Beckett, Ghelderode, Genet and the rest. My plays have not been "officially" translated in Russia.

Playbill: What about "unofficial" or boot-leg translations?

Albee: Some drama and university teachers have read my plays somehow, which might be the reason that their students are not exposed to them. In general, it appears that there is little awareness of the entire off Broadway theatre in Russia.

Playbill: What can you report on Soviet actors?

Albee: The acting level is excellent, often extraordinary. Theatre groups are subsidized in general, and many actors get a full subsidy. Playwrights attached to theatres also receive government stipends, which are linked to the acceptability, volume and success of what they write.

Playbill: What about the theatres themselves?

Albee: There are forty or fifty legitimate houses in Moscow alone. Some are very well equipped, while others are not quite as well equipped as Broadway theatres. There is never an empty seat in Moscow or Leningrad.

Playbill: Why is that?

Albee: As I suggested, the Russians take theatre seriously. This applies to all levels of the urban population, not just the elite. They literally *believe* the plays. They don't go to the theatre for escapist entertainment, as many Western audiences do. That may be one reason why the Soviet government can utilize the theatre for propaganda when it desires.

Playbill: What do tickets cost?

Albee: They seem to range between fifty cents and three dollars.

Playbill: I assume that makes the theatre more accessible to students and others with limited incomes. Did you talk to any Soviet college students?

Albee: Yes, through officially-supplied translators. I also retained some Russian from a U.S. Army language course that I took in the service. The students were intelligent, but tended to talk in stock phrases and dialectics. They asked questions such as "Don't you agree that the playwright must be the servant of The People?"

Playbill: What did you reply?

Albee: I told them that they were probably correct, but that The People must also be the servant of The Playwright. Frankly, I found the professional theatre people more stimulating.

Playbill: Did you speak with Soviet dramatists?

Albee: Yes, with three of the younger playwrights. They were courteous and knowledgeable, but seemed a bit careful. They kept away from politics—perhaps out of politeness—and we talked theatre "shop," as I also did with actors and directors.

Playbill: Had *you* been briefed by the U.S. government on avoiding controversy?

Albee: Not quite. Ed Murrow, then head of the U.S. Information Agency, spoke to Steinbeck and me before we left. He told us to criticize our country or anything else. "Say what you please. Raise Hell!," he advised.

Playbill: Did you raise any Hell?

Albee: A little. We spoke out freely all the way, and when our hosts in Leningrad asked us to toast the Berlin Wall we flatly refused. That generated a few sparks. We were not looking for conflict, of course, but we found some as might have been expected.

Playbill: Will you return to the Soviet Union?

Albee: I certainly hope to. The hospitality was generous, but next time I'll go as a private citizen at my own expense. Russia, the Russian people and their theatre are extremely interesting.

Playbill: The State Department is now exporting ice reviews under the cultural exchange program, but no American drama groups. Does this make sense to you?

Albee: No. None at all

Playbill: I hear that you're working on a new play since you've returned. How do you work?

Albee: I usually discover—yes, *discover*—that I have gotten an idea. I toss it around privately—in my mind—for anywhere between six and eighteen months. When I am ready and it is ready, I go to my typewriter and work steadily. That's four hours a day, five or six days a week. Perhaps in my place in Manhattan, or in my house on Long Island. Then I pencil in corrections and retype.

Playbill: How long is this process?

Albee: I've written the short plays in about three weeks each, and *Virginia Woolf* took seven.

Playbill: I've noticed dramatists hate to talk about works in progress—but what can you tell about your current project?

Albee: I'd rather not go into it. Well . . . it's called *The Substitute Speaker*. Two acts, about an hour in length in all, seven characters. The toughest one on which I've ever worked.

Playbill: What is the difficulty?

Albee: It's tough to write because I'm trying to join naturalism and considerable stylization. It is basically naturalistic—but with hallucinatory elements.

Playbill: Where is it set?

Albee: Contemporary America. A suburban living-room. I hope to finish in June.

Playbill: Do you rewrite much?

Albee: Very little. I cut a bit. I only took nine pages out of *Virginia Woolf*.

Playbill: There are frequent articles about the ills of the American stage. Would you comment?

Albee: Everybody talks about the alleged illness, but there is more experimental theatre all over the United States every day. I believe that this is healthy. I'm disturbed by lazy audiences that only want to be assured that their lives and values are valid. For me, the theatre must be educating and *upsetting* as well as just plain entertaining. It is especially important to reach young people, and I'm pleased that young America knows me.

Playbill: Finally, what about future developments?

Albee: The only real danger now that culture is "in" is that so-called serious theatre may become fashionable and settle for middle-brow works. If this happens, it may not hit as high as it could or should. That is the threat.

Albee Asks and Albee Answers

R. H. Gardner/1964

From *The Baltimore Sun*, 24 October 1964, sec. D, 16. Reprinted by permission.

Edward Albee's much-discussed-and-awarded play *Who's Afraid of Virginia Woolf?* will be presented for four days at the Stanton Theater, beginning November 15.

The cast will consist of Vicki Cummings and Kendall Clark, in the roles of the older couple, and Bryarly Lee and Donald Briscoe, as the younger one. Evening performances will start at 8 and the Wednesday matinee at 2 P.M.

The show, which last season toured much of the East including neighboring Washington, has been largely responsible for the overnight conversion of its young author into an international celebrity—with interesting side effects, as evidenced by an article written by Albee himself and passed on to me by a press agent. The article reads as follows:

I have been invited to write a piece on "How *Who's Afraid of Virginia Woolf?* has changed my life." The subject, as put, is in a faintly silly but sweet way rather like that of a child's theme, and I suspect that it is for this reason that I don't mind doing it.

At the same time, it is not my habit to write about myself often—in my infrequent non-fiction, at any rate—so I shall have to approach it in the manner I am most usually accosted—in the form of an interview. I shall consider myself in the third person, and ask myself the question. Albee on Albee.

Q: In what way are you, or is your life, different now that you have written *Who's Afraid of Virginia Woolf?*

A: I do know what you mean. I was just hoping that if I played it cool you'd go on to another question.

Q: Why?

A: Because people should be more interested in a writer's work than in the person of the writer. Writers, in other words, should be heard and not seen. It is dangerous for a writer to become a public personality. I can think of one American novelist, recently dead, who became so convinced that he was, in fact, the public image of himself that it did serious damage to his work. And the better the writer, of course, the more interesting the work in comparison to himself.

Meaning Of Play

Q: All right, tell me about *Who's Afraid of Virginia Woolf?* What did you mean when you wrote the play?

A: That's a stupid question. If I could tell you what I meant by the play in any fashion other than reading you the play from beginning to end then I should have written the play in a different fashion.

Q: I see . . .

A: What I mean, really, is this: It's dangerous, too, for a writer to dwell too much on "what he meant," on the implications of what he has written. There's little enough spontaneity as it is, and if the writer doesn't dredge up pretty exclusively from his unconscious without super imposing anything more than formal control and intuitive reasoning, he's more likely to write a tract than a play, say. When a writer says that he gives his characters their heads and that he doesn't know exactly what they're going to say, he means that he is relying on both levels of his mind. What a writer "means" by a play he writes is the total experience of the play on an audience, or, to put it more accurately, on the first audience—the audience of himself. And, too, it's curious: I find for myself that maybe six months after I've completed a play I can no longer recall either the experience of writing the play or the motivations for writing it.

Q: An exorcism of devils?

A: You say it, I don't.

Things Change

Q: Surely, though, having *Who's Afraid of Virginia Woolf?* a big hit on Broadway must have altered the patterns of your life.

A: Well, of course, some things have changed. I'm, busier. I have less privacy. I'm solvent. I travel a great deal more. I meet more people. But there are more interesting things that I've discovered about having a success on Broadway.

I've discovered, for example, and to my sadness, that people just don't take the off-Broadway theater as seriously as its importance deserves. When my first three plays—*The Zoo Story, The American Dream, The Death of Bessie Smith*—were done in New York, off-Broadway (each running over a year), while the critics were generous in their comments and the audiences enthusiastic, it was not until *Who's Afraid of Virginia Woolf?* appeared on Broadway that I was admitted into the fraternity. In this regard I find it most depressing when people come up to me now and say, "I saw the play, and I loved it (or, hated it)." On these occasions it is my snippy habit to answer, "Which play?" A brief look of puzzlement crosses these people's faces, and then they reply to me, as if I were mad, "Why, *Who's Afraid of Virginia Woolf?* of course." It is the "of course" that gets me down. Off-Broadway does many more good plays than Broadway any season and is, in my pure aestheic sense, much more "big time."

The Art of the Theatre IV:
Edward Albee: An Interview

William Flanagan/1966

From *Paris Review*, 10 (Fall 1966), 93–121. Interview with Edward Albee reprinted in *Writers at Work: The Paris Review Interviews, Third Series*, ed. George Plimpton. © 1967 by The Paris Review, Inc. Reprinted by permission of Viking Penguin Inc.

The interview happened on a scalding, soggy-aired Fourth of July in a sunny room in Albee's small, attractive country house in Montauk, Long Island. Keeping in mind his luxuriously appointed house in New York City's Greenwich Village, one finds the country place dramatically modest by comparison. With the exception of a handsome, newly built tennis court (in which the playwright takes a disarmingly childlike pleasure and pride) and an incongruously grand Henry Moore sculpture situated high on a landscaped terrace that commands a startling view of the sea, the simplicity of the place leaves one with the curious impression that the news of the personal wealth his work has brought him has not quite reached the playwright-in-residence at Montauk. Still, it is in his country house that he generally seems most at ease, natural, at home.

Albee was dressed with a mildly ungroomed informality. He was as yet unshaven for the day and his neo-Edwardian haircut was damply askew. He appeared, as the climate of the afternoon demanded, somewhat uncomfortable.

The interviewer and subject have been both friends and composer-writer collaborators for about eighteen years. But Albee's barbed, poised, and elegantly guarded public press style took over after the phrasing of the first question—though perhaps it was intermittently penetrated during the course of the talk.

Interviewer: One of your most recent plays was an adaptation of James Purdy's novel *Malcolm*. It had as close to one hundred per cent bad notices as a play could get. The resultant commercial catastrophe and quick closing of the play apart, how does this affect your own feeling about the piece itself?

Albee: I see you're starting with the hits. Well, I retain for all my plays, I suppose, a certain amount of enthusiasm. I don't feel intimidated by either the unanimously bad press that *Malcolm* got or the unanimously good press that some of the other plays have received. I haven't changed my feeling about *Malcolm*. I liked doing the adaptation of Purdy's book. I had a number of quarrels with the production, but then I usually end up with quarrels about all of my plays. With the possible exception of the little play *The Sandbox*, which takes thirteen minutes to perform, I don't think anything I've done has worked out to perfection.

Interviewer: While it doesn't necessarily change your feeling, does the unanimously bad critical response open questions in your mind?

Albee: I imagine that if we had a college of criticism in this country whose opinions more closely approximated the value of the works of art inspected, it might; but as often as not, I find relatively little relationship between the work of art and the immediate critical response it gets. Every writer's got to pay some attention, I suppose, to what his critics say because theirs is a reflection of what the audience feels about his work. And a playwright, especially a playwright whose work deals very directly with an audience, perhaps he should pay some attention to the nature of the audience response—not necessarily to learn anything about his craft, but as often as not merely to find out about the temper of the time, what is being tolerated, what is being permitted.

Interviewer: Regarding adaptations in general, can you think of any by American playwrights that you admire at all?

Albee: No, I can't think of any that I admire. I've done adaptations for two reasons; first, to examine the entire problem of adaptation—to see what it felt like; and second, because I admired those two books—*The Ballad of the Sad Café* and *Malcolm*— very much and thought they belonged on the stage; I wanted to see them on the stage, and felt more confident, perhaps incorrectly, in my own ability to put them on the stage than in most adapters'.

Interviewer: One of the local reviewers, after *Malcolm* came out, referred to it as Edward Albee's "play of the year," rather as if to suggest that this is a conscious goal you've set for yourself, to have a play ready every year.

Albee: Do you remember the Thurber cartoon of the man looking at his police dog and saying, "If you're a police dog, where's your badge?" It's the function of a playwright to write. Some playwrights write a large number of plays, some write a small number. I don't set out to write a play a year. Sometimes I've written two plays a year. There was a period of a year and half when I only wrote half a play. If it depresses some critics that I seem prolific, well, that's their problem as much as mine. There's always the danger that there are so damn many things that a playwright can examine in this society of ours—things that have less to do with his artistic work than have to do with the critical and aesthetic environment— that perhaps he does have to worry about whether or not he is writing too fast. But then also, perhaps he should worry about getting as many plays on as possible before the inevitable ax falls.

Interviewer: What do you mean by the inevitable ax?

Albee: If you examine the history of any playwright of the past twenty-five or thirty years—I'm not talking about the comedy boys, I'm talking about the more serious writers—it seems inevitable that almost every one has been encouraged until the critics feel that they have built them up beyond the point where they can control them; then it's time to knock them down again. And a rather ugly thing starts happening: the playwright finds himself knocked down for works that quite often are just as good or better than the works he's been praised for previously. And a lot of playwrights become confused by this and they start doing imitations of what they've done before, or they try to do something entirely different, in which case they get accused by the same critics of not doing what they *used* to do so well.

Interviewer: So, it's a matter of not being able to win either way.

Albee: Actually, the final evaluation of a play has nothing to do with immediate audience or critical response. The playwright, along with any writer, composer, painter in this society, has got to have a terribly private view of his own value, of his own work. He's got to listen to his own voice primarily. He's got to watch out for fads, for what might be called the critical aesthetics.

Interviewer: Why do you think the reviews were so lacerating against *Malcolm*—a play that might simply have been dismissed as not being very good.

Albee: It seemed to me the critics loathed something. Now whether they loathed something above and beyond the play itself, it's rather dangerous for me to say. I think it's for the critics to decide whether or not their loathing of the play is based on something other than the play's merits or demerits. They must search their own souls, or whatever.

Interviewer: When you say that the play was badly produced—

Albee: I didn't like the way it was directed particularly. It was the one play of mine—of all of them—that got completely out of my hands. I let the director take over and dictate the way things should be done. I did it as an experiment.

Interviewer: What do you mean as an experiment?

Albee: As a playwright, one has to make the experiment finally to see whether there's anything in this notion that a director can contribute creatively, as opposed to interpretively.

Interviewer: Do you believe that a director has any creative vitality of his own?

Albee: Well, that's a very "iffy" question, as President Roosevelt used to say. I imagine as an axiom you could say that the better the play the less "creativity" the director need exert.

Interviewer: Have you ever had the experience of finding out that the director's way was a certain enlightenment?

Albee: I can't answer that honestly, because something very curious happens. In rehearsals I get so completely wrapped up with the reality that's occurring on stage that by the time the play has opened I'm not usually quite as aware of the distinctions between what I'd intended and the result. There are many ways of getting the same result.

Interviewer: Well, you talk about keeping complete control of your plays. Let's say that you'd envisioned in your own mind a certain scene being done a certain way.

Albee: I'm not terribly concerned about which characters are standing on the right-hand side of the stage.

Interviewer: That's not the point I'm trying to make. In the preparation of the early Kazan-Williams successes, Williams was in constant conflict with Kazan, and yet Kazan would come up with the one thing that would finally make the play work.

Albee: Do we know that it was better than Williams's original idea?

Interviewer: According to his own alleged view of it, yes.

Albee: Some writers' view of things depends upon the success of the final result. I'd rather stand or fall on my own concepts. But there is a fine line to be drawn between pointing up something or distorting it. And one has always got to be terribly careful, since the theater is made up of a whole bunch of prima donnas, not to let the distortions occur. I've seen an awful lot of plays that I'd read before they were put into production and been shocked by what's happened to them. In the attempt to make them straight-forward and commercially successful, a lot of things go out the window. I'm just saying that in the theater, which is a sort of jungle, one does have to be a little bit careful. One mustn't be so rigid or egotistical to think that *every* comma is sacrosanct. But at the same time there is the danger of losing control and finding that somebody else has opened a play and not you.

Interviewer: Why did you decide to become a playwright? You wrote poems without notable success, and then suddenly decided to write a play, *The Zoo Story*.

Albee: Well, when I was six years old I decided not that I was *going* to be, but with my usual modesty, that I *was* a writer. So I starting writing poetry when I was six and stopped when I was twenty-six because it was getting a little better, but not terribly much. When I was fifteen I wrote seven hundred pages of an incredibly bad novel—it's a very funny book I still like a lot. Then, when I was nineteen I wrote a couple hundred pages of another novel, which wasn't very good either. I was still determined to be a writer. And since I was a writer, and here I was twenty-nine years old and I wasn't a very good poet and I wasn't a very good novelist, I thought I would try writing a play, which seems to have worked out a little better.

Interviewer: With regard to *Zoo Story*—was its skill and power and subsequent success a surprise and revelation to you?

Albee: A lot interests me—but nothing surprises me particularly. Not that I took it for granted that it was going to be skillful and

powerful. I'm not making any judgment about the excellence or lack
of it in the play. But it did not come as a *surprise* to me that I'd
written it. You must remember I've been watching and listening to a
great number of people for a long time. Absorbing things I suppose.
My only reaction was, "Aha! So this is the way it's going to be, is
it?" That was my reaction.

Interviewer: The biggest news about you at the moment, I
expect, would be the success of the film *Virginia Woolf.* The
Production Code approval came hard, but apparently you approved
of it yourself.

Albee: When the play was sold to the movies I was rather
apprehensive of what would happen. I assumed they would put
Doris Day in it, and maybe Rock Hudson. And I was even a little
apprehensive about the actual casting. Especially Elizabeth Taylor. I
wasn't apprehensive about the idea of Richard Burton being in the
film, but it did seem to be a little odd that Elizabeth Taylor, who is
in her early thirties, would be playing a fifty-two-year-old woman.

Interviewer: At one time you were apprehensive about Mike
Nichols, the director.

Albee: I was curious as to why they chose a man who'd never
made a film before and had made his reputation directing farces on
Broadway, why they chose *him* as a director to turn a serious play
into a movie. I think I learned the answer: being innocent to the
medium he doesn't know how to make the usual mistakes. I had a
number of other reasons for apprehension. One always knows what
is done to a script when it goes to Hollywood. When I saw the film
in Hollywood about two or three months before it was released, I
was startled and enormously taken with the picture, partially
through relief I imagine. But more than that, I discovered that no
screenplay had been written, that the play was there almost word for
word. A few cuts here and there. A few oversimplifications.

Interviewer: Oversimplifications?

Albee: Yes, I'll go into those in a minute. Ernest Lehman, who is
credited with the screenplay, did write about twenty-five words. I
thought they were absolutely terrible. So really there wasn't a
screenplay, and that delighted me. It was a third of the battle, as far
as I was concerned. So that was my first delight—that the play was
photographed action for action. The camera didn't stay thirty-five

feet from the actors and it wasn't done in one set, it moved around a good deal. It behaves and acts very much like a film. In fact, it *is* a film. There are some shots, close-ups, lots of things you can't do on the stage. Then my second delight, after finding that the play was intact, was to appreciate that the director, Mike Nichols, understood not only the play, my intentions (pretty much, again with a couple of oversimplifications), but also seemed to understand the use of the camera and the film medium, all this in his first time around. Third, I was happy that Elizabeth Taylor was quite capable of casting off the beautiful-young-woman image and doing something much more than she usually does in films. And the rest of the cast was more or less fine too, Dennis and Segal. I have a few quarrels with their interpretations, but they're so minor compared to what could have happened. I found that it made an awfully good picture.

Interviewer: The play as a film seems to be generally better understood by film reviewers than it was by drama critics. Is it possible that these oversimplifications you're talking about, that you blame Mike Nichols for, or somebody, are responsible for the fact that the play comes over more clearly?

Albee: I suppose if you simplify things, it's going to make it easier to understand. But without placing blame, I'd say there *was* an oversimplification, which I regret to a certain extent. For example, whenever something occurs in the play on both an emotional and intellectual level, I find in the film that only the emotional aspect shows through. The intellectual underpinning isn't as clear. In the film I found that in the love-hate games that George and Martha play, their intellectual enjoyment of each other's prowess doesn't show through anywhere nearly as strongly as it did in the play. Quite often, and I suppose in most of my plays, people are doing things on two or three levels at the same time. From time to time in the movie of *Who's Afraid of Virginia Woolf?* I found that a level or two had vanished. At the end of the film, for example, with the revelation about the nonexistent child and its destruction, the intellectual importance of the fiction isn't made quite as clearly as it could be. In the film it's nowhere near as important as the *emotional* importance to the characters. In my view, the two of them have got to go hand in hand. But this is quibbling, you see.

It's a really very good film. There are a few things that I wish hadn't
happened—that enormous error in accepting somebody's stupid
idea of taking the action away from the house to the roadhouse.
That's the open area of the film where somebody decided to
broaden it out for film terms. Yet it was the one part of the film,
curiously enough, that all the film critics thought was the most
stagey.

Interviewer: Incidentally, when did the title *Who's Afraid of
Virginia Woolf?* occur to you?

Albee: There was a saloon—it's changed its name now—on
Tenth Street, between Greenwich Avenue and Waverly Place, that
was called something at one time, now called something else, and
they had a big mirror on the downstairs bar in this saloon where
people used to scrawl graffiti. At one point back in about 1953 . . .
1954 I think it was—long before any of us started doing much of
anything—I was in there having a beer one night, and I saw *Who's
Afraid of Virginia Woolf?* scrawled in soap, I suppose, on this
mirror. When I started to write the play it cropped up in my mind
again. And of course, who's afraid of Virginia Woolf means who's
afraid of the *big bad* wolf . . . who's afraid of living life without false
illusions. And it did strike me as being a rather typical university,
intellectual joke.

Interviewer: With the filming of *Who's Afraid of Virginia Woolf?*
the oft-repeated evaluation of it as a play about four homosexuals
recurs. I cannot recall any public statement or comment being made
by you on this interpretation of the play.

Albee: Indeed it is true that a number of the movie critics of
Who's Afraid of Virginia Woolf? have repeated the speculation that
the play was written about four homosexuals disguised as
heterosexual men and women. This comment first appeared around
the time the play was produced. I was fascinated by it. I suppose
what disturbed me about it was twofold: first, nobody has *ever*
bothered to ask *me* whether it was true; second, the critics and
columnists made no attempt to document the assertion from the text
of the play. The facts are simple: *Who's Afraid of Virginia Woolf?*
was written about two heterosexual couples. If I had wanted to write
a play about four homosexuals, I would have done so.
Parenthetically, it is interesting that when the film critic of *Newsweek*

stated that he understood the play to have been written about four homosexuals, I had a letter written to him suggesting he check his information before printing such speculations. He replied, saying, in effect, two things: first, that we all know that a critic is a far better judge of an author's intention than the author; second, that seeing the play as being about four homosexuals was the only way that he could live with the play, meaning that he could not accept it as a valid examination of heterosexual life. Well, I'm sure that all the actresses from Uta Hagen to Elizabeth Taylor who've played the role of Martha would be absolutely astonished to learn they've been playing men. I think it is the responsibility of critics to rely less strenuously on, to use a Hollywood phrase, "what they can live with," and more on an examination of the works of art from an aesthetic and clinical point of view. I would be fascinated to read an intelligent paper documenting from the text that *Who's Afraid of Virginia Woolf?* is a play written about four homosexuals. It might instruct me about the deep slag pits of my subconscious.

I believe it was Leslie Fiedler, in an article in *Partisan Review*, who commented that if indeed *Who's Afraid of Virginia Woolf?* did deal with four disguised homosexuals, the "shock of recognition" on the part of the public is an enormously interesting commentary on the public. To put it most briefly, *Who's Afraid of Virginia Woolf?* was *not* written about four homosexuals. One might make one more point: had it been a play about four homosexuals disguised as heterosexuals, the only valid standard of criticism which could be employed would be whether such license of composite characterization was destructive to the validity of the work of art. Again we come to the question of the critics' responsibility to discuss the work of art not on arbitrary Freudian terms but on aesthetic ones. Only the most callow or insecure or downright stupid critic would fault Proust's work, for example, for the transposition that he made of characters' sexes. It would be rather like faulting Michelangelo's sculptures of the male figure because of that artist's reputed leanings. So, if a play should appear, next year, say, which the critics in their wisdom see as a disguised homosexual piece, let them remember that the ultimate judgment of a work of art, whether it be a masterpiece or a lesser event, must be solely in terms of its artistic success and not on Freudian guesswork.

Interviewer: It's been said by certain critics that your plays generally contain no theme; others say that you've begun to wear the same theme thin; and still others say that with each play you bravely attack a new theme.

Albee: I go up to my room about three or four months out of the year and I write. I don't pay much attention to how the plays relate thematically to each other. I think that's very dangerous to do, because in the theater one is self-conscious enough without planning ahead or wondering about the thematic relation from one play to the next. One hopes that one is developing, and writing interestingly, and that's where it should end, I think.

Interviewer: You've spoken frequently to the effect that your involvement with music has influenced your writing for the theater. Can you elaborate on that in any way?

Albee: I find it very difficult. I've been involved in one way or another with serious music ever since childhood. And I do think or rather I *sense* that there is a relationship—at least in my own work—between a dramatic structure, the form and sound and shape of a play, and the equivalent structure in music. Both deal with sound, of course, and also with idea, theme. I find that when my plays are going well, they seem to resemble pieces of music. But if I had to go into specifics about it, I wouldn't be able to. It's merely something that I feel

Interviewer: Which contemporary playwrights do you particularly admire? Which do you think have influenced you especially, and in what ways?

Albee: The one living playwright I admire without any reservation whatsoever is Samuel Beckett. I have funny feelings about almost all the others. There are a number of contemporary playwrights whom I admire enormously, but that's not at all the same thing as being influenced. I admire Brecht's work very much. I admire a good deal of Tennessee Williams. I admire some of Genet's works. Harold Pinter's work. I admire Cordell's plays very much, even though I don't think they're very good. But on the matter of influence, that question is difficult. I've read and seen hundreds of plays, starting with Sophocles right up to the present day. As a playwright, I imagine that in one fashion or another I've

been influenced by every single play I've ever experienced.
Influence is a matter of selection—both acceptance and rejection.

Interviewer: In a number of articles, mention is made of the
influence on you—either directly or by osmosis—of the theater of
cruelty. How do you feel about the theater of cuelty, or the theories
of Artaud generally?

Albee: Let me answer it this way. About four years ago I made a
list, for my own amusement, of the playwrights, the contemporary
playwrights, by whom critics said I'd been influenced. I listed
twenty-five. It included five playwrights whose work I didn't know,
so I read these five playwrights and indeed now I suppose I can say
I have been influenced by them. The problem is that the people
who write these articles find the inevitable similarities of people
writing in the same generation, in the same century, and on the
same planet, and they put them together in a group.

Interviewer: The point was that the influence may not have
been directly through Artaud, but perhaps, as I said, by osmosis.

Albee: I've been influenced by Sophocles and Noel Coward.

Interviewer: Do you aspire to being more than a playwright . . .
to being a sort of complete man of the theater? You've involved
yourself in the production of plays by other writers; you've toyed
with the idea of doing a musical; you've written a libretto for opera;
you've been an articulate interpreter of the American theater as an
institution; and even a public critic of professional drama critics. In
retrospect, do you feel that you may have overextended yourself in
any of these areas?

Albee: I've certainly done myself considerable damage, though
not as an artist, by attacking the critics, because they can't take it.
As for involving myself with the production of other people's plays, I
consider that to be a responsibility. The playwrights' unit we've been
running, Playwrights 66, encourages thirty or thirty-five writers. The
plays we've put on in the off-Broadway theater, the Cherry Lane,
and other places, are primarily plays that I wanted to see: other
people weren't putting them on, so we did. It seems to me that if
one finds oneself with the cash it's one's responsibility to do a thing
like that. There's certainly no self-aggrandizement. I have done
adaptations because I wanted to. I don't like the climate in which

writers have to work in this country and I think it's my responsibility to talk about it.

Interviewer: Do you feel that in your own particular case, on the basis of a single big-time commercial hit, you have been raised to too high a position? For your own creative comfort.

Albee: I really can't answer that. I have no idea. As a fairly objective judgment, I do think that my plays as they come out are better than most other things that are put on the same year. But that doesn't make them very good necessarily. The act of creation, as you very well know, is a lonely and private matter and has nothing to do with the public area . . . the *performance* of the work one creates. Each time I sit down and write a play I try to dismiss from my mind as much as I possibly can the implications of what I've done before, what I'm going to do, what other people think about my work, the failure or success of the previous play. I'm stuck with a new reality that I've got to create. I'm working on a new play now. I don't believe that I'm being affected by the commercial success of *Who's Afraid of Virginia Woolf?* to make this one more commercial; I don't think I'm being affected by the critical confusion over *Tiny Alice* to make this one simpler. It's a play. I'm trying to make it as good a work of art as I possibly can.

Interviewer: To talk a little about *Tiny Alice*, which I guess is your most controversial play—during your widely publicized press conference on the stage of the Billy Rose Theater, you said the critical publicity had misled the audiences into thinking of the play as a new game of symbol-hunting . . . which was at least to some degree responsible for the play's limited run. Still, you have also said that if audiences desert a play, it is either the fault of the playwright or the manner in which it was presented. With a year to reflect on the matter, how do you feel about all this now as it pertains to *Tiny Alice?*

Albee: I feel pretty much what I said on the stage. I keep remembering that the preview audiences, before the critics went to *Tiny Alice*, didn't have anywhere near the amount of trouble understanding what the play was about; that didn't happen until the critics *told* them that it was too difficult to understand. I also feel that *Tiny Alice* would have been a great deal clearer if I hadn't had to make the cuts I did in the third act.

Interviewer: In view of the experience you had with *Tiny Alice*, the critical brouhaha and the different interpretations and the rest of it, if you were to sit down and write that play again, do you think it would emerge in any terribly different way?

Albee: It's impossible to tell. A curious thing happens. Within a year after I write a play I forget the experience of having written it. And I couldn't revise or rewrite it if I wanted to. Up until that point, I'm so involved with the experience of having written the play, and the nature of it, that I can't see what faults it might have. The only moment of clear objectivity that I can find is at the moment of critical heat—of self-critical heat when I'm actually writing. Sometimes I think the experience of a play is finished for me when I finish writing it. If it weren't for the need to make a living, I don't know whether I'd have the plays produced. In the two or three or four months that it takes me to write a play, I find that the reality of the play is a great deal more alive for me than what passes for reality. I'm infinitely more involved in the reality of the characters and their situation than I am in everyday life.

The involvement is terribly intense. I find that in the course of the day when I'm writing, after three or four hours of intense work, I have a splitting headache, and I have to stop. Because the involvement, which is both creative and self-critical, is so intense that I've got to stop doing it.

Interviewer: If one can talk at all about a general reaction to your plays, it is that, as convincing and brilliant as their beginnings and middles might be, the plays tend to let down, change course or simply puzzle at the end. To one degree or another this complaint has been registered against most of them.

Albee: Perhaps because my sense of reality and logic is different from most people's. The answer could be as simple as that. Somethings that make sense to me don't make the same degree of sense to other people. Analytically, there might be other reasons—that the plays don't hold together intellectually; that's possible. But then it mustn't be forgotten that when people don't like the way a play ends, they're likely to blame the play. That's a possibility too. For example, I don't feel that catharsis in a play necessarily takes place during the course of a play. Often it should take place afterward. If I've been accused a number of times of writing plays where the endings are ambivalent, indeed, that's the way I find life.

Interviewer: Do *The Zoo Story* and *Virginia Woolf* both begin and continue through the longest part of their length on an essentially naturalistic course, and then somewhere toward the end of the play veer away from the precisely naturalistic tone?

Albee: I think that if people were a little more aware of what actually is beneath the naturalistic overlay they would be surprised to find how early the unnaturalistic base had been set. When you're dealing with a symbol in a realistic play, it is also a realistic fact. You must expect the audience's mind to work on both levels, symbolically and realistically. But we're trained so much in pure, realistic theater that it's difficult for us to handle things on two levels at the same time.

Interviewer: Why did you pick the names George and Martha? As in Washington? What did you make of Arthur Schlesinger's discovery that with those names you'd obviously written a parallel of the American sociopolitical dilemma?

Albee: There are little local and private jokes. Indeed, I did name the two lead characters of *Virginia Woolf* George and Martha because there is contained in the play—not its most important point, but certainly contained within the play—an attempt to examine the success or failure of American revolutionary principles. Some people who are historically and politically and sociologically inclined find them. Now in one play—*Virginia Woolf* again—I named a very old Western Union man "Little Billy"—"Crazy Billy" rather. And I did that because as *you* might recall, Mr. Flanagan, you used to deliver telegrams for Western Union, and you are very old and your name is Billy. Things like that—lots of them going on in the plays. In *Zoo Story*, I named two charactrers Peter and Jerry. I know two people named Peter and Jerry. But then the learned papers started coming in, and of course Jerry is supposed to be Jesus . . . which is much more interesting, I suppose, to the public than the truth.

Interviewer: Going back to those "levels of understanding," in *Virginia Woolf* the audience questioned the credibility of George and Martha having invented for themselves an imaginary son.

Albee: Indeed. And it always struck me as very odd that an audience would be unwilling to believe that a highly educated, sensitive, and intelligent couple, who were terribly good at playing reality and fantasy games, *wouldn't* have the education, the sensitivity, and the intelligence to create a realistic symbol for themselves. To use as they saw fit.

Interviewer: Recognizing the fact that it was a symbol?

Albee: *Indeed* recognizing the fact that it was a symbol. And only occasionally being confused, when the awful loss and lack that made the creation of the symbol essential becomes overwhelming— like when they're drunk, for example. Or when they're terribly tired.

Interviewer: What you're saying is something which I guess is not really too commonly understood. You're suggesting that George and Martha have at no point deluded themselves about the fact that they're playing a game.

Albee: Oh, never. Except that it's the most serious game in the world. And the nonexistent son is a symbol and a weapon they use in every one of their arguments.

Interviewer: A symbolic weapon rather than a real weapon. In the midst of the very real weapons that they do use.

Albee: Indeed, yes. Though they're much too intelligent to make that confusion. For me, that's why the loss is doubly poignant. Because they are not deluded people.

Interviewer: I see. Then what you're trying to suggest now is that the last act of *Virginia Woolf* is in no way less naturalistic than the first two acts.

Albee: I don't find that the play veers off into a less naturalistic manner at all.

Interviewer: Well, if not into a less naturalistic one, certainly into a more ritualistic, stylized one. With the Requiem Masses and all that.

Albee: Well, going into Latin, indeed. But that's a conscious choice of George's to read the Requiem Mass which has existed in Latin for quite a number of years. I like the sound of the two languages working together. I like the counterpoint of the Latin and the English working together.

There's one point that you've brought up that annoys me. It really annoys the hell out of me. Some critics accuse me of having a failure of intellect in the third act of *Who's Afraid of Virginia Woolf?*, merely because *they* didn't have the ability to understand what was happening. And that annoys the hell out of me.

Interviewer: I can see that it would. A critic recently wrote the following paragraph: "Mr. Albee complained with *Tiny Alice* that people asked questions and would not let the play merely occur to them. He complains of those critics who judge a play's matter and do not restrict themselves to its manner. Both of these statements tend to a view much in vogue—that art consists principally of style, an encounter between us and the figurative surface of the work. This view reduces ideas to decoration, character to pageant, symbol and feeling to a conveyor belt for effects. It is to shrink art to no more than a sensual response, one kind or another of happening. To some of us this modish view is nihilistic, not progressive." Now the critic in question has come fairly close to defining a theory that might be got out of, say, Susan Sontag's *Against Interpretation* or her essay on style. I wonder how closely the critic's interpretations of your remarks—of the remarks, I guess, that you made most specifically at the *Tiny Alice* press conference—are true to your own understanding of them.

Albee: Well, this critic is a sophist. What he's done is to misinterpret my attitudes, Miss Sontag's attitudes, and the attitudes of most respectable creative people. What I said is that I thought it was not valid for a critic to criticize a play for its matter rather than its manner—that what was constituted then was a type of censorship. To give an extreme example, I was suggesting that if a man writes a brilliant enough play in praise of something that is universally loathed, that the play, if it is good and well enough written, should not be knocked down because of its approach to its subject. If the work of art is good enough, it must not be criticized for its theme. I don't think it can be argued. In the thirties a whole school of criticism bogged down intellectually in those agitprop, social-realistic days. A play had to be progressive. A number of plays by playwrights who were thought very highly of then—they were very bad playwrights—were highly praised because their themes were intellectually and politically proper. This intellectual morass is very dangerous, it seems to me. A form of censorship. You may dislike the intention enormously but your judgment of the artistic merit of the work must not be based on your view of what it's about. The work of art must be judged by how well it succeeds in its intention.

Interviewer: In other words, what you're saying is that a critic should separate what he takes to be the thematic substance of a play from the success or lack of success that the author brings to its presentation.

Albee: It's that simple. And critics who do otherwise are damn fools and dangerous, even destructive people. I don't think it can be argued.

Interviewer: You have said that it is through the actual process of writing that you eventually come to know the theme of your play. Sometimes you've admitted that even when you have finished a play you don't have any specific idea about its theme. What about that?

Albee: Naturally, no writer who's any good at all would sit down and put a sheet of paper in a typewriter and start typing a play unless he knew what he was writing about. But at the same time, writing has got to be an act of discovery. Finding out things about what one is writing about. To a certain extent I imagine a play is completely finished in my mind—in my case, at any rate—without my knowing it, before I sit down to write. So in that sense, I suppose, writing a play is *finding out* what the play is. I always find that the better answer to give. It's a question I despise, and it always seems to me better to slough off the answer to a question which I consider to be a terrible invasion of privacy—the kind of privacy that a writer must keep for himself. If you intellectualize and examine the creative process too carefully it can evaporate and vanish. It's not only terribly difficult to talk about, it's also dangerous. You know the old story about the—I think it's one of Aesop's fables, or perhaps not, or a Chinese story—about the very clever animal that saw a centipede that he didn't like. He said, "My God, it's amazing and marvelous how you walk with all those hundreds and hundreds of legs. How do you do it? How do you get them all moving that way?" The centipede stopped and thought and said, "Well, I take the left front leg and then I—"and he thought about it for a while, and he couldn't walk.

Interviewer: How long does the process of reflection about a play go on?

Albee: I usually think about a play anywhere from six months to a year and a half before I sit down to write it out.

Interviewer: Think it through, or—

Albee: —think *about* it. Though I'm often accused of never thinking anything through, I think about it. True, I don't begin with an *idea* for a play—a thesis, in other words, to construct the play around. But I know a good deal about the nature of the characters. I know a great deal about their environment. And I more or less know what is going to happen in the play. It's only when I sit down to write it that I find out exactly what the characters are going to say, how they are going to move from one situation to another. Exactly how they are going to behave within the situation to produce the predetermined result . . . . If I didn't do it that way, I wouldn't be able to allow the characters the freedom of expression to make them three-dimensional. Otherwise, I'd write a treatise, not a play. Usually, the way I write is to sit down at a typewriter after that year or so of what passes for thinking, and I write a first draft quite rapidly. Read it over. Make a few pencil corrections, where I think I've got the rhythms wrong in the speeches, for example, and then retype the whole thing. And in the retyping I discover that maybe one or two more speeches will come in. One or two more things will happen, but not much. Usually, what I put down first is what we go into rehearsal with; the majority of the selections and decisions have gone on before I sit down at the typewriter.

Interviewer: Could you describe what sort of reflection goes on? Do whole scenes evolve in your mind, or is the process so deep in your subconscious that you're hardly aware of what's going on?

Albee: I discover that I am thinking about a play, which is the first awareness I have that a new play is forming. When I'm aware of the play forming in my head, it's already at a certain degree in development. Somebody will ask, Well, what do you plan to write after the next play? And I'll suddenly surprise myself by finding myself saying, Oh, a play about this, a play about that—I had never even thought about it before. So, obviously, a good deal of thinking has been going on; whether subconscious or unconscious is the proper term here I don't know. But whichever it is, the majority of the work gets done there. And that period can go on for six months or—in the case of *The Substitute Speaker*, which is a play that I hope to be able to write this coming summer—it's a process that has been going on for three and a half years. Occasionally, I pop the play up to the surface—into the conscious mind to see how it's coming along, to see how it is developing. And if the characters seem to be becoming three-dimensional, all to the good. After a certain point, I make experiments to see how well I *know* the characters. I'll improvise and try them out in a situation that I'm fairly sure *won't* be in the play. And if they behave quite naturally, in this improvisatory situation, and create their own dialogue, and behave according to what I consider to be their own natures, then I suppose I have the play far enough along to sit down and write it.

Interviewer: That's not an answer.

Albee: It really is. There's a time to go to the typewriter. It's like a dog: the way a dog before it craps wanders around in circles—a piece of earth, an area of grass, circles it for a long time before it squats. It's like that—figuratively circling the typewriter getting ready to write, and then finally one sits down. I think I sit down to the typewriter when it's time to sit down to the typewriter. That isn't to suggest that when I do finally sit down at the typewriter, and write out my plays with a speed that seems to horrify all my detractors and half of my well-wishers, that there's no work involved. It *is* hard work, and one *is* doing all the work oneself. Still, I know playwrights who like to kid themselves into saying that their characters are so well formed that *they* just take over. *They* determine the structure of the play. By which is meant, I suspect, only that the unconscious mind has done its work so thoroughly that the play just has to be filtered through the conscious mind. But there's work to be done— and discovery to be made. Which is part of the pleasure of it. It's a form of pregnancy I suppose, and to carry that idea further, there are very few people who are pregnant who can recall specifically the moment of conception of the child—but they discover that they are pregnant, and it's rather that way with discovering that one is thinking about a play.

Interviewer: When you start, do you move steadily from the opening curtain through to the end, or do you skip around, doing one scene, then another? What about curtain lines? Is there a conscious building toward the finale of each act?

Albee: For better or for worse, I write the play straight through— from what I consider the beginning to what I consider the end. As for curtain lines, well, I suppose there are playwrights who do build toward curtain lines. I don't think I do that. In a sense, it's the same choice that has to be made when you wonder when to start a play. And when to end it. The characters' lives have gone on before the moment you chose to have the action of the play begin. And their lives are going to go on after you have lowered the final curtain on the play, unless you've killed them off. A play is a parenthesis which contains all the material you think has to be contained for the action of the play. Where do you end that? Where the characters seem to come to a pause . . . where they seem to want to stop—rather like, I would think, the construction of a piece of music.

Interviewer: You think of yourself then as an intuitive playwright. What you're saying in effect now is that superimposing any fixed theme on your work would somehow impose limitations on your subconscious imaginative faculties.

Albee: I suspect that the theme, the nature of the characters, and the method of getting from the beginning of the play to the end is already established in the unconscious.

Interviewer: If one worked expressly by intuition, then, doesn't the form get out of control?

Albee: When one controls form, one doesn't do it with a stop watch or a graph. One does it by sensing, again intuitively.

Interviewer: After writing a play in this sort of intuitive way, do you end by accepting its over-all structure (which must also be something of a revelation to you), or do you go back and rewrite and revise with the idea of giving it cogent shape?

Albee: I more or less trust it to come out with shape. Curiously enough, the only two plays that I've done very much revision on were the two adaptations— even though the shape of them was pretty much determined by the original work. With my own plays, the only changes, aside from taking a speech out here, putting one in there (if I thought I dwelled on a point a little too long or didn't make it explicit enough), are very minor; but even though they're very minor—having to do with the inability of actors or the unwillingness of the director to go along with me—I've always regretted them.

Interviewer: Your earlier work, from *The Zoo Story* to *Virginia Woolf*, brought you very quick and major international celebrity, even though today at . . . thirty-eight—

Albee: —thirty-seven.

Interviewer: When this is published it will be thirty-eight—you would otherwise be regarded as a relatively young growing writer. Do you feel this major renown, for all the doubtless pleasure and financial security it has given you, is any threat to the growth of the young playwright?

Albee: Well, there are two things that a playwright can have. Success or failure. I imagine there are dangers in both. Certainly the danger of being faced with indifference or hostility is discouraging, and it may be that success—acceptance if it's too quick, too lightning quick—can turn the heads of some people.

Interviewer: I was thinking less in terms of what the personal effect on you would be. In terms of what you said before, there seems to be a certain pattern that's acted out in the American theater, if not exclusively in the American theater, of elevating new playwrights to enormous prestige, and then after a certain time lapse, arrived at arbitrarily, the need comes to cut them down to size.

Albee: Well, the final determination is made anywhere from twenty-five to one hundred years after the fact anyway. And if the playwright is strong enough to hold on to reasonable objectivity in the face of either hostility or praise, he'll do his work the way he was going to anyway.

Interviewer: Since I guess it's fairly imbecilic to ask a writer what he considers to be his best work or his most important work, perhaps I could ask you this question: which of all of your plays do you feel closest to?

Albee: Well, naturally the one I'm writing right now.

Interviewer: Well, excepting that.

Albee: I don't know.

Interviewer: There's no one that you feel any special fondness for?

Albee: I'm terribly fond of *The Sandbox*. I think it's an absolutely beautiful, lovely, perfect play.

Interviewer: And as for the play you're writing now. . . .

Albee: A *Delicate Balance*, which I am writing now. *The Substitute Speaker* next, and then in some order or another, three short plays, plus a play about Attila the Hun.

Interviewer: You say three short plays. Do you hold forth any prospect of going off-Broadway with anything?

Albee: Well, considering the way the critical reaction to my plays has been going in the past few years, I may well be there shortly.

Interviewer: I was thinking out of choice rather than necessity.

Albee: I'm talking about that too.

Is the American Theatre in a Vacuum, Part II
Dorothy Gordon/1966

This is a transcript (prepared by the Zimmer Reporting Service) of
an interview done by the Dorothy Gordon Youth Forum program
broadcast on WNBC TV on 2 January 1966 and aired on WNBC
Radio on 9 January 1966. All rights reserved. Used with permission of NBC, producers of the Dorothy Gordon Youth Forums,
and Mr. Edward Albee.

The Announcer: The Dorothy Gordon Youth Forum is on the air.
WNBC presents the award-winning Youth Forum, in which students
meet to exchange ideas on vital issues in the news. Today, in a
spontaneous discussion, students will take up the topic, "Is the
American Theatre in a Vacuum (Part II)." The expert guest is
Edward F. Albee, playwright and author of *Who's Afraid of Virginia
Woolf?* As always, Dorothy Gordon, founder and moderator of the
Youth Forums, will direct the discussion. Now, here is Miss Gordon.

    Miss Gordon: Thank you, and greetings, everybody. We often
get requests that we continue a discussion, with a feeling that the
programs are too short, and at times the requests are quite strong
and overwhelming, and this was one of them. We had a discussion
on the theatre about a month ago with Edward Albee, and since we
have this many requests to continue, we are giving you Part II
today. We rounded up a new panel of youth, but we kept the guest,
who, as *The New York Times* said, and I am quoting now, "is the
first new important playwright to shake Broadway from its lethargy,"
the author of *Who's Afraid of Virginia Woolf?* And I present, with
great pleasure again, Edward Albee.

    Before you say a word, Ed Albee, I want to announce that your
new play *Malcolm* is in previews.

    Mr. Albee: It is in previews right now.

    Miss Gordon: Yes, in previews right now, and opens officially
January 11th.

    Mr. Albee: It's supposed to. I wonder sometimes though.

    Miss Gordon: Don't you think it's going to happen?

Mr. Albee: I think sometimes one should keep right on previewing and never open.

Miss Gordon: Well, treating everything as a preview. Well, let's preview by having our young people introduce themselves and then we'll continue with the discussion.

Mr. Reilly: I'm Robert Reilly from Most Holy Trinity High School in Brooklyn.

Miss Young: I'm Dianne Young, from New York University.

Mr. Davis: I'm Buddy Davis, from Jersey Prep School in Paterson.

Miss Faber: I'm Leona Faber, from City College.

Miss Gordon: This is a cross section of young people. I know how I want to start the discussion. We were discussing "Is the American Theatre in a Vacuum?" I want to quote two questions that were asked by Howard Taubman in a recent article, in which he said (1) Where are the fresh visions without which the theatre is an empty light? And (2) Where are the new plays that can quicken a theatre-goer's pulse and intensify his perceptions?

Now we are here. Does anyone on the panel want to take the first one? Where are the new plays that can quicken a theatre-goer's pulse and intensify his perceptions? That is Question 2. Of course, we'll eliminate Ed Albee on that question. Who wants to take it? Yes, Buddy Davis.

Mr. Davis: I think that the shows right now are in the same general area. It is either that it is fast-moving or that it is very slow, such as *Golden Boy* or *Fiddler on the Roof*. These plays are very fast-moving, and it takes a minute to understand them, and I think this is where the new plays are starting.

Miss Gordon: You know, he went on further to say, "Can these questions be answered, or is the American theatre really lost?" Now, how do you young people feel about this? Leona Faber, go ahead.

Miss Faber: I really think the American theatre is reforming. A lot of the playwrights have been crushed, or the activity has been crushed by the commercialism of Broadway at the moment, and there seems to be a reforming, a re-thinking, to try to bring in more repertory or to try to bring in more companies across the country, and I think if you have that sort of feeling, you have more of an

avenue to experiment. You have a more exciting theatre on
Broadway.

Miss Gordon: You have thrown out very challenging questions.
Speak up so we all can hear you. All right, Dianne.

Miss Young: Well, I personally feel that the American theatre
hasn't really begun. I mean, if we consider the United States in
retrospect with the other nations and their theatres, after all, the
United States is only 200 years old, and our first big playwright,
Eugene O'Neill just died in 1953, so I think we are really just
beginning, and we have a great deal of energy which is bound to be
expressed sooner or later—sooner, I think.

Miss Gordon: All right, let's hear from Robert over there.

Mr. Reilly: Well, I feel that the theatre is on its way up now, but
I think that one of the main reasons is that right now people don't
appreciate the theatre. They don't actually know the full value of the
theatre.

Miss Gordon: Why don't they?

Mr. Reilly: Well, because, in school you start off learning about
the theatre, but you don't really get the full value that you should in
order to appreciate it. You just go over it. You scan it. You take
certain points out of it. But in order to appreciate it, you have to see
the inside of a theatre, the meaning behind it.

Miss Gordon: All right, Ed Albee, you've heard these four
young panel members. How would you take these questions?
Where are the fresh visions without which the theatre is an empty
light? And where are the new plays that can quicken a
theatre-goer's pulse and intensify his perceptions? As I said before,
we are eliminating you because, according to all the reviews of
Who's Afraid of Virginia Woolf?, and I hope the same thing
happens with *Malcolm*, you were the great new Shakespeare of the
American theatre.

Mr. Albee: That's a terrible responsibility. Why not the second
question first?

Miss Gordon: All right.

Mr. Albee: Where are the plays that Mr. Taubman wonders
where they are? Well, they show up each season, about two or
three of them, but they are usually killed pretty quickly by the critics.

There are always two or three interesting plays that are new and
valuable to the theatre each season, but for some reason or another
they perhaps aren't as expert to their intention as other plays are,
and they don't get as long a run, and off Broadway, in the café
theatres which are taking over from off Broadway now, there are
lots of young vital playwrights who are experimenting, and these are
the plays that people who are interested in the theatre should see.
They should go off Broadway. They should go to the cafe theatres
and see the experiments that are being made. I agree with you that
practically everybody under 30 in the United States now is writing
plays, and inevitably some of them are going to be good.

Miss Gordon: Something must happen, yes.

Mr. Albee: But on the other question, where are the fresh
visions, as Mr. Taubman puts it, without which the theatre is an
empty light. I wonder exactly what he means by "fresh visions." It is
a playwright's responsibility to reflect and comment on his time as
accurately as he possibly can. These, it seems to me, are the fresh
visions—honest critical comment on the times. I find that with the
newer playwrights, the younger ones, there is a certain amount of
honesty and search, but for honesty you've got to search off
Broadway usually.

Miss Gordon: There must be something wrong, because
Broadway certainly should have theatre which—why must it all be
relegated to off Broadway? Perhaps a point that Robert Reilly made
is a very important one, that in the schools the emphasis on drama
should be greater than just sort of a scanning. Now, Dianne, you're
at New York University, and I believe you have quite a theatre
group there, haven't you?

Miss Young: Yes. There is a new school we are getting at NYU.
You may have heard of the School of Arts.

Miss Gordon: Yes.

Miss Young: And the program for the School of Arts is to train
people who want to go into the theatre, professional people, just as
we have professional doctors, and there is no reason why not. I
think it is very important that the American theatre should have
some professionally trained people—actors immediately come to my
mind, and I think there is a dirth of training for actors in the United
States. The repertory movement is exciting and expanding, but my

question is, where are we going to get the people to fill up these repertory theatres who are capable of putting across the new visions, as Mr. Albee says.

Miss Gordon: I notice you're nodding your head. What did you want to say, Leona?

Miss Faber: I'm in complete agreement with her. We have only one professional training school in all our high school level of New York for performing arts that is free, whereas many other countries have schools that go right through the college level and train their people for a full creative career. They consider it a career in itself. I don't think until very recently the people began to look upon the arts with respect and the idea that we should have a trained elite for the theatre or for all the arts.

Miss Gordon: Buddy?

Mr. Davis: After your training, where do you go from there? There are many, many local theatres in New Jersey, there are many fine actors and actresses, but I think it is experience more than it is training to get in. I would like to ask Mr. Albee, how do people who have this training break into the theatre?

Mr. Albee: Now you're talking about performers?

Mr. Davis: Yes.

Mr. Albee: There are always going to be more actors than anybody can ever use. Right now in New York City, I think in the last report from Equity, it must have been that there were 10,000 actors in New York City. There is never work for more than 1,000 of them. I agree with you that there should be specific training for actors so they will know how to act in the contemporary plays. It seems to me the necessary training is not so much with actors as it is with audiences, which is the point that you were making that it is the responsibility of schools and colleges to teach people how to read plays, to make them understand. In school a long, long, long time ago, if we were taught anything about plays, I think the theatre stopped with Bernard Shaw. But I went back up to the prep school that I went to last year, and I was very surprised to learn that Samuel Beckett was being taught like he was a respectable, grown-up author, which I think is very nice. It is that particular trend, I think, of the training of the audience and how to respond to the truly contemporary that is most important.

Miss Gordon: You know, there is something else I want to get into, and that is speech, because you are talking about the theatre. You were talking about learning about the theatre and being trained, and so forth—and this is directed to you, Edward Albee, because when you did your first plays, you took them over to England because you were not satisfied with the speech of our American actors.

Mr. Albee: That's not true.

Miss Gordon: That's not true at all. All right, then, you tell us.

Mr. Albee: They took my first plays to Germany, but I didn't take them there. The Germans were the first people who wanted to do them. This subject of my being dissatisfied with the speech of American actors was actually a misquote of a remark that I made in answer as to why, in *Tiny Alice*, the two main roles were played by British actors, and I said something to the effect that I was concerned about actors primarily who could speak the lines, and it so happened that the two actors that I thought could best speak the lines happened to be British, and I got a lot of criticism that I was knocking the American theatre and criticizing American actors. As we all know, they shouldn't be knocked and they can't be criticized.

Miss Gordon: I'll turn this over to the panel members before we go out to the audience. Do you young people feel that the American youth speak well? Robert Reilly, what would you say?

Mr. Reilly: Well, they follow the pattern that has been set, I think. It's common. They follow the common talk, as you would say, but I think you don't find too many individuals who can go off into a play and speak as if they know how to speak or know how to read poetry, or things like that. It just seems that they speak commonly.

Miss Gordon: You think that there is a place in the schools to teach young people how to speak, whether they are going to speak lines in a play or whether they are just going to speak?

Mr. Reilly: Yes. I feel that in high school they should give courses for speech and also, say, forming dramatic clubs in high schools, so that they get the experience needed in speaking and in acting.

Miss Gordon: All right. What about you young people here? Buddy Davis.

Mr. Davis: I feel the same way that Robert does, that the school should give courses in speech, because when you get up on a stage and try to audition for a play, it's very difficult if you don't have the right amount of training.

Miss Gordon: How about you, Leona? Are you young people all interested in the theatre personally?

Miss Faber: Yes.

Mr. Davis: I'm in it.

Miss Gordon: You're in it. That's how we got you. Oh, I have a very good assistant. All right, Leona Faber.

Miss Faber: I think the lack of speech training is indicative of the lack of interest or shying away from any type of classical training in dramatics. There is a tendency to feel, let it be natural, but when you get on a stage and you have to project to an audience, if you do it in a natural tone you're not going to get anywhere, and there are certain types of plays which must be spoken with a great deal of detailed enunciation, and there is a terrible tendency to say, you know, "Well, let's not stress it. It's not that important." But I think if they did, more people would be able to express themselves better with friends, and also in the United States you do need to train your voice, and there's no getting away from it, and I think our dramatic schools would be better off if they began to realize they need technical training as well as the Stanislavsky method.

Miss Gordon: All right, Ed Albee, and then I'm going to the audience.

Mr. Albee: I think you are almost defeating your point by having four panel members who use the English language quite nicely. I suppose for actor's training one of the problems, of course, is that up until quite recently the American theatre has been concerned with naturalistic plays, in which people don't have to use anything except the most usual language. But do you think it is a responsibility for people to teach and for people to learn the proper use of the language, or else how can one build it and make a change in the way it must to be a vital language?

Miss Gordon: Yes, English is a vital language, and certainly I personally feel that everybody, whether they are training for the theatre or whether they just should project every word in just speaking ordinarily as you move along in our activities, should

speak well, because I find a great difference when I'm having an
international broadcast, for instance, where we hear the speech of
the young people in other countries and many of our young people
here, even some who have been on the panels. All right, we have a
very attractive young lady standing up there in the audience. Let's
hear what she wants to say or ask.

Miss Green: My name is Carol Green, from Columbia
University. A statement was made before about the role of the
critics. I think someone said the critics killed plays. I would like to
address the question to the panel. What do you think the role for
the critics should be, especially because there has been so much
criticism of the critics in New York City in the past month?

Miss Gordon: Well, you know Mr. Albee took that question in
Part I of this program. Maybe we'll ask the young people what they
think about it. Buddy?

Mr. Davis: I think the critics take much responsibility on
themselves. They don't want the responsibility. This has been stated
in many shows that the critics have been on. I think that there
should be, though, a set of critics on various newspapers or
television so that they have an overall opinion, not just one opinion,
where it either kills a play, such as maybe David Susskind's play, or
makes a play a hit.

Miss Gordon: I don't quite understand what you mean, that all
critics should have the same opinion?

Mr. Davis: No, no. They should have some more critics on the
Daily News, not just Chapman himself.

Miss Gordon: Well, now you'll have to take this, Ed Albee.

Mr. Albee: I'm just laughing. You were suggesting, I believe, that
the critics don't want the responsibility they have. Maybe they don't
want the responsibility they have. If they don't want it, why don't
they educate their audiences into thinking for themselves? And then
they can get rid of all of this responsibility.

Miss Gordon: Would you do away with critics altogether?

Mr. Albee: Well, I would let them live, yes. A critic seems to be
essential as a reporter, but the audience, it seems to me, must use
its mind a great deal more and make more decisions for itself. I
mean the critic really can't be anything more than in the function
that he wants to serve in—he can't be anything more than a

reporter, to give people a basis of judgment on which to make their own judgment.

Mr. Davis: Miss Gordon?

Miss Gordon: Go ahead.

Mr. Davis: The people aren't financially [able]—they can spend some $15 for a show. They rely on the critics a lot. There is a reason why they should be there.

Miss Gordon: But at the same time, Buddy, there have been many, many plays that have been successful despite the critics.

Mr. Davis: Yes.

Miss Gordon: And have fallen by the wayside in spite of the critics, so that in the end the audience really is the greatest judge of all. Don't you agree?

Mr. Albee: It must be, and that's why it must be more responsible.

Miss Gordon: Yes, I know. Well, let's get the young lady.

Miss Frankel: My name is Randy Frankel, from City College. I would like to address my question to Mr. Albee. Mr. Albee, do you think that a government subsidized theatre would act as a controlling influence or a liberating influence on young talent?

Miss Gordon: Oh, I'm so glad you asked that question. We never got into it before.

Mr. Albee: What do you mean exactly by "young talent"?

Miss Frankel: People such as yourself, so that when they are studying, they think that they are studying to have a place to go.

Mr. Albee: Right. I suppose it is the government's responsibility to subsidize education, and certainly informing an audience of the history of the theatre so they can understand that the contemporary theatre is a form of education. So long as the government can subsidize education without merely subsidizing buildings or subsidizing repertory companies, and certainly so long as the government doesn't exert any control over what plays are put on, then I think it is the responsibility of the government, and I would imagine that more and more theatres will have to be subsidized in this country. The truly experimental theatre, the off-Broadway theatre, is almost totally subsidized privately right now, because it can't be commercially feasible.

Miss Gordon: Dianne?

Miss Young: Yes. Well, you remember that a new bill was just passed, the first one I guess of its kind, $63 million for the arts.

Mr. Albee: I'll bet it all goes into buildings.

Miss Young: I bet it all goes into buildings too. That's why I want to make my comment, because it seems to me that the atmosphere is we have a healthy theatre going because we are making buildings, and it seems to me it would be very fatal to the United States theatre to think because we have new buildings and equipment that our theatre is in a very healthy state.

Mr. Albee: That's called an edifice complex.

Miss Gordon: Well, let's get to the young gentleman in the audience.

Mr. Boboly: Paul Boboly from Trinity High School in Brooklyn. I would like to ask Mr. Albee if there is any special kind of play that, you know, young people of high school or college age can have in order to learn more about the theatre, you know, just by seeing the theatre, seeing the play.

Mr. Albee: I think there are two phases for really knowing about the theatre. One is what you do at home primarily is to educate yourself as much as you can to what's been going on in the theatre from Sophocles on up to the present, reading plays, and then the most exciting theatre to see fortunately is the least expensive, the work that is being done off-Broadway and in the café theatres, the work of very young playwrights—the two phases together, finding out what has been going on before 1965, as quite a bit has, and then what's really going on. The truly contemporary plays aren't the commercial plays for the most part that are being done on Broadway, but the plays that are being written today by the kids, off Broadway and cafe theatres—that's where you should go.

Miss Gordon: Do you think that they will continue to exist, or are they just a little part of the contemporary scene and then will die out?

Mr. Albee: Oh, no. Perhaps even only out of perversity, but I imagine they will continue. They had better continue or there's no point in writing for the theatre.

Miss Gordon: Otherwise we'll remain in a vacuum.

Mr. Albee: Exactly.

Miss Gordon: All right, the young gentleman.

Mr. Capelle: My name is Charles Capelle from Most Holy Trinity High School. I would like to address my question to the panel. Do you think that poetry should go into much depth in high school?

Miss Gordon: Buddy?

Mr. Davis: Yes, I think it should, because this sets you up. If you can understand poetry or—well, let me take Shakespeare, for example. This is a sort of poetry. I think if you can take this and correct speech by it, and understand it and comprehend it, you're ahead of the game, and I think it should go into a lot more detail than it is right now.

Miss Gordon: Wouldn't you say almost that all good drama is poetry? Leona.

Miss Faber: Well, all good drama is very literate usually, and it has depth, and in reading poetry or any classical writer or any good writer, you learn to have depth, to be able to understand the written language. I remember in my high school we didn't have much poetry. We had one Shakespeare play for my whole high school career, and I think it was terrible because it's not right to get out of high school when you're 18 having read *Macbeth*, period.

Miss Gordon: You know, we must talk about the Arts Council in England, because there they have plays of Shakespeare and the very best actors for the youngsters at prices that the youngsters can afford regularly all the time. Now, what's the matter with the United States of America? All right, Robert Reilly.

Mr. Reilly: In high schools now they do give student discount prices for a group of students to go see a play produced.

Miss Gordon: What plays?

Mr. Reilly: Well, most of them they will simply [go to plays]—in Lincoln Center, or go to the colleges to see them put on their own productions.

Miss Gordon: Not the Broadway things.

Mr. Reilly: Not the Broadway theatre.

Miss Gordon: That's why I asked about the word "plays." It's a question of plays. Out to the audience. All right, yes, have you another question?

Miss Frankel: I don't understand why people such as yourself are so afraid of going into government subsidized theatre. Isn't there the same sort of control exercised by private people? You have to get your money from somewhere, don't you? Don't the people you get your money from influence and have as much control over you as, let's say, your government would? Are you afraid of the government?

Miss Gordon: He didn't say he was afraid of government subsidies. I thought it was just the other way.

Mr. Albee: I would be delighted. I'm not afraid of anything.

Miss Frankel: You seemed to stress the training part and the students should get the subsidization, but once you put things on, it is out of the hands of—

Mr. Albee: No, I was merely trying to suggest that it is the government's responsibility to provide a subsidized theatre in order to educate people into the nature of the theatre, but it is also the responsibility of the government to keep its aesthetic hands off of what's presented in the theatres. I will agree with you that theatre is a very large attempt at control over what playwrights write in this country through sheer commercialism, and perhaps government subsidy would free playwrights a little bit from that pressure. I'm afraid of subsidy only if it is concerned only with buildings or if it tries to stifle the creative impulse, as much as commercialism stifles the creative impulse

Miss Gordon: Have any of you young people, or you too, Ed, seen the story about National Education Television providing money for the development of plays for television that are going to be developed at the Lincoln Center of Performing Arts? What do you think about that? What do you think about television as a media to introduce plays to the audience? All right, Dianne.

Miss Young: Well, I think it is probably a good thing as far as educating a mass public into the theatre, but as for the vital contact that you get in the theatre when a play is produced, that is impossible when you have everyone sitting in his separate home.

Miss Gordon: You feel that nothing takes the place of flesh and blood.

Miss Young: No, it doesn't. The vital quality of the theatre can't be brought across in television. I don't think.

Miss Gordon: I'm going to give the rest of the program right over to you, Edward Albee, to finish and wind up. Say anything you want to.

Miss Faber: You know, many of your interviews talked about theatre for entertainment and theatre for diversion, and I wonder if you didn't think this makes some kind of a schism in the theatre which really shouldn't be. Isn't theatre for entertainment and theatre for some kind of fun the same thing?

Mr. Albee: Exactly.

Miss Gordon: All right, this is a very good thing for you to wind up with.

Mr. Albee: All right. That was actually the point that I have been trying to make, trying to redefine the nature of entertainment. It seems to me that entertainment means engagement, and the assumption that so many people make that a play is entertaining only if it is escapism rather than engagement seems to me a false assumption to make.

Miss Faber: The word "entertainment" means "to enter into."

Mr. Albee: Exactly, and if people are willing to admit that they were being entertained by something that drew them into it rather than take them out of it, then the theatre would be a much healthier place. I'm lamenting the schism.

Miss Faber: Yes, I am too.

Mr. Albee: And I don't think it should exist.

Miss Gordon: Well, I'm sure now I'm going to get requests to continue, and we'll have to have a Part III. Thank you very much, Edward Albee, and thank all of you again. I want to remind the listening audience that Mr. Albee's new play, *Malcolm*, is now in previews and will open on January 11th.

The Private World of Edward Albee

Adrienne Clarkson/1967

From *The Montrealer*, 41 (October 1967), 42–49. Originally broadcast as a CBC program on "Take Thirty," hosted by Adrienne Clarkson, 31 May 1967. Used with permission of the Canadian Broadcasting Corporation/Société Radio-Canada.

In seven years Edward Albee has moved from off-off Broadway to the top of the admittedly undistinguished heap of significant playwrights who are attempting to work outside the Zelda and the Zulu circuit. With plays such as *Tiny Alice, The Death of Bessie Smith, The Zoo Story* and *Who's Afraid of Virginia Woolf?* he has brought to the US stage a brilliant facilty for upturning the smooth stone of society to reveal the slimy multi-legged horrors that lie underneath.

It is done with tooth and claw and a macabre obliqueness that implies unspoken, and perhaps unspeakable, inter-relationships. As with Pinter, the lines that lie unsaid are the significant ones.

Such skill does not need mileage from the kitchen sink. A suburban coffeeklatch becomes an incipient orgy, and the home life of an Ivy League professor—as in *Virginia Woolf*—a miasmic, caterwauling hell on earth.

Albee has not endeared himself to the spurs and stetson mentality that runs strong in the States; which may explain why he and people like Truman Capote are rarely, if ever, seen on US television. Capote's first extensive interview ran on television in this country, as did Albee's recently on the excellent CBC programme "Take Thirty," a late afternoon show.

The following is an edited transcript of Albee's conversation with one of the programme's hosts, Adrienne Clarkson. The producer, Cynthia Scott, wanted to hold the interview in front of the zoo in Central Park, New York (this was the setting of *The Zoo Story* and animals figure large in his plays) but the author demurred, opting instead to hold it in the Playwrights Unit, a small off-Broadway theatre which he runs with a group of associates.

80

Q: Why?

Albee: For a number of reasons. First of all, the zoo at Central Park is a fairly public place and I'm sort of a private person. And while it is true *The Zoo Story* was set in Central Park, it wasn't a literal Central Park, it was a Central Park of the imagination. . . . also I like this theatre. A very good 199 seat theatre with a totally flexible stage. I've had some rather good times here. We've put on 73 plays here; experimental plays, the work of young playwrights who have a rather curious distinction and happen to write work that's alive.

Q: Who is the "we" who put on the plays?

A: My partners Dick Barr, Clinton Wilder, and I. We put this organization together but its been run by a man named Chuck Innasue. He more or less manages the entire unit for us. In this past year a little group called The Rockefeller Foundation has come in and decided to give us a little money to help run it, which is nice too. So, between us and the Rockefellers we're keeping going.

Q: Is there anything especially different about this theatre?

A: Yes, aside from the distinction I mentioned before, that we do plays that have a certain life to them, the major distinction is that this is a workshop, in a sense that actors are not paid, directors are not paid, nobody is paid. And the audience is invited, and they don't pay either. The major advantage of this is that young playwrights can see their work before audiences without the commercial pressure of having a heavily financed production, or having those curious types, the crtitics, in to see what they are doing.

Q: What do you mean, that their plays are alive?

A: The further you get away from the commercial theatre on Broadway, as a general rule, the more life plays have. Most of what's done in commercial theatre is dead before it starts. And what isn't, two thirds of that is killed by the time it opens. Then you move off-Broadway, where the plays are a little more alive, because the commercial pressures aren't so great and the playwrights are younger and more adventurous. And if you move further off Broadway, to off-off-Broadway, to a place like this, a sort of cafe theatre where nobody's in it for the money and everybody is terribly young or pretends that they're terribly young—one or the other—

you find a certain amount more life, adventurousness, and excitement. Quite nice.

Q: What do you think of as life, adventure and excitement in the theatre?

A: Taking a chance. Being willing to create your own style. Or if you're going to imitate somebody else's style, at least imitate Sam Beckett instead of Neil Simon. I always mention Neil Simon. And I've got absolutely nothing against him at all personally. He's a very nice, easy-going man. He said some very nice things about me and he writes the kind of play that he writes very expertly indeed. The only reason I keep bringing him up—and I always do in lectures I make in universities—is that there is something wrong with a theatre setup where a man like Simon, according to his press agent, earns about $50,000 a week and Sam Beckett's lucky if he earns that in two years. So that's why I always bring Neil Simon up. Not that there is anything wrong with Neil Simon. But there's something wrong with our theatre setup.

Q: Is it important that the playwright make money?

A: No, it's not important *per se* that the playwright make money, though I do think any artisan should be paid a living wage. However, in a capitalist society, I'm afraid there is a considerable confusion between aesthetics and commerce. And too many people think that the play in the largest theatre and making the most money is automatically the best play. Including a man like Walter Kerr for example.

Q: Does this deaden creativity—does it make it harder for young playwrights to start writing because of the risk?

A: It doesn't deaden it. You can't stop a playwright of any quality from doing what he wants to do. He'll find a stage to have his plays put on. Of course, it makes it a great deal more difficult. The theatre is an area of compromise, if nothing else, and it's a tough fight to have your play put on exactly the way you want it put on without having other people trying to tell you what to do. It makes it tough for the playwright. But it won't stop him, no.

Q: What about your own experience? You started off Broadway.

A: I started way off Broadway in West Berlin. What happened to me is a special case. It usually takes, I think, about five years from

the writing of the first play to the first production for the average
young playwright. But I, through a curious set of circumstances,
had my first play, *The Zoo Story*, put on about six months after I
wrote it, and in Berlin. But it was done here in New York at the
Provincetown Playhouse about six months after that. Since then
each of my plays has been put on shortly after I've written it. So
what happened to me isn't average.

Q: Have you had to fight to keep your integrity?

A: There are some people who say I haven't fought. And some
people who say I haven't kept it. However Dick Barr and Clinton
Wilder, who are my producers, are very strange men. They have
the concept, now almost unheard of, that the theatre belongs to the
playwright, and that he should have his own way, make his own
mistakes, be burnt with his own errors, and also take his own credit.
So they pretty much let me do what I want to do. It's worked out
pretty disastrously in a couple of cases, and then fairly well in some
others. I can't answer the question about integrity because you can
never answer that for yourself.

Q: Your plays have had an enormous public and critical success.
Take *Who's Afraid of Virginia Woolf?* Were you pleased about the
kind of production it got on Broadway—because it was a full-blown
treatment which was made into a huge money making movie?

A: Well it didn't get the full-blown treatment. The script wasn't
changed: none of the actors asked for their parts to be rewritten so
they'd be more sympathetic; we didn't have a director who wanted
to be terribly creative and change all of the author's lines. No, it
wasn't the usual full-blown treatment at all. It was a sneaky little low
budget production. But it managed to have damned good actors
and a good director. It was put on pretty much exactly the way I
wrote it . . . as I wanted it done. Then again, the film that was
made of it was rather extraordinary too. Think what could have
happened to the film. On its own level, it's not a bad picture—it's a
pretty good picture. But they could have written it for someone like
Esther Williams. They could have made it into a swimming flick for
example. They could have put it in technicolour on a big wide
screen. They could have done all sorts of things that they didn't do.
They cut out about fifteen minutes and took out the entire historical-

political argument and de-intellectualized the characters a little bit, but compared to what they could have done it was almost if it hadn't been done in Hollywood.

Q: When you've seen your plays go through the metamorphosis from play to hit movie does that change your view of it. Does it give you a different feeling than you would have towards perhaps a smaller play?

A: I don't think so, but for a very curious, rather strange reason. About a year and a half after I have finished writing a play I discover that I can no longer recall specifically the experience of having written it. In other words, I could never revise a play of mine because I couldn't put myself into the same frame of mind I was in when I wrote it. And so there is a curious kind of loss. Anybody could have written it. I go to see it with a certain objective fascination and so there's no sense of loss. It's almost as if somebody else had written it, somebody whose work I find fairly interesting, I'll grant, but not specifically mine.

Q: Does this mean that at this point, you don't feel any sensitivity to criticism of it?

A: Unfortunately, in the United States at least, about the only thing you can learn from critics is how long your play is going to run. I wish we did have a college of critics who could tell playwrights something about their art and craft. But unfortunately we don't. You learn a great deal more from the critics about what the audience expects than you do about the value of the play you've written. The playwright's sensitivity over critics ought to be over their (the critics) insensitivity and nothing else.

Q: You're never hurt by the critics?

A: No. I don't really think so. The playwright has to develop . . . how can I phrase this accurately without sounding ridiculous . . . a certain amount of confidence in what he's done. And he's got to learn that what a critic says unfortunately more often than not, reflects the state of the theatre rather than the state of a particular playwright's craft. At the same time you shouldn't put yourself in the position where you are cut off totally and can't learn anything from critics. But the only really good critics are playwrights themselves. And we are not usually hired to do that work. We should be.

Q: Do you think it's a good thing for playwrights to talk to other playwrights about their work?

A: You learn a great deal more. There's this great unfortunate division in the theatre between the play as an art form, and the play as a commodity. The only time you get much of a discussion of it as an art form is among other creative people. There are exceptions to this of course. There are a few critics in the United States whose opinion I respect almost completely; people that are like Harold Kremen and Elliot Norton for example. They are first rate critics, which is probably the reason they're not critics of the *New York Times.*

Q: Do you feel that all your plays have running through them a certain theme?

A: Well, we all know about critical oversimplification. If they (the critics) oversimplify, it does make it easier for them to understand. Doubtless, there is a theme running through my work. I don't know what it is, probably because I find it best not to examine that terribly carefully. If, for example, I'm at work on a play and somebody says to me "What's it about?" I just have to say, well I really don't know. I won't know until I finish it. Because too much careful examination of what you're doing, while you're doing it, removes the necessity for doing it—totally. You know, one isn't naive or a primitive. But at the same time, it is very bad to become so self-conscious that you're examining your themes, the implications of what you're doing and all the rest of that jazz. That's for those people who are paid to be critics.

Q: Are you interested in what the critics find in your plays?

A: Yes, I'm always interested in what a critic, whose opinion I respect, finds in a play. But you will notice, I think, that the critic whose opinion you can respect doesn't usually tell you too much about what a play is about—merely how good it is, or how bad it is, and how it relates stylistically to the history of the theatre as an art form. Most of the good critics don't tell you plots.

Q: Why do you write plays, and why don't you write novels or poetry?

A: I started writing poetry when I was six years old because when I was six, I decided that I was a playwright, and a poet, and a

novelist. In other words, I decided I was a writer. So I wrote poetry
for twenty years and by the time I stopped, when I was twenty-six, it
was getting a little better. It was better than it was when I was six
years old, though not all that much better. And I wrote two novels,
one when I was fifteen, one when I was seventeen. I don't know if
they're the worst novels ever written by a teenaged American, or by
anybody for that matter, but they're pretty close to it. What was
there left. Essays? Since I have a terribly disorganized mind, I
couldn't write essays. So there was not much to do except plays. I
started that when I was twenty-nine with *Zoo Story*, and so far I
believe that's worked out a little better than the poems and novels
did. I also decided that when I was eleven and a half that I was
going to be a composer.

Q: What happened to that?

A: I couldn't learn how to read music, and that stopped me.

Q: Once you've finished a play, do you have to go away and
rest?

A: I have to go away and lie down a lot, just generally. Probably
more often when I'm not writing a play than when I am, because I
don't find writing exhausting. I find it rather exhilarating. I get a
headache after writing for about four hours at the stretch. But no,
it's a great deal more interesting than not writing.

Q: You've produced one play a year for the past seven or eight
years. How long does it take you to write one? For instance *A
Delicate Balance?*

A: I thought about that—or what passes for thinking with me—for
maybe a year. Then it took about two months to write it. That's
specific writing time. So I don't know what the answer is. Two
months, or a year and two months.

Q: Do you change things for your director in the way, for
instance, Tennessee Williams has changed things for Elia Kazan?

A: I change things very little, not much. You know, a line here
and there. I don't imagine in *Delicate Balance* I took out a page or
two and added a page here and there. It's pretty much the way I
wrote it.

Q: One of the most interesting facets of your playwriting has been
the woman figures you have created. Martha of *Who's Afraid of*

Virginia Woolf? has now become a kind of myth figure. Then
there's Alice in *Tiny Alice* and the latest, the middle-aged woman in
Delicate Balance. These women are perfectly terrifying. What do
you feel about them? Do you hate them, love them, are you
interested in them, want to watch them? What's your attitude
towards them?

A: I've been accused a lot of writing about terrible women:
Martha in *Who's Afraid of Virginia Woolf?*, and Miss Alice in *Tiny
Alice* and Agnes in *Delicate Balance*, not forgetting the nurse in
Death of Bessie Smith who is considered one of the real monsters.
But what is there to write about? Men, women, children and
animals. Other animals rather. I suppose one can write about
terribly content people, or what Herbert Gould was asked to write
about by the television executive: Happy problems. I guess you can
do that. I suppose my men and my women both tend to be a bit
more argumentative than placid, to be a bit more discontent than
content. But then again, to choose a few other examples throughout
playwriting history, so was Lady Macbeth so was Clytaemnestra.
Serious plays have got to be based on a certain amount of conflict,
discontent, and argument. What really bugs me is the accusation
that my women aren't an accurate representation of the female kind
in this world. I guess if I were insane, they wouldn't be. But the
thing that interests me also is the fact that people don't see
themselves in my characters. They see their friends and neighbours.
I couldn't write about a character only with hatred. I feel ambivalent
about most of the characters and then again most of the characters I
create are ambivalent themselves. Ambivalent towards each other
and towards their role in or out of society. I'm very fond of Martha
in *Who's Afraid of Virginia Woolf?* for example. I think she's a real
gutsy three dimensional well rounded woman who can play the
monster when she's thrust into that role. A lot of people
misunderstand about a lot of the women I write. Usually the men
misunderstand; women seem to be a little more tolerant of the
women I create, which leads me to suspect they aren't monsters.
The men seem to object to them because they don't want to see
women represented in that fashion whether it's true or not. I think
my lady characters are quite nice.

Q: Are you then interested in the way it's put on? Or does the objectivity you mentioned earlier make you detached so that you can just leave it?

A: Well, the only production I can get particularly involved in is the original production. And I do try to have the play look as I imagined it would look when I was writing it. But something curious happens even there. Once you get actors on stage, and a director moving around, you get a physical construction and that reality begins to take over a little bit from what you remember as being your original line of thought. So you just muddle through the best you can. For me the experience with the play is finished when I finish writing it, because plays can be read and as often as not you'll see as good a production of the play by reading it as you will by looking at it.

Q: Do you have a consciousness of the people you are writing for? Your audience?

A: Oh. I thought for a moment you meant the people I was writing about. Well, that's who I'm writing for, the people I'm writing about. But no, not as an audience. Except the audience is me. When I'm writing a play I've got to be interested in it. I've got to be involved and I guess I make the assumption that if I am, other people will be.

Q: Therefore you don't say "I'm writing this play to be aimed towards. . . . " You don't have an idea, for instance, of aiming towards the middle class?

A: I think that would be just as dangerous as writing for any particular actor. The actor can very easily drop dead two weeks before you finish the play and there you'd be with a play for a dead actor. Which is quite often the case in general. Or the entire middle class might drop dead for example.

Q: Not likely though.

A: Unfortunately not. And there you'd be without an audience. I think you've got to create the reality for yourself and if it interests you, make the assumption that it interests other people. Make the assumption that what concerns you and what fascinates you is going to involve the rest of the world. It's a difficult assumption, but one must make it.

Q: Does your attitude as a playwright affect your social attitudes in your own life? Are you interested for instance in what young people are doing . . . the 'in' thing of tuning in and dropping out and all that?

A: I suppose I listen a great deal more than most people do. I let other people talk. I sometimes think that other people think I'm a psychiatrist rather than a playwright because I find that they love to talk to me. Or maybe it's because I sit very quietly and listen, I hear a great deal more and I learn more than when talking myself. I know, more or less, what I think.

Q: Maybe they think they are feeding you?

A: No, I think that would shut them up totally. They must think that I'm a psychiatrist.

Q: You have said that you don't think of your plays in terms of scenes.

A: Well, naturally, you can't write a play without an idea behind it, though I have been accused of doing it, and so have lots of other people. But there are didactic playwrights who create a theatrical reality on a premise of a polemic. And there are others whose polemical ideas are most subtly disguised. They find out what the ideas are after they have finished the play. Rather, they let the unconscious do more of the work. I guess I'm the second kind.

Q: That's something like what Robert Frost said about poetry: That it's going somewhere by a crooked road and you don't know you've got there until you have finally arrived.

A: I wouldn't write a play if I knew exactly what all the characters were going to be saying or exactly how it was going to reach the end point that it does. There'd be no interest. Then I could just think about it and not bother to write it down.

Q: When you say you're waiting for things to come out, this does not imply that you are just an automatic writer . . .

A: No. When you start talking about how playwrights get ideas and build inspiration and all the rest of it, it's dangerous and always sounds ridiculous. All I can say is that I don't get ideas for plays. I discover that I have been thinking about a play; that somewhere in the unconscious the idea has been formulating. And when it pops up into the conscious mind, a certain amount of the work has already been done.

Q: In all your plays I almost wait for the part when somebody describes their relationship with an animal.

A: Well wait until the next play, the one that I'm writing now. There are very few people in it, mostly animals.

Q: Are they going to be played by animals?

A: Unfortunately no; they will be played by other actors.

Q: Are animals more interesting than people?

A: I don't make that distinction usually. People do, between themselves . . . and other animals.

Q: I think most people like animals.

A: I like animals too, but everything's got to exist on two levels, a real level and a symbolic level. A play, to be at all interesting, has got to move on two or possibly three or four levels.

Q: Do you like animals?

A: Yes. I think they like me too. At the moment I have five cats and two dogs. I grew up around horses and dogs and cats. I was in England a couple of weeks ago and in Harridges and they had a tame puma which I wanted very much. But somebody had bought it already so I couldn't have it.

Q: Does it help you to place life away from yourself, so that you are looking at it rather than being involved in it?

A: I think a writer has got to learn the trick of being involved in the situation, and at the same time being objective about his involvement. Some people call that schizophrenia. Other people call it very useful for the creative process.

Q: Does this take the passion out of living?

A: No, I don't think it takes the passion out of living. It doubles the intensity I suspect.

Q: Why?

A: Because you're doing two things at the same time. There's passion in doing, and passion in the observation of what you're doing.

Q: And this holds true even though you're not writing about your own life in any way?

A: I would guess that any writer is writing about his own life in a sense that he's filtering what passes in reality through his own prisms. So obviously one is writing about one's own life. Can't avoid it. Whether you're writing specific and strict autobiography or not, everything is filtered through your own view of reality so that you are writing about your own life. You are creating your own life as you write about it.

Q: Do you specifically recreate certain tensions or contradictions in order to resolve them?

A: I can't answer that specifically. It's part of the area I don't like to think about terribly much. People do say that writing, by its very nature, is an act of aggression and that one is getting something out of one's system. But fortunately one always finds there's a great deal more in the system. Each time one gets something out, there's something else coming in to get out.

Q: That's the personal aspect of writing. We were talking earlier about the didactic writer, and then the writer who works a secondary way, in which something comes out after he has written it.

A: I think they're both doing the same thing. It's just a difference in approach. All writing inevitably is didactic.

Q: What about political commitment? Are you committed in any way, or do you stay apart from that?

A: Yes. I'm deeply committed. But I'm hesitant about stating political specifics. I've seen too many playwrights and too many writers in general lessen the artistic intensity of what they were doing in order to make intense, immediate, passionate political points.

Q: What do you feel about the war in Viet Nam?

A: I'm thoroughly disgusted with the United States, and with the Soviet Union and China for making the Vietnamese people, north and south, into a metaphor. This war has absolutely nothing to do with the slaughter of people in Viet Nam. It is geo-politics played at the highest level between the three super powers, and it's disgusting. But it's disgusting for all three, not just the United States.

Q: What do you feel you can do about it? Or do you feel helpless?

A: I don't necessarily feel helpless. I'm suspicious of just about every point of view. Intellectually and emotionally suspicious. Perhaps I can't reconcile myself to the notion that geo-politics have got to be all that immoral.

Q: How does the problem of morality enter into it?

A: I like to assume that governments are run according to morality as well as people's lives. Alas it may not be true. I find almost every point of view too simplistic.

Q: Does this mean that you have walked away from doing anything political?

A: No. I'm trying to think it through before I start carrying placards either as a hawk or a dove.

Q: Your latest play, *Delicate Balance*, has cooled off after the white heat of *Virginia Woolf*. It's like looking at love two thousand years later. It's cool; it's got a kind of elegance that comes from order, from a pattern that is in it.

A: The play is about the death of passion. The play is after the fact, and is about people realising that they no longer have freedom of choice any more and so naturally the play has got to seem cool because it is about a cooling off. I don't necessarily suspect that means my own passions have cooled. If you're writing about people whose passions have cooled then you've got to give that impression.

Q: You won the Pulitzer Prize for that play. What did that mean to you?

A: It meant that I won the Pulitzer Prize for it.

Q: Are you excited by laurels and accolades?

A: No. I suppose if they exist you might as well win them. I don't see any point in resisting.

Q: Is this the first one you've won?

A: I don't think so. In 1963 the Pulitzer Prize jurors voted *Who's Afraid of Virginia Woolf?* the prize and then the trustees, all 15 of them, got together. They were wheeled and carted in, and they had decided by an eight to seven vote that *Who's Afraid of Virginia Woolf?* was too controversial, or too dirty, or something. And so they overrode the jurors. And then it turned out—which I found the only interesting thing—that of the eight who voted against it, four had neither read nor seen it. So I don't know whether this is my first Pulitzer Prize or my second. I don't really think it's terribly important.

Q: Is it important to you to be an American playwright? To live and work in the United States?

Q: Why not?

A: I don't like it very much. But I don't like it much anywhere else. I am an American I suppose, and I'm an American playwright. And my point of view is specifically American, but my plays don't seem to be particularly exotic. In fact I've seen productions of them all over Europe, Eastern Europe and Western, and they seem to resemble each other, and the critics seem to come to more or less the same conclusions about them; if perhaps slightly more intelligent conclusions in Europe than in the United States. One has to live somewhere. I don't know if I'd write the same kind of plays in a different environment or not.

Edward Albee Returns to View *Zoo Story*

The Choate News/1968

From *The Choate News*, 17 December 1968, 1, 3. Reprinted by permission.

The Choate Dramatics Club presented Edward Albee's *The Zoo Story* under the direction of Ken Bartels, last Friday, December 13. Edward Albee returned to Choate for the second time since 1946 to see the performance.

Mr. Albee is currently writing the screenplay for *The Death of Bessie Smith*; he is also halfway into two other plays, "one of which is vaguely about evolution, the other . . . gives the illusion of being a naturalistic play concerning how much anguish and pain we will permit anyone before we destroy them."

A one act play combining humor with tension, Albee's *Zoo Story* is basically a confrontation between two men of different ways of life. Peter, portrayed by David Rather, is a successful $18,000 a year businessman who is naive to the problems outside of his middle-class environment. Sitting unobtrusively in the park one Sunday afternoon, his quiet way of life is upset by a conversation with Jerry (Paul Zaloom), a sarcastic recluse, who tries desperately to relate to people.

After the performance, Mr. Albee spoke individually with the actors and the director; he then held an informal discussion with several interested students and masters. He offered comments— some serious, some facetious—on Bartels' production, the theatre in general, its critics, and Choate.

"The production tonight was totally different and refreshing for me. I am used to seeing the play done in an infinitely quieter fashion."

"In the *Zoo Story* I suppose my enthusiasm may be for Jerry but my sympathies are equal for both characters."

"I guess the original intention of the play was to examine cross-pollination or the intent to transfer the continuing awareness of life from one person to another."

"The value of people like the Living Theatre is that they are expanding the horizons of the theatre—allowing the people who write for the theatre a greater opportunity."

"The Theatre of the Absurd is nothing more than the truly contemporary theatre, and it belongs to the playwright . . . . Most people unfortunately prefer theatre which uses basically the nineteenth century concept of the theatre. They go to the theatre to have values not examined, but reaffirmed."

"I have always been interested in the fact that theatre audiences have always been offended by hearing or seeing on a stage the same behavior that they themselves indulge in privately. It is a curious double standard which is a holdover from the hypocrisy of our Puritanical beginnings. Of course there is a lot of exploitation going on because we are a Puritanical society, which means we are a great deal more obscene than we admit to be."

"I've always found that nudity is a great deal less exciting than partial dress. But this may be my hangup . . . . Within a year or two, people are going to be going to the theatre and shouting. 'Put it on!' "

"What most people mean by comedy is a play in which everything ends up the way each individual member of the audience is most comfortable with. Our present definition of a serious play is a play in which things end up the way they really are and most people don't want to face. So, I prefer the serious play."

"They are having a hippie experience. It is refreshing because it lets some fresh air into the theatre."

"The plays that the young people are writing today have one thing in common: they are not dead on the page; they are full of thoughts, but they are alive."

"LeRoi (Jones) has turned into so much of a propagandist that he has let his responsibility as a creative artist go straight down the drain."

"There is nothing to be gained in Diahann Carroll's program except dismay for the blacks in this country. If Diahann Carroll wants to do a television program, then damn well let her do something worthwhile and serious instead of being a black Doris Day."

"There is only one proper critic of an art form, and that is someone who deals with the art form himself."

"Critics in general should be mistrusted and despised. They are people who live off the works of their betters . . . I wish I could learn something from our critics."

When asked about Choate, Albee noted that the "most interesting things about Choate were, first, the only important thing that I think any educational institution can ever teach you: how to educate yourself; and, second, I was encouraged to be as much of a pretentious fool as I could possibly be."

"I wouldn't mind sending my son to Choate. If it's anything the way it used to be when I was here, I can't imagine not sending him here. But maybe you know something about that I don't.

"When I was at Choate, the theatre ended with Bernard Shaw."

"All Choate graduates end up smoking."

Albee Looks at Himself and at His Plays

Irving Wardle/1969

From *The London Times*, "Arts," 18 January 1969, 18-19.
Reprinted by permission.

Edward Albee has no particular reason to like London. Before he
hit the jackpot with *Who's Afraid of Virginia Woolf?* ours was the
only city, of the many it visited, that failed to appreciate his first
play, *Zoo Story*; and he got the cold shoulder a second time when
the Royal Court took a dutiful stab at the two short plays that
followed it. I got a five-minute audience with him at that time: a
soft-spoken boss relaxing under the eyes of a looming bodyguard,
and confiding that the happiest time in his life was when he was
delivering telegrams for Western Union.

Now he is here again for the Aldwych production of *A Delicate
Balance*. Broadway saw it three years ago, since then Albee has
moved on to fresh territory with a pair of plays designed for
simultaneous performance ("Eventually I think I'll write a play that
has to be conducted") and is well into another piece featuring a pair
of French-speaking amphibious fish. He is forty: not a man to take
liberties with. Looking at that tight, closed face it is easy to imagine
him as an unhappy little boy. More than Osborne, more even than
Edward Bond, he is the dramatist of Western cannibal customs, of
what we do to each other in private. " 'I wanna know why Miz
Amelia and Marvin gonna kill t'other.' 'Because they know each
other, that's why.' " But he himself seems barricaded against
unwanted intrusions. He is armour-plated with professional
confidence, and has organized his career so as to secure the
maximum control over his work. He is the joint head of a
production company (Albar) that is now branching out from the
theatre into films, and he co-produces his own plays so as to
acquire power over budgeting, advertising, and choice of theatre.

"I'll probably end up directing my own plays, too. By contract the
playwright has every single protection that he needs: he needn't pay

attention to anybody except himself. But most neophyte playwrights do give in to what they incorrectly assume to be greater wisdom and it's usually just greater ego. It's much nicer to go with your own mistakes and your own successes. Of course, it's always better to have a first-rate actor than a second-rate actor. You can gain insights into your intention, and if they're good enough insights you pretend you intended them.

"I've written 12 plays now, and done three adaptations. In the case of James Purdy's *Malcolm* and Carson McCullers' *The Ballad of the Sad Café*, I felt they ought to be on stage and I'd rather get at them before somebody else did. With Giles Cooper's *Everything in the Garden*, one of my producers thought it would be a grand commercial success and wouldn't I like to tinker with it. My original thought was just to change a few words here and there and not even take any programme credit. But it's very difficult just working on the surface: so in changing the speech rhythms, I also changed the nature of the characters and the dramatic structure.

"In my own work I find that the characters' speech rhythms have to come naturally before they can carry out the structural intentions. Before I really sit down to write, I take the characters and put them in situations in my head: and if they can behave on their own in situations that will not be in the play, I know that I can put them into the play. It's rather similar to what actors do when they improvise. Of course there has to be a structural intention: but I use the author's necessary self-deception of pretending that the characters are taking over for themselves. I try to let the unconscious mind do as much work as it possibly can.

"Writing a play doesn't take terribly long—maybe two months for a full-length piece. I wait until I know what I want to do well enough for the writing to be semi-automatic. Once I've popped a play down into the unconscious it keeps germinating. Right in the middle of playing tennis or talking, having dinner, making love, the reality of the play will pop right up and I'll know it's making some sort of progress and I'll push it back down again.

"I only feel the play's going well when it's moving like a piece of music: in the sense of both structural order and the interweaving of voices. I wanted to be a composer when I was 11, and I'd still like to be one but I don't suppose I ever will. Naturally, content and thematic material have to interrelate all the time. The problem—and not only in the United States—is getting people to listen to the words. They will listen only to what they want to hear and then translate it into something they can live with. I don't like to let them off the hook: which is one of the reasons I get criticized for not having the catharsis in the body of the play. I don't think that's where the catharsis should be any more. I think it should take place in the mind of the spectator some time afterwards—maybe a year after experiencing the play. One thing I don't like about the naturalistic theatre in general is that it usually gives answers instead of asking questions.

"I've never been a politically didactic writer, though it must be fairly clear from my plays that my sympathies are far more to the Left than with the reactionaries. How people exist in their society and how they cheat themselves—that's my basic concern. And I'd like to think that my plays don't look exotic when they get outside the United States. It's still an enjoyable game—though rather a dangerous one just now—for people to do the anti-American business.

"Of course, the East European Party Press is quick to see the plays as an attack on United States values; but I haven't noticed any great difference of response from one country to another. Or too much difference in performance style—though there was a terribly funny version of A Delicate Balance in Oslo where the bar was set in the rear wall and designed as an altar: so that when Julia was protecting it you saw a female crucifixion. The only reception I pay any attention to is the breathing response of an audience when I'm in a theatre.

"So far as Britain is concerned, I do prefer the rehearsal system here; and your theatre isn't quite as bad as theatre in the United States—but it's getting there.

"It's true that animals crop up in my plays from Zoo Story onwards. You can judge a fair amount about the human being from the way his animals respond to him. I'm fond of animals, all kinds; people too. At the moment I have cats and dogs, and birds and fish, and sheep. And I'd like to get a horse to have out at Long

Island—there's a marvellous wide beach that goes on for about 50 miles. Will I write a play for animals? You'll have to see what I do after the fish play. I wouldn't be surprised. Nothing I do surprises me. Some of it interests me, and some of it doesn't; but none of it surprises me."

Edward Albee Fights Back

Guy Flatley/1971

From *New York Times*, 18 April 1971, Arts & Leisure, sec. 2, 1, 10. © 1971/75/76 by The New York Times Company. Reprinted by permission.

All Over is what Edward Albee calls his new play, now struggling valiantly for life at the Martin Beck Theater. And "all over" is what wisecracking woe-wishers are saying about the career of the 43-year-old playwright who, just nine years ago, shattered conventions, nerves and possibly a few marriages with his scalding portrait of a carnivorous couple named Martha and George in *Who's Afraid of Virginia Woolf?*

Albee still has his fervent fans—Clive Barnes and Harold Clurman among them—but his efforts in recent years have left a great many viewers feeling befuddled, bothered and belligerent. Where have Albee's powers gone, they want to know—where's the white-hot passion of *Virginia Woolf*, and where's the riveting tension of his early one-acters, *The Zoo Story* and *The American Dream*? By comparison, *Tiny Alice* and *Box-Mao-Box* seemed inscrutable puzzles, or painful put-ons.

But the critical dams burst a couple of weeks ago with a fury that was unprecedented. The occasion, of course, was the calamitous premiere of *All Over*, a mystifying drama in which a man—famous, but unseen and unidentified—lies dying a gruesome death while the shadowy, nameless figures of his wife, his mistress, his grown children and his best friend talk and talk and talk about how much or how little the perishing patient has meant to them.

All Over impressed most critics as a bloodless but bloody bore and the lacerating language employed by some of them to describe their disappointment would have brought a blush to the cheeks of Martha and George. But who's afraid of critical wolves? Not Edward Albee, judging by the boldness of the comments he made a few days after the butcherous night at the Martin Beck.

101

The scene is Albee's house on a cliff overlooking the ocean at Montauk—a serene refuge, complete with swimming pool, sauna bath, tennis courts, Henry Moore sculpture and a den with glass paneled doors that slide open to let in the sound of the surf washing over the private beach below. The day is bright and pure, and Albee is spending it with close friends: Richard Barr, his partner in the Playwrights Unit, an artist named Patrick and a pale young Greek who is named Constantin but sometimes called Tino. It is a peaceful Sunday, with plentiful sunshine and sea breeze and food and drink. But Albee is not at peace.

"There is a syndrome in this country," he is saying in an even, clipped voice that borders on British. His unruly hair is not quite shoulder-length, he is wearing boots and jeans and a turtleneck sweater, and there are circles beneath his brooding green eyes. "The critics set somebody up, maybe too soon— underline *maybe*—and then they take great pleasure, the only pleasure critics *do* take— except possibly with their wives and mistresses—in knocking them down."

"The reaction to Edward's play has been exceptional," says Barr. "A major work by a major playwright—you don't just kick it down the toilet that way."

"The majority of our critics are best qualified to cover brush fires in New Jersey," Albee elaborates. "There *have* been good reviews for this play—Elliot Norton and Clurman and Clive—but the vituperation of the *bad* reviews exceeds any *rational* opinion of the play. It's hard not to get paranoid in the theater, but I think I've succeeded."

"Certainly," agrees Barr.

"Most American critics think play-writing stopped with Ibsen," Albee says. "Walter Kerr thinks it stopped with Pinero. Then there are those critics who think that the agitprop theater of the thirties, applied to the seventies, is a valid art form. Like Ted Kalem writing in *Time* magazine about *The Trial of the Catonsville Nine*, which is not even a play."

Albee rattles the ice cubes in his glass and frowns. "And of course we have John Simon and Martin Gottfried and Robert Brustein— men who are basically concerned with themselves and a redefinition of theater that they can control. There is no excuse for John Simon, except his own need to create a John Simon. As for Martin Gottfried, I have a collection of letters from him in which he is absolutely hysterical about homosexuality—a gratuitous correspondence that clearly indicates he has hang-ups on the subject. If Gottfried is ever offered a job as critic on a *responsible* newspaper, I will see to it that those letters are published.

"Do you know what my nightmare is? I dream that I'm going to wake up one morning and find that the critic for the *Times* is Martin Gottfried, the critic for the *Post* is John Lahr, the critic for *Time* is John Simon, and the critic for *Newsweek* is Jerry Tallmer. Tallmer, as you know, is just waiting around for Watts to fall down.

"The truth is that in this country we just do not have a theater culture. Forget that crap that Maxwell Anderson and Robert Sherwood were writing. And forget Odets, who has dated so badly. Theater didn't get serious until around the end of the Second World War, with Tennessee Williams and late O'Neill. Richard and I and Chuck Woodward down at The Playwrights Unit wonder if it's really possible to have a serious commercial theater. Especially when you consider the dross that's been put on over the past several years. Things like *J.B.*, *The Great White Hope*, *A Man for All Seasons*, *Rosencrantz and Guildenstern*, *All the Way Home*.

"And we ourselves did a little thing down at The Playwrights Unit called *The Effect of Gamma Rays on Man-in-the-Moon Marigolds*. I didn't think very much of it then, and I don't now. It's such an old-fashioned play, without any resonance. It's only about what it seems to be about. At any rate, I was horrified when it went on to win the best play of the year award."

Nor is Albee particularly pleased with British attempts to pump blood into the sagging Broadway scene. Christopher Hampton's *The Philanthropist*, starring Alec McCowen, for example. "I walked out on it. It's a fifth-rate British director with third-rate British actors."

Revivals of the classics, such as Stephen Porter's current production of Moliere's *School for Wives*, also leave him cold. "Why did the actors have to keep coming right up to the footlights? I was sitting close to the stage, and I felt so *imposed* upon. And Brian Bedford's mugging was inexcusable!"

"Yes," says Barr, "and Brian is usually such a good actor. He was much better in *Private Lives*. Well, at least he was much better than *Tammy*."

"God," moans Albee, "wasn't *she* awful? I once saw Tallulah do it—when she was still capable of giving a performance—and she was splendid."

But to get back to the criticism of *All Over*, what about the accusation that nothing really *happens*? Albee's eyes narrow and the corners of his mouth droop. "There is no more nor less action in *All Over* than in *Virginia Woolf*. There is never any physical action in my plays. Think about it; what *really* happened in *Virginia Woolf*? All of the action took place in the *spectator*. People are objecting to what they've accepted before. My God—in *All Over* there's a hemorrhage. I've never had a hemorrhage in a play before!"

But perhaps the thing that disturbs Albee most is the complaint that *All Over* is remote and exotic—it is set among extraordinarily wealthy people— and that its action, or lack of action, has no relevance to current political realities.

"There is a misunderstanding about what political theater really is. That's why I object to people like Richard Schechner going back to the agitprop of the thirties. In 1968, I went around campaigning for McCarthy, and during my speeches I talked in *specific* political terms. But when I write a play, I'm interested in changing the way people look at themselves and the way they look at life. I have never written a play that was not in its essence political. But we don't need an attack on the specific or the conscious. We need an attack on the *un*conscious.

"I daresay I could write a play attacking Nixon. But we all hope that he will go away in '72, so it would be a play with no interest after '72. And why write a play about the shooting of Martin Luther King? Isn't it better to write about the mentality which allows that shooting to take place? When you've got a society that's so uptight that all it cares about is self preservation, it's far more important to write about *that* situation than to make specific attacks on Nixon and the ghettos. Nixon and the ghettos are *particular* horrors that have come about because people are so closed down about themselves. If we can get them to be open about themselves, the rest will come automatically.

"Serious theater is meant to change people, to change their perception of themselves. And there is a change that takes place in *All Over*. At the end, when Jessica Tandy says, 'All we've done is think about *ourselves*.' And she says it quite regretfully, doesn't she? You see, I write plays about how people waste their lives. The people in this play have not *lived* their lives; that's what they're screaming and crying about.

"One of the points of the play is to make us aware of our mortality. And that bothered the critics. In *Virginia Woolf*, they saw people they knew, not themselves. But this play is not about others. It's about us, because it's about death, and you can't fob off death.

"I was recently talking to a psychiatrist who told me that most people are not willing to accept the fact of death. I had an awareness of death when I was 15, but when I turned 36 or 37 I became aware that *I*, Edward Albee, was going to die. The realization did not fill me with dread. I simply became aware of the fact that this is the only time around for me. I'm going to be alive for a certain time, and then I won't exist any more.

"Do you take acid? Neither do I, but I'm told that when people do take acid, things become infinitely more real. The knowledge that you are going to die should present this same intense awareness of life. I'm so much more aware of things around me now. I find that I make love more often, and much better than before. I'm more aware of colors, of seasons, of textures."

It has grown chilly, and the sound of the wind blends with that of the surf and the clinking of ice cubes.

"Here I am, Edward Albee, entering into my middle age," says America's foremost bruised playwright, "and I think of it as a *beginning*. Life is absolutely super and wonderful. There shouldn't be any sadness in it. People should be aware of all things at all times, they should experience the extremities of life, fulfill themselves completely. Why does everyone want to go to sleep when the only thing left is to stay awake?"

Albee on the Real Thing
(Theatre) Versus a Film

Tom Donnelly/1973

From *The Washington Post*, 28 October 1973, sec. L, 1, 2. ©
1973 by *The Washington Post*. Reprinted by permission.

Katharine Hepburn met Dick Cavett to plug The American Film
Theater program, but other participants in the series (playwrights,
actors, and directors) met the print media. Sample scenes from the
films *(Luther, The Iceman Cometh, A Delicate Balance, Lost in the
Stars, The Three Sisters, Rhinoceros, The Homecoming*, and
Butley) were shown, and then some of the celebrities talked to small
groups of reporters in relays. Edward Albee talked to (or with) one
small group.

The American Film Theater series ("Its purpose is to create a
national theater on film—to bring the entire nation the excitement of
legitimate theater at its finest") has its gala premiere with *The
Iceman Cometh* on Monday, Oct. 29, "at a motion picture theater
near you."

While we wait for the curtain to go up (or the film to unroll) let's
get on with the interviews. The first question asked of Edward Albee
was whether or not he made Katharine Hepburn, Paul Scofield,
Lee Remick and the other players in the film version of *A Delicate
Balance* so nervous they asked him to stop visiting the set. This
question didn't come out of thin air. I can tell you; it came out of a
press release. It was asked nervously. Albee is not renowned as the
world's most easy-going interviewee. It is said he does not suffer
fools gladly.

Albee smiled affably and said, "Sure." It was true. He did that
and they did that. The movie was filmed not on a stage set but in a
real suburban home (outside London) and this, he indicated, may
have helped to make his presence seem a bit intrusive, a bit
unsettling. He said, "Besides, *these* actors were concerned with
trying to get the words right."

106

Albee remained affable through the interview, but then why shouldn't he have? The press kept a respectful tongue in its head. Nobody pressed him to explicate the mysteries of *Tiny Alice* and nobody brought up the fact that in the seven years since *A Delicate Balance* he has written nothing but losers (*Everything in the Garden, All Over,* etc.)

Of the movie version of *Who's Afraid of Virginia Woolf?* (the only other Albee work to have been filmed), the playwright said, "There the *intention* may have been to get the words right." After a moment he said several actors have told him that Albee dialogue demands an uncommon degree of precision. It's not just a matter of getting the sentences right, "they have to get the paragraphs right or the sentences themselves tend to fall apart."

Albee wanted either Ingmar Bergman or Tony Richardson to direct *A Delicate Balance*. He got Richardson. He said, "Tony and I would go over alternate—what do you call those things?—takes. We'd go over four or five takes and agree on the best. What we've wound up with is an accurate representation in film terms of what I wrote for the stage. It is *not* a photographed play." No, he wouldn't say he'd functioned as a co-director.

There are time sequences that are acceptable on stage but "just don't work on film," Albee said. In the play version of *A Delicate Balance* a woman character invades the home of her best friends and announces that she's terribly frightened; it's some nameless terror that drives her. Albee said, "Two minutes later she says 'Can I go to bed now?' That kind of transition can work in the theater, but not in a movie." He said that apart from adjusting the time sequences and other minor matters he has left his text substantially intact.

Albee said, "Of course I don't think a film ever has the same impact as a play. I think subconsciously everybody knows that film is an unreal experience. Though not if you compare it with television, of course. But anyone who's ever been to the theater, even street theater, knows that's where the real thing is." (A few million cinema-minded youths could tell Albee he's got it exactly wrong, but I doubt if he'd be swayed. Not even if they spoke with one voice.)

If our friends flee from their own premises do we have to take them in for months or years, or maybe forever? That's one of the questions that *A Delicate Balance* asks, or seems to ask. Instead of asking Albee what kind of label should be pinned on his play I said, "Your plays certainly aren't naturalistic, but what degree of stylization would you say . . . ?" and let the question trail off.

Albee said, "I think all my plays are realistic. Though some may be more stylized than others. I think *every* experience we have is both real and a metaphor. I don't see why this shouldn't be true in art. Most authors write in the hope that the problems they write about will disappear one day. What I hope is that my plays will encourage people to participate in their own lives more."

Albee said it seems apparent that the majority of people want to be left alone with their own little status quos. "How else do you explain the existence of a Republican administration? A recent poll showed most people would give up the Bill of Rights in the interest of their own security. How do you combat that? Now my plays aren't simple-minded. I doubt if I'd ever write a specifically political play; I've seen how agit-prop plays dry up and disappear. What I do is write about the states of mind that make these things—the anti-Bill-of-Rights poll, Watergate, and so on—possible."

Albee said that he is never suddenly visited by an "idea" for a play. "I never have a light bulb turning on over my head the way they used to in the funny papers. First I get a notion of people who are having something happen to them. Then I think about the thing that's happening. Then I flesh it out."

What about that new play of his, the one that's been announced for the Kennedy Center, the one called *Seascape*? Albee said. "Oh, that will be coming along sooner or later. It's not so easy to cast a play these days. So few people want to work in the theater." He said that the new work has four characters, a middle-aged couple at the beach, and "two giant lizard-like creatures." He said some of it takes place on land and some of it takes place under the sea. I gathered that the lizards take the humans to the ocean floor for a discussion of various vital topics. I asked, hesitantly, what the theme might be. Albee said, "It's about whether or not evolution has taken place."

The press subsided momentarily into an awed silence. Then someone asked how Albee felt about Hepburn's performance as Agnes, the elaborately articulate heroine of *A Delicate Balance*.

Albee said, "It is indeed fortunate that the character of Agnes is very much like Katharine Hepburn. Of course if she played King Kong it would still be Katharine Hepburn. Fortunately there is room enough in Agnes to contain Hepburn. In fact, I never realized till I saw her do it how close to Agnes Katharine Hepburn is."

Albee said his *All Over*, a failure on Broadway in 1971, is now in its second year in Vienna. "American playwrights are relying more and more on Europe for an audience," he said. "We don't have a theater culture in the United States. It's depressing for a playwright to find that his work is not reviewed intelligently in his own country and that audiences don't understand it."

Jeanne Wolf in Conversation with Edward Albee

Jeanne Wolf/1975

This is a transcript of an interview done on 30 March 1975 for the program "Jeanne Wolf in Conversation with . . . " produced by WPBT TV (Miami), Community Television Foundation of South Florida, Inc., and broadcast on the PBS network on 22 June 1975. Transcribed by Scott Nations. Used with the permission of WPBT TV.

The following program, made possible by a grant from the Ben Tobin foundation, is a production of WPBT, public television in South Florida.

"The most valuable function of theatre as an art is to tell us who we are, and the health of the theatre is determined by how much we want to know about that." Words of playwright Edward Albee. I'm Jeanne Wolf at the Society of the Four Arts in Palm Beach where Mr. Albee will be lecturing and will be my guest for this program.

Edward Albee is determined to share his insights through the theatre in plays that bear the mark of his telling dialogue and controversial themes. If audiences and critics didn't love the impact they felt from *The Sandbox, American Dream, The Zoo Story, The Death of Bessie Smith*, they couldn't stop spinning from the jolt. Those who sensed his extraordinary talent were not at all surprised at the overwhelming success of *Who's Afraid of Virginia Woolf?*, and *Tiny Alice* revived the flood of Albee analysis, and *A Delicate Balance* won the Pulitzer Prize. There's a new play of his on Broadway called *Seascape*, starring two people and two lizards. I want to get the inside story about the meaning of that play from its director and author Edward Albee.

Jeanne Wolf: Edward Albee. Am I pronouncing your name wrong? Is it Albee or Albee?

Edward Albee: I thought you meant the first name. It's Albee. Well at least I say Albee. Most people say Albee and you're in the majority.

110

Jeanne Wolf: All right. So now it's Albee for the rest of the program. There's a new play of yours on Broadway. Here I live in Florida and I'm heading for New York and I think "Should I go see *Seascape* or not?" The experts will tell me. Now I already know that Clive Barnes says it's an event.

Edward Albee: That's not true. He says it's an important major event.

Jeanne Wolf: All right. Okay. I believe in Clive Barnes, but I probably don't get the *New York Times*; I'm more likely to get something like the *New Yorker* and *Time*.

Edward Albee: That would confuse you very much, to get the *New Yorker* and *Time*.

Jeanne Wolf: Right. Let me show how much it's going to confuse you. If I pick up *Time*, in the middle of the review I'm going to read something like "*Seascape*; it's not a hateful play, it's blind and inaccurate, a two hour sleeping pill of aimless chatter."

Edward Albee: I wish we could say that about that critic.

Jeanne Wolf: But it's okay. I don't believe him. And I'm going to read the *New Yorker* and feel very good because it says "Of all Mr. Albee's plays, *Seascape* is the most exquisitely written. He's calculated not only every immaculate line of dialogue but every word." And the review goes on and on with praise.

Edward Albee: You know it's interesting. *Seascape* is my thirteenth or fourteenth play. Every single one of them, from the ones that have run the longest like *Who's Afraid of Virginia Woolf?* and *The Zoo Story* through the ones that have had the shortest commercial life, has split the critics right down the middle. In other words, I've never had unanimously good praise or unanimously bad praise. Every one of them is fifty-fifty.

Jeanne Wolf: Have you tried to analyze why after all these years of living with that?

Edward Albee: Well, I don't seem to please everybody and I don't seem to make everybody hate what I do. I must be doing something wrong.

Jeanne Wolf: Yes, but when you say they are split they are not; they are not mediocre or well-I'm-not-sure reviews; they are hateful.

Edward Albee: Some critics are so ambitious that they try to climb up on other people's prostrate bodies. Some of them think that they have an important function in the theatre (they like to be kingmakers) and if you're not nice to them, if you don't kow-tow to them, and if they think they can't control you, they get pretty vicious.

Jeanne Wolf: So you think that sometimes the reviews are a reflection of just a personal feeling against you, and not a view of the play.

Edward Albee: I hope this doesn't come across as personal paranoia, as opposed to the natural paranoia that's necessary if you're going to be a playwright. People come up to me about a review like the one by T. E. Kalem in *Time* all the time and they say, "What does this man have against you?" Now, they don't say, "He doesn't like your play."

Jeanne Wolf: Or didn't understand it.

Edward Albee: The point was critics do themselves a disservice by being so obvious in what they do. Now if he were a cleverer man he would disguise his dislike of my work by being rational. But he doesn't.

Jeanne Wolf: And give the reasons why.

Edward Albee: But they don't have any reasons; that's why they're not rational about it. There's nothing you can do about people like that. If you're in a tough thing like the theatre you take your friends where you can get them. There are a whole group of critics who are learned, intelligent, good men like Clive Barnes; Brendan Gill at the *New Yorker*; Richard Watts at the *New York Post*; Elliot Norton in Boston; Harold Clurman on the *Nation*; and George Oppenheimer at *Newsday*, a whole bunch of critics who all know a good deal about the theatre, men without axes to grind. Those are the men whose opinions I value.

Jeanne Wolf: Does it hurt you when in fact one of them doesn't like your work?

Edward Albee: No, but I'm interested in their opinion if they don't like what I do because it's an informed opinion; it's an objective, honest, informed opinion and these men don't have an axe to grind. And so what they say is not going to be colored by anything terrible in their own personality.

Jeanne Wolf: I don't like to read a critique of a play before I go and see it. It kind of ruins it for me.

Edward Albee: And you're in the minority, aren't you?

Jeanne Wolf: I suppose. But I like to review the critiques afterwards because it's like having a conversation with someone. But there are, as you know, a few very important effects of reviewing which is why I started out with this topic. One is keeping people away from the theatre and the other is whether or not reviews ever will change something that you do in the future.

Edward Albee: Well, the function of criticism is to give people some information on which to make up their own minds about things, but unfortunately most people use what a critic says not as an opinion but as a fact. And that's laziness. And that's why so many good things disappear so quickly because people don't make up their own minds. I can't let either good or unfavorable criticism affect what I do, because then I'd be writing for people rather than for myself. And though one does like audiences in the theatre, and it's nice if people like what you do, you better write for yourself and hope that other people come along for the ride.

Jeanne Wolf: When you write for yourself, though, do you envision an audience's reaction? Is there something in you that goes, "Oh, boy. This will get them." or "They'll laugh at this."

Edward Albee: I don't think so. No, you can't do that. You know when something is dramatically effective on its own terms. The danger is if you try to do it and expect an audience reaction from something you're going to be mistaken half the time. It's just like the danger of writing a role for an actor. You make the role so tailored to that actor that if the actor doesn't want to do it, or dies, then you're left with a role that nobody else can play.

Jeanne Wolf: And then, perhaps, if you focus on a New York audience, you're going to leave out what's become a good part of your audience, the performances of the plays all over the country, and in fact, all over the world.

Edward Albee: Yes. The audiences that seem to like my work are by and large young people and old people much more.

Jeanne Wolf: Why?

Edward Albee: I don't know. Young people haven't made up their minds about everything yet and old people realize the decisions they've come to are probably not right. So, they're an open-minded audience. At least, I've found the most alert and interested audiences in my work to be young people.

Jeanne Wolf: Have you ever noticed a response from Albee groupies who say they find your plays a little bit obtuse and so by liking your work this puts them in an inner circle.

Edward Albee: I've never found my work obtuse. I'm surprised at your question. It's possible, of course. But you can't kid the college students too much. They don't put up with much nonsense, and they turn off very quickly.

Jeanne Wolf: You say you don't believe any of your work is obtuse, but literary critics have called it abstract. This is the kind of analysis— pulling apart and gluing back together, again—that almost all of your plays, except the brand-newest ones, have been subjected to. What does that type of criticism do to you?

Edward Albee: The mind boggles. It really does. I read these analyses coming out in book form and magazine articles and newspapers about my work and it makes me feel dead. Most of what is said has very little to do with what I intended. And it all seems so beside the point. A discussion of the work of art is always less interesting than the work of art itself. I suppose it's a necessary thing to happen, but I find it very curious and sort of unreal.

Jeanne Wolf: It's almost as if they'll do anything but go to the heart of it.

Edward Albee: Let me give you an example. About two months after my first play, *The Zoo Story*, opened in New York, I got an article by a nun in Brooklyn. Very nice girl and very interesting article. It discussed a whole pattern of Christian symbolism in *The Zoo Story*, that Peter was indeed Peter and denied Jerry, who was Christ, three times and all that. There was all sorts of marvelous Christian symbolism in the play. Now I was raised in the Episcopal Church which I left, in my head at least, when I was six. And indeed I suppose that Christian symbolism did creep into *The Zoo Story*, but I wasn't aware of it and I didn't use the Christian symbolism when I was writing the play. But when I finished reading her article I felt so bright. And what I did, probably half consciously, whenever people after that would ask me questions about what I meant in *The Zoo Story*, I would pretend that I had meant all this symbolism. And it made me feel so good and look so good.

Jeanne Wolf: I have visions of English classes magic-marking your plays, and making cross references.

Edward Albee: But plays ultimately say what they mean and mean exactly what they say. And the experience of a play itself is the only thing that's important—reading it or seeing it, and not reading about it. And I'd rather, or just as soon, have a play of mine read than seen in a not very good performance. You get a great deal out of reading the plays. I wish more people would read them. But I think that's changing now with paperback books. More people are reading plays. Did you know that Sam Beckett's play *Waiting for Godot* has sold half a million copies in paperback? Isn't that extraordinary?

Jeanne Wolf: I like to read plays, but there's something just a little bit left out of the whole work unless you have the actors performing.

Edward Albee: Yes, but you have to know how to read them. You create your own stage and your own set when you read a play. I find it a very invigorating experience.

Jeanne Wolf: As a playwright, you've been involved in *Seascape* on Broadway now as a director; your reputation is that you've taken more of the control of the elements of the play than most other modern playwrights ever had a chance.

Edward Albee: I suppose that's true. And that's by choice not chance. Because by contract a playwright has all the controls that I exercise. But a lot of playwrights don't bother to exercise the controls they have. After all, it is my work. And I want to see it done accurately, as close to my intention as possible. I'd rather take my own blame and my own credit rather than the blame and credit of other people.

Jeanne Wolf: But wouldn't it be tougher for an actor to work with someone who's both the director and playwright? Is there any room left for an actor to create?

Edward Albee: Well, a creative actor is not going to do any better at working with a director who is not the playwright than he or she is with a director who is the playwright.

Jeanne Wolf: Is there a little more room for you to listen to an actor's interpretation when it's not your work that he or she is trying to change?

Edward Albee: I watched twelve of my plays directed by other people and I looked at *Seascape* directed by me and I don't think that anybody else has come any closer to my intention than I do as a director. And certainly actors that I've worked with don't seem unhappy to work with me.

Jeanne Wolf: And they enjoy the experience?

Edward Albee: You should ask Deborah Kerr if she's had a good time. If I didn't know how to direct my own work and if I wasn't being cooperative with the actors, they'd complain about it. And I, as author and coproducer, would have replaced myself as director.

Jeanne Wolf: Would you have had that kind of objectivity?

Edward Albee: I think so, yes. One thing that people did notice about the direction of this play, even the people that didn't like it, is that the direction is very good. In fact, one of the worst reviews of the play said a paradoxical, interesting thing about this play: it's directed so well that we can see how lousy it is.

Jeanne Wolf: What you're accomplishing is that it's directed well enough to let us see the play.

Edward Albee: Right.

Jeanne Wolf: Do you think audiences in general miss a lot of your humor? Do they take you too serious?

Edward Albee: No. You can never be taken too serious. You can be taken too humorously. And too glumly, I think. A lot of audiences find a good deal of humor in plays of mine. Sometimes, since I do have a bit of a reputation of being a serious playwright, they will come into the theatre and sit there very glum and resist laughing for a while. But then they realize that they're supposed to laugh and then give in to it and have a good time.

Jeanne Wolf: I mean, do you like being grouped with the theatre of the absurd?

Edward Albee: I don't like any labels. Here's an example. The producers wanted to call *Seascape* a comedy. I said no. I don't want to call it a comedy because the only plays that are advertised as being comedies are commercial plays that aren't very good. It's a cheap selling point. So I won't let it be called a comedy, even though it's funny. It's a serious play which happens to be very funny. People tend to think that they shouldn't be laughing and shouldn't have a good time at plays that are any good. It's a terrible attitude.

Jeanne Wolf: Is part of the device of using lizards in *Seascape* your way of waking an audience up and saying something about the silliness of the life condition?

Edward Albee: Oh, sure. The play is about whether or not evolution has taken place. Sometimes I've got my doubts.

Jeanne Wolf: You're not sure if we're growing?

Edward Albee: I don't share the view that we're on our way up, anyway.

Jeanne Wolf: What would be the way up? Where should we go?

Edward Albee: I don't know, but the whole assumption that we're at the top of the pile just because we're the most recent animal strikes me as being a fallacious assumption. I think we're making sort of a mess of it. Maybe we'll stop being one of the two or three animals that kills its own kind, for example. We're the only animal that is polluting its atmosphere so that it can't survive anymore. No other animal does that. And this can't be high intelligence that creates global suicide.

Jeanne Wolf: Is it your intention then to call our attention to this predicament?

Edward Albee: In this play I'm certainly concerned with whether or not we shouldn't look to see whether we're as splendid as we think we are and if we don't have something to learn from our theoretical inferiors. I'm always trying to examine something different in every play.

Jeanne Wolf: Is it really something different each time, because there is a theory that perhaps great authors really are trying over and over again to say the same thing?

Edward Albee: There are only a couple of things you can write about ultimately. First of all, interpersonal relationships; whether people, to the extent that they will or are able to, deal honestly and completely with each other. Communication is the only thing that is really viable to write about. That's the only thing you can write about.

Jeanne Wolf: And writing about that, have you found that you deal with people more honestly?

Edward Albee: You never know. I hope so, but you can never know whether you're lying to yourself. It's impossible to tell. I try not to. I try not to compromise, to give in. I try to be as honest as I know how to everytime I sit down to the typewriter or, as I'm sure a lot of old playwrights did when they sat down to the quill, but you never know. You can't tell whether you're kidding yourself.

Jeanne Wolf: Talking of interpersonal relations, I had read a lot of your plays, and seen them performed, but I really didn't know much about you until I looked up Edward Albee in the *Oxford Companion to the Theatre* and found Edward F. Albee.

Edward Albee: My grandfather.

Jeanne Wolf: I would love you to talk about your upbringing and your grandfather.

Edward Albee: I didn't know my grandfather because he died when I was about a year and a half old. The family had a great number of theatres around the country. The Keith-Albee circuit was an enormous set of theatres, vaudeville in its heyday. It was a national booking organization and would give performers for the first time a job fifty weeks a year and send them all over the circuit, performing from one place to another. The great vaudeville performers were with them. It was an enormous empire. And so, as a result of it, I started being sent to the theatre when I was four or five years old, which was an enormously valuable thing for me. Whether that pushed me directly into being a playwright, I don't know, because I became a poet first and a lousy novelist and then didn't start writing plays until I was in my late twenties.

Jeanne Wolf: Was it always in the back of your mind that you wanted to write plays?

Edward Albee: No, I didn't know. I couldn't have known it because I tried other things first. But certainly, I suspect, that being allowed and encouraged to go to the theatre at such a young age must have made a deep impression on me.

Jeanne Wolf: And from what I have read you had a rather stormy relationship with your parents over the years.

Edward Albee: I was a brat.

Jeanne Wolf: Are you still?

Edward Albee: I don't think so. I don't know. I'm not sure. I doubt it.

Jeanne Wolf: As you look back, do you think that rebellion was necessary for you?

Edward Albee: Oh, I think that any kid who has any intelligence, any individuality, has a responsibility to rebel against everything. It's a necessary thing. Everybody tries to create his own universe, and if you accept the fact that everybody who knows better, knows better, you're not going to find out for yourself. Everybody's got to try it on his own. And disagree with everything. It's a natural function of being young to rebel.

Jeanne Wolf: Is that still a necessary function for you?

Edward Albee: Rebellion turns into questioning. I question everything. You have to set some guidelines for yourself.

Jeanne Wolf: Is that just a milder form of the same thing?

Edward Albee: It's not milder, it's different. It's a more mature form. Rebellion is clearing the ground and saying, "Look, I've got to create my own structure, my own identity, my own individuality, my own sense of values. And therefore, I've got to clear away everything else, no matter how good it is." And you start building your own. But, you don't build a structure completely around you that closes yourself in from everything else. You build a structure that you can exist in, and at the same time, see everything and be aware of everything, and question it, and rebuild it if you have to.

Jeanne Wolf: Do you ever reach a place where you do find out? Would that be fun if you did?

Edward Albee: No, I don't think it would be. Most people, or a lot of people, build a structure around them that is without windows, without air, and close themselves in completely.

Jeanne Wolf: Is that because they're scared?

Edward Albee: I don't know. Maybe it's easier and keeps the cold winds out, the rain. But more and more people, I think, are aware now that always asking questions is a lot better than having easy answers.

Jeanne Wolf: You've been accused over the years of being anti-woman, of writing characters that were very unflattering to women. They are always tough and emasculating. How do you reply to that criticism?

Edward Albee: I think I've written just as unpleasantly about men. I don't think I've written any more unpleasantly about

anybody than anybody else has. Take a rather good playwright
named Shakespeare. Lady Macbeth, lots of these lady characters.
Or take Ibsen. Take Chekhov. You can't write a play without conflict
and you can't write a successful serious play about people without
problems.

Jeanne Wolf: You don't have any strong anti-women feelings?

Edward Albee: Heavens, no. It's a fiction that has come up.
Actually, the women in my plays are stronger and more able to deal
with life than the men are. That's exactly the way it is in Ibsen's
plays. The men tend to be passive; the women, active. The only
people who've perpetuated this fiction about women in my plays
being unpleasant are people who themselves can't accept women as
being strong and vital and vocal people.

Jeanne Wolf: Being a star playwright there must be an aspect of
your life that's very tough. People wondering "Did he use all of his
energy up in *Who's Afraid of Virginia Woolf?* Does he still have
another play in him?" Don't you go through that yourself without
them doing that to you? Do you ask, "Can I do it again?"

Edward Albee: No. As long as I know that I've always got two
or three plays in the back of my head, I make the assumption that if
they turn out not to be any good that I won't let them be seen. I will
be concerned when I don't have any ideas. I think I'm objective
enough to know when I would write a lousy play.

Jeanne Wolf: We have only thirty minutes for a TV show, and
time is up. Thanks.

Edward Albee: Okay.

Edward Albee Takes to the Air

Alan Rich/1976

From *Radio Times* [London], 27 March-2 April 1976, 12.
Reprinted by permission of Radio Times.

To most Americans, the news that Edward Albee has written a play for radio is a little like having General Motors announce the revival of the hand-cranked automobile. As far as the vast bulk of American radio is concerned, original drama is the thing of the distant past, while radio itself has become an adjunct of the wallpaper industry: a background, mostly musical, against which other activities can take place unimpeded by any serious demands upon the attention.

Yet even in the American radio wasteland there have been some small attempts to restore to broadcast sound some measure of the artistic self-respect it once enjoyed in that country, and which it still enjoys in Europe. Albee's new play—called, appropriately enough, *Listening*—is the direct result of one such attempt. "I was lecturing in the small university town of River Falls, Wisconsin," Albee recalled in New York last month, "when a nice lady came up and asked if I would write a radio play. I agreed, rather casually, and then put it out of my mind. Six months later I began to think about it again, and here we are."

The "nice lady" had turned out to be a representative of Earplay, a non-commercial organization founded in 1972 by a University of Wisconsin professor of communication arts named Karl Schmidt. It produces some 30 original American radio plays a year and makes them available, on records, to nearly 200 educational broadcasters in the US, mainly stations maintained by colleges.

Sitting in a New York hotel room prior to final rehearsals of his play, Edward Albee—slight, intense, given to slouching, his new moustache imparting a donnish look like a somewhat-too-young understudy for George in *Who's Afraid of Virginia Woolf?*—waxed unwontedly voluble on the subject of everything but the play itself.

121

About the latter: "Oh, it's just another of those things about people's failure to communicate. It's about three people who talk, but who don't say anything, and so all their talking merely becomes absurd."

Does writing for voices only impose some special discipline? "Not really," Albee replied. "I think I always write for voices first of all. Many of my plays—*The Zoo Story* certainly, and *A Delicate Balance*, and *All Over*—would work just as well on radio as on the stage. Perhaps *Tiny Alice* wouldn't: that has quite a lot of visual virtuosity. But I think that a great many plays today would benefit greatly by *not* being staged. Take O'Neill's *Long Day's Journey*, for example, or many of the plays of Lanford Wilson. If we had the radio drama here they have had in England, those plays would probably have been written for radio."

What about *Virginia Woolf?* "Well, that's a special case. It has been recorded, and produced on BBC radio, but I imagine that most people who hear the play have either seen it on stage or on film, so they know the action. Look: most plays of a generation ago spend their first half-hour or so just giving information, so that even if you don't see the action you know everything that has happened, or is about to happen. When some of these plays are revived today, you can go crazy with impatience until all that exposition has been gone through. Today—and *Virginia Woolf* is a case in point—we have learned how to give that information much more subtly. Writing for radio is based on the assumption that people will listen with intense concentration. But that's not the writer's problem; it's the listener's."

Enter, at this point, Irene Worth who, along with James Ray and Maureen Anderman, makes up the cast of *Listening* (Albee himself will speak a few stray lines). She is now an Albee veteran, having played Alice in *Tiny Alice* both in New York and London; she has been captivating New York this season as the "Princess" in a revival of Tennessee Williams's *Sweet Bird of Youth*. She is also, of course, a veteran of BBC radio drama, and regards radio work as the ultimate refinement of the actor's art.

"To me, radio is *it*. Working just with the sound of your voice means getting back to the absolute purity of the original as the author set it down. It's terribly hard work, of course; it demands complete control over both the voice and the thought behind it.

When I'm on the stage, I can distort a line here and there, because I have the stage movement to give it colour. But before the microphone, anything even slightly off true becomes totally false.

"I think the persistence of radio drama in Europe, and the signs that it's coming back in America, are extremely important. It isn't a transitional art, you know, or something that's just a substitute for the real thing. People listen to radio, and are doing so more and more, partly out of dissatisfaction with the banality of so much television. It's better to hear *something*, after all, than to watch *nothing*.

"I know Edward doesn't want us to talk in detail about his new play, so I'll just say that, to me, it's an absolutely brilliant piece. In a sense, it is the realization of something T. S. Eliot said to me when I was in *The Cocktail Party* and I made the mistake of asking him what the play was about. Eliot said that, for him, the horror of life at that time was the absolute breakdown in the ability of people to reach one another. We make noises, he said, and think we're talking. We look at one another, and think we're seeing. And we're wrong."

"Let me make one final point," Albee said. "I told you before that writing *Listening* for radio took no special technique or discipline on my part. That's true, but at the same time I can see now that radio writing can be valuable to any writer, because of the flexibility of the medium and the chance it gives for trying things out. Writers in America don't have nearly enough opportunity to test out the *sound* of their words before they get to the stage. Radio gives us that opportunity.

"As for *Listening*, I wrote it for radio, but that doesn't mean it couldn't be staged some day. As far as my immediate plans for London are concerned, I've been approached by Peter Hall about my last stage play, *Seascape*, but nothing has been settled. Beyond that, my plans are in the best possible shape: nothing and everything."

Edward Albee Speaks

Brooks von Ranson/1977

From *Connecticut* (February 1977), 38-39. Reprinted with permission from *Connecticut Magazine*.

Two new plays by Pulitzer Prize-winning playwright Edward Albee had their American stage premiere at the Hartford Stage Company on January 28 and will run through March 6. *Counting the Ways* and *Listening*, despite the titles, are about lack of communication between and among people. *Listening*, a self-described chamber piece, is musical in form, with recurring themes and arias. *Counting the Ways* is a series of vaudeville-style blackouts involving a husband and wife. Angela Lansbury appears in both plays; she is directed by Albee himself. In view of this important theatrical event, the rapidly increasing importance of regional theatre, and Edward Albee's past association with Hartford, *Connecticut* interviews Albee for his views on the state of the art and the state of Hartford.

Q: I understand you're interested in music. What kind?

A: Serious music.

Q: What's serious music?

A: I have extreme catholicity of taste. I suppose I listen to everything from as early as I can find to as present as I can find. I guess I like eighteenth-and twentieth-century music more than nineteenth century, generally speaking. And there's some very good jazz.

Q: What about reading?

A: I do it.

Q: What have you read most recently?

A: *The Ordeal of Gilbert Pinfold* by Evelyn Waugh, a novel about his madness; one of Kawabata's novels, the Japanese novelist; two late plays by John Osborne; a book of Kenneth Tynan's dramatic criticism; and autobiography by Louise Nevelson. That's in the past couple of weeks.

Q: What about criticism, do you read much of it?

124

A: Not too much.

Q: Who stands out?

A: You see, the problem with answering your questions about what I listen to and what I read is that I never bother to remember because it all happens so naturally.

Q: You do impressively well citing titles.

A: I read lots of poetry, too.

Q: What poets do you like?

A: I like lots of poets.

Q: Have you ever considered working in the movies?

A: Very difficult.

Q: Why?

A: Because you're not in control. You're not your own man. I will take a movie assignment from time to time, to keep the wolf from the door, but I don't do it with any great joy or enthusiasm because I know that some halfwit of a director is going to want to revise everything I do, and then some quarterwit of a producer is going to do the rest.

Q: It seems as if movies are becoming increasingly more the contemporary art form.

A: I dare say they are, but I'm not sure that's good, however.

Q: Why not?

A: Because it's a passive experience.

Q: What's wrong with a passive experience?

A: It's synthetic, fundamentally. It's also a synthetic experience. One knows that it's jerry-built, and put together, and one is safe in everything one experiences during the course of it. It's George Orwell time.

Q: What about television?

A: I think public television is fine. Television is one of the most extraordinary educational things ever invented. It's misused. And it's doing more damage than good at the moment, and furthermore, I don't see any way of correcting it. What I object to in television is that it invades one's privacy far too much.

Q: You can always turn it off.

A: Yes, but most people don't.

Q: We haven't talked about what probably should be the most important thing, and that is regional theatre. I understand that you are very interested in regional theatre, that you think that's where the action is.

A: I never said that.

Q: No? Then why are you having plays premiered at the Hartford Stage Company?

A: *Counting the Ways* had its world premiere at the National Theatre in London on December 6. Therefore, *Counting the Ways* is having its American premiere at the Hartford Stage Company. *Listening* was commissioned as a radio play and was broadcast all over the United States and all over Britain and Europe.

Q: Why did you want to do a radio play?

A: I didn't. I was writing the play, and I was given a commission to do a radio play, and I realized that since almost all of the action in *Listening* was interior, it would work just as well or almost as well on the radio as it would on stage. So it is having its world stage premiere at the Hartford Stage Company. So neither one of them is actually a world premiere. They are both having their American stage premiere.

Q: All right, but why not New York?

A: Hartford is a congenial environment.

Q: It's congenial for premieres? Why?

A: Because one is given a subscription audience, a guaranteed run. These are not the easiest plays in the world.

Q: Nor was *All Over* [Hartford Stage Company, 1975].

A: True. Well, that lasted longer in Hartford than it did in New York.

Q: Because you had a subscription audience?

A: That's right. And I don't have to be subject to that make-or-break commercial situation that exists even in the off-Broadway theatre in New York. These are not ideal plays for the Winter Garden Theatre.

Q: Why?

A: Because they are intimate, difficult, avant-garde plays.

Q: What do you mean difficult, avant-garde?

A: Well, you read them and see. They're not your usual commercial fare.

Q: Why does somebody like you want to write difficult, avant-garde plays? Because you don't care about success?

A: I don't particularly want to write them, but every play comes out in its own way. Some of them are more commercially successful than others.

Q: Do you worry about that at all?

A: No. That's the way it is. *All Over* is less commercially accessible than *Who's Afraid of Virginia Woolf?*

Q: Obviously, if you say movies are passive and synthetic, and that's why you're a playwright and aren't interested in movies, etc. the interplay of the audience and your play becomes terribly important. I saw *All Over*, and I went with someone who fell asleep during it.

A: Well, you know, it's not a law that people have to pay attention.

Q: Does that worry you, though?

A: I suppose it raises a few questions as to whether one is communicating clearly, but if you reexamine the work and decide that you are, to the terms of the work . . .

Q: You use the word communicating. I don't think anybody knows what that word means.

A: It comes from the word "to commune." I think the word is clear in its meaning.

Q: Communication professors would differ with you.

A: Well, then maybe they're using the word differently than it was intended originally. All right. Then I will change it to "commune with the audience."

Q: You went to Trinity. You must know Hartford very well. What do you think of Hartford?

A: I wish there were some way to stop spending all the money on those awful buildings and give enough money for the museum [Wadsworth Atheneum] to stay open decent hours. That's the primary reason for me to go to Hartford.

Q: The museum?

A: I mean except for the Hartford Stage Company, of course.

Q: And of course when it has your plays.

A: Especially then, Not only then, but especially then. But I think it's shocking that such a wealthy community as Hartford treats its museum shabbily. Wouldn't you think all those enormous insurance companies could spend a little bit of money to keep the museum open? Or do they try to help? When I was there, I guess a year ago, one had to race from section to section in the hour it happened to be open. The last time I appeared on stage as an actor was at that museum. There is that auditorium, the Wadsworth. We used to do our Trinity College plays there.

Q: So you were active in the theatre at Trinity?

A: Yes, I was. Until they stopped me because I wouldn't go to classes, you see, and they told me I couldn't be in the theatre if I wouldn't go to classes. I didn't go to chapel either.

Q: I understand that you're interested in college theatre.

A: Yes, you see some good productions in college theatre. Clear productions, because they haven't learned to be failed actors yet. They haven't learned how to be bad actors yet.

Q: Are you active in college theatre at all?

A: No, but I go and lecture in colleges from time to time.

Q: Do you ever teach?

A: No, I don't like to teach.

Q: Why not?

A: I wouldn't mind—if I had a group of six extremely gifted young playwrights, I'd like to do a workshop with them and see their works [through] to production. Also, I don't like to commit myself for a year or a semester. But why should I limit myself to teaching six people when I can reach thousands by doing my own work?

Q: Are you rehearsing the Hartford plays in New York?

A: Probably, for the first two weeks. The museums in New York are open. I think we'll rehearse in New York for the first two weeks because the actors will be based in New York. Why should everybody go to Hartford? Not that there's anything terrible about going to Hartford, but they live in New York. Actors are happier, and so are authors and directors if they live at home.

Q: Can we talk a little about what you remember about Hartford?

A: I liked the Heublein [hotel and restaurant] very much. Why did they tear it down? I used to go to the museum, and I used to go to the Heublein. I like them both very much. That's all I remember about it. My God, that's 1946, 47.

Q: What courses did you take at Trinity?

A: I remember taking ones that I wasn't supposed to take and that I would go to the classes I thought I should go to that were not required [such as] philosophy and French and various other things, creative writing, literature at any rate. You know, interesting survey courses that interested me, but I did not go to chapel or athletics or mathematics or science, which were all required.

Q: Did you make any friends there, either among faculty or students?

A: Nobody that's lasted through the thirty years. There was a nice man who taught aesthetics. I can't remember who he was, except that he was British.

Q: Rumor has it that *Who's Afraid of Virginia Woolf?* was based on a Trinity couple.

A: Well, every place I go to lecture has that rumor. No, it's not based on any college. I didn't spend that much time with the faculty or with anybody.

Q: What I love most about your work is the ear you have for dialogue. How does one go about getting that absolutely pure sound of how people really talk?

A: Just listening.

Q: You've never used any particular devices? You just listen to the people who are around you? You don't make an effort to get beyond that circle?

A: Not a conscious one.

Q: Like listening to people on the subway?

A: Oh, I listen to everything.

Q: And you have the capacity to retain it?

A: Well, I listen to the shape of a conversation and to what's happening, as well as the content.

Q: You don't really like to talk about your work per se.

A: My feeling is that if a play can be discussed adequately without seeing it, then you haven't done your job with the play.

Edward Albee "If the Play Can Be Described in One Sentence, That Should Be Its Length"

Allan Wallach/1979

From *The Times-Picayune*, 10 January 1979, 4. © 1979 Newsday.
Reprinted by permission of Newsday.

In the 20 years that he has been writing plays, Edward Albee has elicited enormous praise and indignant condemnation. But whatever the reaction to a new Albee play, there is widespread agreement that it is a major theater event.

Albee has been accorded serious attention since his early one-act plays stamped him as one of the country's most talented young playwrights—and one of the angriest. In an oft-quoted preface to his 1960 *The American Dream*, he called the play a condemnation of the "complacency, cruelty, emasculation and vacuity" that characterize much of our society. Although his plays have become more subtle and metaphorical since then, his view of the society has not softened significantly.

It was not until his three-act *Who's Afraid of Virginia Woolf?* was produced in 1962 that Albee achieved international fame. The Pulitzer Prize that was denied him for that scathing work was awarded to him for two later plays, the 1966 *A Delicate Balance* and the 1975 *Seascape*. In addition to several adaptations, his longer plays have included the metaphysical *Tiny Alice* (1964) and *All Over* (1971).

Born 50 years ago in Washington, Albee was adopted as an infant by Mr. and Mrs. Reid Albee, heirs to the Keith-Albee vaudeville chain. At the age of 30 he wrote his first one-act play, *The Zoo Story*. Albee was named last month's company playwright of Lincoln Center's Vivian Beaumont Theater, which will reopen by 1980. He recently directed three programs of his one-act plays. He was interviewed as a national tour of the plays began.

Question: I head that your next play, *The Lady From Dubuque*, is somewhat in the style of *Virginia Woolf*.

130

Albee: I don't know whether it is or not. I can't get that objective about my own work. It probably gives the illusion of being as naturalistic a play as *Who's Afraid of Virginia Woolf?* I don't think that's a particularly naturalistic play either. None of my plays is, and all of them are, depending on the approach you take to it. It's not a highly stylized play like *The American Dream*; it's not a terribly experimental play on the surface of it like *Quotations From Chairman Mao Tse-tung*; it's not vaudeville like *Counting the Ways*; it's not theoretically opaque like *Listening*. It's a fairly devious play with a fairly easy-going surface to it.

Question: Can you say more about it?

Albee: I'm terrible about giving that one-sentence description of the play because, as I've said before, if the play can be described in one sentence, that should be its length. It's about, I suppose, the fact that our reality is determined by other people's view of it. The old argument between Descartes and various other people, Bishop Berkeley and others. I don't want to get very specific about the play.

Question: In directing your one-act plays, including some you may not have looked at in a while, did you find any changes in style as you progressed from the earlier to the later ones?

Albee: I can never find any direction in my work whatever. I do not think I'm getting a bit more in control of my material. I can't go back and rewrite any of them—not that I really want to; I think they hold up rather well. I think *The American Dream* may be a trifle slapdash; that was written with a certain youthful enthusiasm and it's occasionally fairly ham-handed in its effects, and its metaphors are hardly as subtle as the metaphors are in the later work. I think I probably handle structure a good deal better and I'm probably more in command of my material. But as to what they're about, I can never draw a straight line there from one to another. This is an interesting group of plays, and since it does take from 1959 through 1977, which is 18 years of my one-act plays, it's fairly interesting. Three early ones, a couple of middle ones and a couple of late ones. Not late; I mean I'm in the middle right now. A couple of early, a couple of middle-early and a couple of middle ones, because I haven't written the last ones yet.

Question: Did you discover any new facets in directing them?

Albee: I am startled by how little I'm able to cut. As a director I do want to cut a great deal. I must have done all the cutting in previous productions because I find very, very little that I can cut in these plays with out taking out tendons. There's very little fat that I can cut, I find. And also, I'm a little leery about cutting my work 10 or 15 years after I've written it. I wouldn't let any other stranger meddle with my stuff, so why should I, as a stranger, meddle with something I wrote 15 years ago?

Question: When you wrote that play, you were labeled by some critics as a playwright of protest. Did you ever accept that label?

Albee: I dismiss all labels. Theater of the Absurd. Angry Young Man. Playwright of Protest. Labels are so facile, and they're a substitute for conscientious analysis so much of the time. I like to think that my plays are out to change people, out to make them more aware of themselves and to point out misuse of consciousness, I suppose, as much as anything. And I certainly don't think my more recent plays are any less concerned with that; they may be concerned more indirectly from time to time.

Question: Do you think the later ones are less angry than the early ones?

Albee: I don't think so. I think they're less strident. I don't think they're any less angry at all.

Question: Would you say there are some things that keep recurring from play to play?

Albee: Oh, I'm sure there are. Again, I'm pretty bad about that. I read about these from time to time. I'm told that I'm concerned with people refusing to communicate rather than being unable to. Since all of my people are terribly articulate, they could communicate if they chose to. But they don't choose to. I'm sure there are recurrent themes.

Question: You once said that one theme was the way people get through their lives, and whether they'd loved one another enough.

Albee: Yes, the old James thing, in that story that Henry James wrote about a man who had a nagging suspicion that something terrible was going to happen to him during his life. And he kept worrying and worrying and worrying about it, and somewhere in his 50s or late 50s he figured out what that terrible thing was: the terrible thing was that absolutely nothing was going to happen to him. He was going to go through his entire life safely, without adventure, without danger, without full participation. And by the time he figured that out it was too late. Yeah, there are a lot of people like that. And that's one of the terrible things about what's going on in our country now: People have pulled back even further into me first, and let-me-get-through-as-comfortably-and-as-asleep-as-possible. That's a very dangerous thing. Maybe it's a sign of a civilization collapsing.

Question: Having reached the milestone age of 50, do you have any feelings like that man in the Henry James story that you'd have done things differently if you had it to do over again?

Albee: No, I don't think I've wasted my time at all, you see. I can't remember any period of my time that I've wasted, really. I do plan to live for a very long time because I have a great deal that I plan to do. I've got another 20 or 25 plays to write, a lot of places to see and things to do.

Question: Do you try consciously to disturb an audience? If you succeed, what do you feel that you've done to the audience?

Albee: I hope, put them in contact with areas of their feelings that they may have gotten out of contact with, or maybe make them see things from a different point of view. To think about things they haven't thought about, think about them differently. Affect them in some way that they'll have to react differently in the future to things.

Question: Some of your plays have dealt with philosophical concepts. Do you feel that's unusual for an American playwright?

Albee: The life of the mind? Yeah, fairly unusual. That may be one of the reasons that a lot of my plays are a lot more popular in Europe than they are in this country.

Question: One other area that's interesting is that you're probably the only well-known playwright around who has written about faith, in a religious sense, in at least one play, *Tiny Alice*. Does that suggest anything about your background?

Albee: Well, I was raised in the Episcopal Church, which I left when I was 6 years old. That was the extent of my formal religious training. But I remember I left the Episcopal Church because . . . Why did I leave it? I was terribly upset about the idea of the Crucifixion. As a child I had to be taken out, crying, from Sunday

school or church during the story of the Crucifixion. I was really a
kid, and that upset me a lot. I think I've always been very interested
in Jesus Christ. About the only substantial and good Marxist I know
about.

Question: Can you recall what your original impulses were when
you began writing?

Albee: No, not really. I was quite startled when I wrote *The Zoo
Story*, but it seemed very natural to be a playwright so I kept right
on with it.

Question: And you had written as a child.

Albee: Oh, yeah, but a lot of lousy stuff.

Question: What was it about theater specifically that attracted
you, as opposed to other forms of writing?

Albee: I guess the major thing about theater more than anything
else was that I did it very well. I didn't do poetry very well, or the
novel very well, and I did theater well. So naturally, you feel at
home in what you do well. Reasonably well, anyway. And there's
something very nice about the magic and the immediacy of theater.
It's not passive, the way the novel is; it's not synthetic, the way film
is. There's something very real and dangerous about theater that I
like. The theatrical event is a real event in the way that many things
aren't. Things can happen unexpectedly. You go to see a film and
you know that everything's planned. There is no reality there; it's all
synthetic experience.

Question: You had once talked about doing some screenwriting,
though.

Albee: Yeah, but they never let me do it the way I wanted to.
You get spoiled in the theater; you end up being your own boss.

Question: Do you get impatient when intellectuals or pseudo-
intellectuals analyze your plays in terms of symbols?

Albee: Well, I wish they'd spend more time in seeing things as
what they are rather than what they're supposed to represent. I
mean, some people go into a dramatic experience determined not
to have the dramatic experience, but merely to have all the allusory
stuff that's connected with it. I mean, the metaphors and the
symbols you're supposed to get afterwards, not sit there with a
notebook not enjoying the emotional content of the plays so you
can seem bright.

Question: Have you seen any plays lately that you've really admired?

Albee: That I've really admired? I see maybe one or two plays a year because I go to an awful lot of theater around the country. I see two or three plays a year that interest me.

Question: You're probably the only major playwright who does adaptations of other people's work. Is there some satisfaction you get in doing them?

Albee: I enjoy doing them very much. Now I've been commissioned to do an adaptation of Nabokov's *Lolita*. That interests me very much . . . it's a totally different kind of experience, becoming somebody else.

Question: What do you like to do when you're not writing?

Albee: Oh, I like to write. I don't consider that work. I like to read, to see friends, to cook, to listen to music, to walk on the beach, to make love, I like to do just about every single thing that everybody else does. I like to drive, I like to shop, I like to sing from time to time. The usual stuff.

Edward Albee: A Playwright Versus the Theatre

Peter Adam/1980

From *The Listener*, 102 (7 February 1980), 170-171. Excerpted from an interview originally transmitted on BBC2 on 8 February 1980 and entitled "Edward Albee—The Playwright versus the Theatre." Reprinted by permission of Peter Adam.

I think a person is born a playwright or a painter or whatever, because it's a way of responding to reality and translating it into something else. If you happen to write plays, that's your way of translating something. Edward Albee

I decided when I was very, very young that I was a writer. I didn't decide that I was going to be a writer, but with this healthy immodesty that is required in the arts in this country I decided that I was. Having no common sense at all, at the age of six I began writing that naked and most complex of all forms—I began writing poetry. I wrote poetry from the age of six to 26, when I stopped.

As for my education, I was put into, and managed to get myself thrown out of, a great number of the better preparatory schools in the northeastern United States, graduating finally from a place called Choate—a prep school where they taught me two things that I remember, two things of value to me. They taught me, first, that the function of an education is to learn how to educate yourself when you get out of school, and secondly—and this lesson is very important to anybody knowing they are not planned to be in the theatre— they taught me how to make a fool of myself in public. If you are in the theatre you do this constantly, and it's wise to learn it early.

When I was 26 I went back to New York City, to Greenwich Village, where I lived for ten years before I hit upon the idea of writing a play. *Zoo Story* was produced in German in West Berlin on a double bill with Samuel Beckett's *Krapp's Last Tape* in the autumn of 1959, and produced off Broadway in January 1960 on the same double bill in English, where it ran for approximately three years.

the same double bill in English, where it ran for approximately three years.

When I'm directing a play of mine I will be more strict with myself as an author than I will allow any other director to be. I see a play when I write it, I know pretty well how it's going to look, sound, feel and smell, and that's what I am interested in seeing the audience receive. I will not necessarily make my plays as effective or flashy as other people will, but I will certainly, since my aim is clarity, make them clearer. And I find that with a good play—anybody's good play—seeing it on stage is merely a proof of what exists on the page and not an improvement on it, not a completion of it, merely a proof of it. A bad play could be improved by production, a first-rate play can only be proved, not improved, by production.

Peter Adam: Do you have the feeling that your characters take over and dictate to you the play?

Edward Albee: All writers who pretend that their characters take over and dictate the play know better, because we all know that we are creating the characters and nothing that they say comes from anywhere other than in our minds. But there is this thing called creativity which resides in the unconscious, and this sense of the character taking over comes from connections that we are making to the unconscious. Sometimes I will be writing along in a play of mine and a character will say something that I didn't know I knew—but obviously I knew it, I just didn't know it consciously. The characters can't know anything that I don't know, but they can inform me of conclusions that I've come to on things that I know without knowing them.

Peter Adam: Does it happen that your characters are more real than the real world?

Edward Albee: Sometimes, after three or four hours of working on a play, involving myself very carefully with the characters, I will look at my friends downstairs or people who are about and they will have a kind of unreality to them, for a few minutes.

Peter Adam: So your characters in your plays are more real to you than reality?

Edward Albee: No, I wouldn't come to that conclusion as a result of it; they are more organised, perhaps.

Peter Adam: Do you write in spurts or great outbursts, or do you reserve a space every day for writing?

Edward Albee: Well, I write for a very long time in my head without putting anything down on paper. I will keep an idea for a play going for a long time—six months, eight years, 15 years—and then I will write it down. When I actually literally write it down, that's fairly concentrated and a play will be literally written down in no more than two months. But I will have thought about it on and off for a long time. Then again, I usually keep three or four plays in my head in various stages of development.

Peter Adam: But what happens when it suddenly gels, and you say: "Now I'm going to write it down"?

Edward Albee: That means to me that it has moved irrevocably into the conscious and won't go back to the unconscious again, so I have to write it down to get it out of my head.

Peter Adam: You make several drafts then?

Edward Albee: No, usually two.

Peter Adam: What happens when you finish writing a play? Is it finished or do you like to go over it and revise it?

Edward Albee: Well, I would never go back to a play that I had written several years before, I mean I won't let anyone else mess with anything I've written, so why should I mess with it a few years later when I am no longer the same person. I would rather get it fairly close to right the first time, which is probably why I wait so long before I write anything down. I trust my own conscious a lot.

Peter Adam: There is enormous opportunity for a talented young playwright in the United States to have his work performed. More opportunity now than ever, because of the regional theatres and off Broadway and off off Broadway.

Edward Albee: At the same time, it's more difficult for a young playwright to have a serious play done in the commercial theatre on Broadway. This week, if I wanted to see a play on Broadway— which is the commercial theatre centre of the United States, and also the theatre centre that fundamentally determines the theatre taste of the rest of the country—I could not see plays by the following playwrights on Broadway this week in New York City. I could not see plays by Shakespeare, Sophocles, Racine, Wilde, Shaw, Ibsen, Strindberg or Chekhov. I could also not see plays by

Beckett, Ionesco, Pirandello, Brecht, O'Neill, Pinter, Tennessee Williams, or, for that matter, by me.

We know that the commercial film in the United States, eager as it is to make money, is producing less and less of any interest to anybody. The live theatre is the only area which has retained some portion of its integrity. What can one do in a society in which commercial success is equated with excellence? What do we do in a society where what the public wants becomes a standard of judgment, and what is done in the large Broadway theatres is considered the standard by which the theatre as an art form should be judged in this country?

It's been stated that in the "Megalopolis" around New York City there is a guaranteed audience for a serious play of around 60,000 people. That's 60,000 out of an enormous population of around 19 million who can get to New York with some regularity. I doubt if more than one per cent care very much about what is called serious theatre.

Peter Adam: Do you think it's more difficult for a serious playwright in America than it would be in Europe?

Edward Albee: I think probably what there is in Europe and Britain is a tradition of going to the theatre as a natural experience that we don't have in this country. As an art form in the United States, the theatre really began to be taken seriously after the Second World War. By the time the theatre started to become a force in the United States consciousness, television was looming and film had really taken over the entertainment nature of our people.

Peter Adam: Is there any particular aspect of your work that you dislike?

Edward Albee: I dislike the fact that one cannot always get the actress that one wants to work in a play because they've been grabbed up or devoured by Hollywood or commercial television. I dislike the fact that there are pressures on almost all playwrights to simplify their work to reach a larger audience. I dislike the fact that most of our critics are stupid. I dislike the fact that most of our audiences are lazy.

Most theatre criticism in the United States is laughable. But then again, most theatre criticism in Europe is laughable too, because, basically, the people who are writing it are not practitioners of the arts and lack the understanding of the creative act. I'm interested in what other playwrights, painters, poets, composers, novelists think about my work. I have my own private views about how well I write compared to other people but I don't think about it very much. That would make me rigid. I just want to get better as a writer. I've written 19 plays, I plan to write at least another 19. By then maybe I will have mastered my craft and we'll find out whether I'm any good or not.

What does amuse me are the critics, especially these people who write books on me, who are making judgments on the nature of my work when they *can't* know anything about the nature of my work because I haven't finished it yet. I've only made half the statement, and they can't make any judgment about the overall art of the work. I read some books where they refer to my "late style," as if I had stopped writing!

Peter Adam: Why are you so fascinated by the ambiguity of life's situations?

Edward Albee: I guess probably because if I limit what I wrote to questions that I had the answers to I would be a very limited and dull playwright. And I am more interested in examing things that I don't have the answers to. I don't find that most things are ambiguous and ambivalent, and I find great fascination in that.

Peter Adam: But don't you think one of the aspects of a playwright or a writer is to give up to us, the audience, some of the answers?

Edward Albee: No, I don't think so at all. I think it's the responsibility of the playwright to say: 'Here are some of the questions, you find the answers.' I've been accused of becoming hermetic in my more recent work, and that my concern with language is getting a bit problematical for some people but that's just tough. They ignore the fact that some of my plays are absolutely straightforward, and the next one will be hermetic and difficult. My last play, which was called *Listening*, was commissioned by the BBC and done on the radio, and was a fairly hermetic piece. My latest play, *The Lady from Dubuque*, which does raise a few metaphysical questions perhaps, is a relatively straightforward piece. *Counting the Ways*, which was produced at the National Theatre in

Edward Albee: I mistrust any rigidity. I go to a university and there is a question-and-answer period, and there are about 19 questions that you hear all the time: why do you write?; how do you write?—you know, all those questions. You can rely on your brain to furnish you with the usual answer to the question. But every once in a while somebody will ask me a question—No 17— and I will begin my answer and, right in the middle of it, I will realise that a) it is no longer true, or b) that I don't believe it any more. So I've learned to mistrust attitudes of that sort. In the same way that I loathe to talk about my work.

Peter Adam: Are you never tempted to repeat commercial success?

Edward Albee: Write *The Son of Who's Afraid of Virginia Woolf?!* I don't know how I'd do it. I wish someone would tell me how I'd do it. And I'd go right ahead and do it. No I wouldn't. I guess it's better to succeed in your intention with a play than fail at it, but at the same time it's pretty useful to try something so difficult that you won't quite succeed, rather than to try something less than you know that you can succeed at.

Peter Adam: You've had failures?

Edward Albee: I've had a number of plays where I've reached too far—thank heavens—and I keep on hoping that I will reach too far. I'd hate to think that I would ever settle for what I can do easily. I'm interested in finding out how my career comes out, and I suspect that unless I try to screw it up somehow by imposing on it, it's going to evolve itself quite naturally, and at the end of it I'll have some sense of what I've been about. I would never try to arbitrarily simplify or popularise, mythologise, or anything. I think it's dangerous to do that because you are no longer your own man, you belong to somebody else. I suppose this question should come up: "Why should anybody bother to concern himself about the state of the arts in this society of ours at this present time?" We've had quite a bit to worry and concern us in America in the last 15 years, things of some magnitude. Why should we care about things so

seemingly ephemeral, so seemingly useless, as the arts. Well, I think
there's only one reason why we should. We are the only animal
who consciously creates art. We are the only animal who attempts
metaphor. It is our distinguishing mark. If we turn out to be the kind
of society that is unwilling to use the metaphor, unwilling to use art
to instruct us about ourselves, then we are this curious kind of
society which is on its way downhill without ever having reached the
top. And indeed, if we are unwise enough not to be instructed by
the arts, then perhaps we do lack the will and the wisdom—the
courage—to support a free society.

Edward Albee: An Interview

Edited by Patricia De La Fuente/1980

From *Edward Albee: Planned Wilderness, Living Authors Series No. 3,* ed. Patricia De La Fuente (Edinburg, Texas: School of Humanities, Pan American University, 1980), 6-17. Reprinted by permission.

Q: The first question is raised by Jean Paul Sartre's death last week: since you have the image of boxes and confinement in many of your plays, were you influenced by Sartre at all, particularly by his *No Exit?*

A: Well, there are certain writers you come across that if you aren't influenced by them you are a damned fool. My first experience with Beckett, Genet, Ionesco, Sartre, Camus—going back further even, my first experience with Gide was a powerful influence. All these things should be influences. I just assume naturally that I've read Sartre and Camus as the novels were coming out; I saw the plays when they were first done. Obviously it must have influenced me.

Q: Were you conscious of influence?

A: I am not conscious of much of anything in the sense that when I read a book or see a play, look at a picture or even listen to a piece of music, I don't recall the experience a week afterwards. It just vanishes into my head, and then I'll discover twenty years later that a character of mine will have figured something out based on something that I had read twenty years ago. So I don't retain things. And so I'm never aware whether I'm being consciously influenced by something or not. It's an osmosis process with me, I think.

Q: When you write plays, do you have an underlying thought or do they emerge and surprise you as much as they surprise the audience?

A: Well, that would depend on the critic you are reading. There are certainly some critics who think I haven't had a thought in my head ever. Obviously there must be something that prompts plays, something that I have been thinking about. When I write a play, I am so much more involved with the three-dimensional reality of the moment that I don't consider the implications. There is nothing more embarrassing than to realize you are writing a metaphor. Just create it and then go away until it's over. Then you go back to your work.

Q: You made a statement this morning to the effect that you saw writing a play as an aggressive act against the status quo. Could you elaborate on that?

A: I wasn't talking about all plays, actually. Obviously. There are a number of plays that are written to aid flight from reality, aid in people's escapism. There are some that are just confected as escapist entertainment. But all serious art, not just plays, is an attempt to modify and change people's perception of themselves, to bring them into larger contact with the fact of being alive. It is the function of art to do that. Art is not pacification. It's disturbance. And since its attempt is to change, even though it works indirectly sometimes, it doesn't work by pacification. It's not the function of it.

Q: Art should shake up then; it should shake up the audience?

A: If we lived in a utopian society, there would be no need for art because the function of art is to make people better. If we lived in a utopian society, everybody would be perfect, so art would vanish; but I think we are a certain distance from that anyway, aren't we? I have noticed.

Q: Talking of audience, how much does your implied or prospective audience influence the way in which you work?

A: I hope not at all.

Q: Not at all? Don't you consider at all the aesthetic experience for the audience in the way you structure your work?

A: I think it's unsafe to anticipate a kind of audience or the nature of an audience response or even the socio-economic nature of an audience that your work is going to reach. It is foolish to do that because you may unconsciously modify what you are setting out to do. I think you have to assume that your theoretical audience is going to bring to what you have done some of the same enthusiasm, perception, information, dedication and open-mindedness that you have put into it.

Q: But at least you hope that this open-mindedness is out there when you are writing.

A: Oh, yes, writing is an act of optimism. You assume there is somebody out there to pay attention. To those people who accuse me of being a pessimist I always say, "Nonsense, I write."

Q: Do you find quite a difference between the audience at large and the critics as a group?

A: Well, one is a group of human beings, one is not.

Q: I think you said in an interview in *The New Yorker* that there is very little relationship between what the critics say you do and what you do. Will you comment on this?

A: I've noticed that there is not necessarily a great relationship between what the majority of critics have to say and what is actually true. Some of them are so busy trying to mold the public taste according to the limits of their perceptions, and others are so busy reflecting what they consider to be the public taste—that view limited again by their perception. You find very few critics who approach their job with a combination of information and enthusiasm and humility that makes for a good critic. But there is nothing wrong with critics as long as people don't pay any attention to them. I mean, nobody wants to put them out of a job and a good critic is not necessarily a dead critic. It's just that people take what a critic says as a fact rather than an opinion, and you have to know whether the opinion of the critic is informed or uninformed, intelligent or stupid—but most people don't take the trouble.

Q: There are critics, then, who have interpreted your works in a way you would agree with?

A: Oh, there are some whom I find more generally on the side of this particular angle than others, yes. But I'm startled sometimes by how one critic can be so bright about one play of mine and so dumb about the next one. I'd say this is my war with the critics, but I've given it all up. I just tell people to ignore them.

Q: Your feeling is based mostly on your New York critics; what about theatre over the country? Perhaps we are not sophisticated enough out here in the boonies to trust what the critics say as much as New York people would.

A: It's hardly sophistication to trust and take as a fact what a critic says. I've noticed that every single one of my plays has received half good and half bad reviews. Every one—from the most commercially popular to the most apparently obscure. But it is also true that many of the plays that are not commercially successful in New York do have considerable life both on campus and in regional theatres and in Europe. In fact, I may be far more popular in Europe than I am in New York.

Q: Will this strangle hold on the critical taste that New York critics seem to have ever be broken by a viable and strong regional theatre?

A: It would be nice to think so, except that so many regional theatres are selling out now and using themselves as try-out houses for the commercial managements . . . and that's a disgrace. That's a terrible thing that's happening. I think it's a violation of the public money that's been poured in.

Q: Mr. Albee, you mentioned this morning that you were doing another adaptation. Why does the adaptation appeal to you rather than writing your own play?

A: It doesn't. I've done nineteen plays and four adaptations, which hardly suggests that it's a preoccupation of mine. But once in a while somebody comes up with an idea for something that strikes me as belonging on stage and I want to screw it up rather than let anybody else do it. I've only done four and three of them were on purpose.

Q: Is an adaptation more difficult, would you say, than your own story?

A: I don't think it's difficult. It's different, because you have to be two people. You have to be both the other author and yourself.

Q: If you had to write dialogue for a particular locale, Southern or something, is that . . .

A: Well, here's a particular example of that: I did an adaptation of Carson McCullers' *Ballad of the Sad Cafe* . . . and one of the New York critics in his infinite wisdom said that Albee didn't really have to do any work when he did this adaptation. All he did was take down the dialogue from McCullers' book and put it on stage. That pleased me a lot because there's not a line of dialogue in Carson's book . . . So I guess I succeeded in my attempt to write, which is what I've done with Nabokov's *Lolita*. I tried to write the play of *Lolita* that Nabokov would have written had he been me, if he had my dramatic sense, and I tried to assume his literary way of thinking. And people who have read this play of *Lolita*, they don't know which line of dialogue is Nabokov's and which is mine. It works as a play very differently than it does as a novel. Obviously, I had to make choices, dramatic choices. What is dramatic in the novel and what is dramatic in the play are quite different. Except people seem to feel that they are getting the essence of the piece and the nature of the piece. So I think that adaptation as much as anything is a set of mediations on *Lolita* rather than an attempt to transcribe the work from one form to another. You can't really do that. You've got to do an equivalency.

Q: Something similar, then, to translation?

A: No, because it's moving from one form to another; that makes it a different story.

Q: How about television, has that affected the theatre audience adversely, would you say?

A: About seven years ago, eight years, or maybe ten, I was at a commercial comedy in New York and somebody said something funny onstage, and where I expected the audience to laugh, they didn't, they applauded. Which meant that this was an audience that had spent its time listening, watching television and hearing canned laughter and canned applause (when people hold up the applaud sign which is off camera), and obviously they have been conditioned by what's going on on televison. I think television is the destruction of the United States. I mean, that and the Republic party . . . And the Democratic party, for that matter, come to think of it.

Q: Are you often called in as a consultant in the stage production of your work?

A: When you have a play done, if you are not directing it yourself, you hire the actors and hire the director and nobody makes any changes and you are there; you run the show.

Q: That's only if you are directing it.

A: No, no.

Q: If somebody else is directing it, you also have that much say-so?

A: Of course. It's in the author's contract—the playwright's contract. Now you can't exert much authority over a production you are not going to be at. Though I do try to control all productions of my plays, and any production within seventy-five miles of a whole list of about thirty cities in this country I get cast approval of.

Q: You have a lot of say-so as to who gets what part?

A: Oh, sure. You have to protect your work to a certain extent.

Q: Is that just the opening run?

A: Any time.

Q: Do you allow changes once rehearsals start? Do you work with the actors and listen if they suggest a change in a line?

A: I usually do. I usually do most of my homework before I let a play go into production but if an actor comes up with something that I think is better than I intended, I'll incorporate it and pretend it was my idea.

Q: I saw a movie with Tennessee Williams—a little documentary on a play he had done—and I noticed that he talked with the actors quite a lot and they responded and they changed quite a few things.

A: Tennessee may have changed his way of working. He used to resent people changing his work; but he may have changed. Is this about a new play?

Q: *Red Devil.*

A: That's a fairly recent play. I think he's changed the way he works. He used to go into rehearsal fairly in control of the situation. But I think Tennessee has lost a little of his sure footedness. I would judge by his last several plays, anyway.

Q: What play do you get the most questions about?

A: Usually *Tiny Alice*. People expect me to remember what I meant by it. And then again there are some apparently obscure ones that nobody seems to understand, like *Quotations from Chairman Mao Tse-tung* and *Listening*, an occasional play like that which seems to bewilder people. I imagine that *The Lady from Dubuque* will fall into that category. Some of them are straightforward and some of them are difficult. Not much to be done about that.

Q: What about *The Lady from Dubuque?* That has been classified as your best work since *Who's Afraid . . .*

A: It was also called, by John Simon, the worst play ever written by anybody, ever. It's one of the two.

Q: Let's assume that it's the first one.

A: Oh, it's likened to *Who's Afraid of Virginia Woolf?* only because it's in the living room and it's late and some people are sitting around drinking and they're insulting each other. But after all, that's Strindberg too, you know.

Q: It's a situation that is rather typical in your plays anyway.

A: Plays are either indoors or outdoors, and it's either two people or people with their friends usually. My people just tend to be fairly articulate in their insults.

Q: Yes, articulate is the word.

A: Let's judge, let's see a hundred years from now.

Q: How do you distinguish, or do you, between an art of propaganda and a more legitimate art?

A: You must remember what, who was it, said that if you wanted to deliver a message, call Western Union. That whole group of agit-prop plays that was written in the thirties—popular movement and propaganda plays, was very interesting. Absolutely no literary value whatever. And delivered its messages rather effectively for the time. But most effective message-delivering in drama is about the public unconscious and that should be done fairly indirectly.

Q: You don't want to frighten the audience; is that right?

A: I don't think you should frighten them, I think you should terrify them.

Q: So you wouldn't write a light comedy, like Neil Simon?

A: I have absolutely no objection to Neil Simon's plays. I wish they had some content every once in a while. I mean, I wish they were not pornographic. You know the legal definition of "pornography" I imagine: that which is without redeeming social virtue whenever they're pornographic. They're escapism without anything of issue other than pure escapism. I think one can accomplish a great deal by indirection. I think laughter caught in the mouth is absolutely marvelous. Most of my plays are far funnier in performance than they read on the page. They are quite funny and people suddenly stop laughing in the middle of a laugh, and I'm delighted when that happens. And any writer without a sense of humor is suspect. That's probably one of the two troubles with O'Neill, no sense of humor. The other one is that he couldn't write. Aside from that, he's a marvelous playwright. And he had tin ears by the way. His sense of overall dramatic form is pretty good, but no sense of humor and a tin ear. And very few writers who lack humor are really ultimately any good. That's why Chekhov is a better playwright than Ibsen. Ibsen was humorless.

Q: Do you see the American theatre as having a viability and a purpose and a life that is lacking in other countries?

A: In theory. I mean, there are all kinds of censorship. The amazing kind of self-censorship that our audiences exert in this country, determining what they will not participate in, can be just as deadly as any totalitarian society telling them what they can participate in. The ultimate results can be the same. I mean, one is enforced self-deception and the other is chosen self-deception.

Q: Is there commercial censorship in N.Y. as well?

A: Well, it is hard to have an obscure, difficult play produced in large commercial theatres, and so most serious playwrights become second-class citizens. But I suppose that is the way it should be in a capitalist democracy.

Q: You mentioned the Latin-American writers this morning. Could you tell us something about what is going on in the theatre down there?

A: Far more than we seem to know about.

Q: Yes, that's for sure. Which particular country are you talking about?

A: I'm talking about wherever the government permits its writers to perform properly; then you have a healthy theatre in Argentina, a healthy theatre in Venezuela, a fairly healthy theatre in Brazil. It depends upon the sophistication of the society usually, and the degree of totalitarianism in the government. It varies from country to country and from time to time, doesn't it?

Q: What are they doing in Argentina right now?

A: It's in a state of flux. I have lots of Argentine writer friends; some of them tell me that all the small experimental theatres have just been closed down because they were all accused of being Marxist.

Q: Yes, that's always the case.

A: Always the case. The only reason that the experimental theatres turn out being Marxist is because somebody is trying to shut them down. If people would leave them open they wouldn't be so Marxist, would they?

Q: Are they writing protest plays?

A: In the sophisticated societies in Latin America, the theatre reaches the middle class and is most sophisticated in areas where there is a middle class to reach, which may be okay, because that's the class that is going to effect change in the social structure and in a society of that sort. There are plays that obviously have learned a great deal from both the European and the American avant garde. They are right up to date. And in some countries you will find that the people work in complete isolation without even knowing what is going on in the next country because of censorship, poverty. They will sometimes invent their own particular kind of folk drama to appeal to a highly parochial audience. I mean, you can't make a generalization about what is going on in the theatre in Latin America.

Q: Have some of these opened in New York City, and if so, how are they received?

A: Very few Latin American plays have been done, are being done in New York. Very, very few. It is something we are trying to change. There have been productions of Latin American plays in Spanish and Portuguese, which obviously reach a terribly small audience since theatre-going in the U. S. is a middle-class experience and the majority of the Spanish-speaking audience that the theatre wants to reach is not middle class. And so it seems to us that you could probably do more good by having the plays translated to reach the theatre-going audience. A number of Spanish-language films create no problem, exhibits of Latin American painting and sculpture create absolutely no problem. American publishers have begun to understand now that there are some Latin-American writers, including one of the probably two or three towering figures among live writers, in Jorge Luis Borges. They have begun to understand that there is a literary life going on in Latin America and that they were damned fools not to be participating in it for quite a long time. Yes. And some of us have known about it but even now it is shocking, the tiny number of Latin-American writers that are known by American readers who fancy themselves as educated people. Those ones who know the Japanese novel and know the Italian novel and the French novel don't know the Latin-American novel.

Q: Mr. Albee, we have some student questions, one of which is: "Was there any particular incident in your life which inspired you to write *Who's Afraid of Virginia Woolf?*"

A: Probably. But I don't know how. I never know the genesis for any of the plays. The best student question I ever got in my life was: "Why don't any of your characters have last names?" It was an interesting question because it set me to thinking and I realized that I don't know the last names of any of them. And the reason I never gave them last names was that it had never occurred to me that they needed last names.

Q: It makes them more universal.

A: I don't know whether it does or not, but they never needed last names.

Q: Is it because you feel so intimate towards them, or because they remain on that kind of level?

A: Even strangers, like in the *Zoo Story*, introduce themselves by their first names. I have never had last names for any of my characters, not at all. I'm convinced that all characters are created out of a whole amalgam of things, people you know, yourself, things you make up. I mean, why ever let a real person limit the characterization that you are drawing? And also most real people aren't believable on stage. They are smaller than life. When you translate them into stage terms, most individuals don't have much universality.

Q: Do you ever include yourself as a character in your plays? Have you ever deliberately done that?

A: No, certainly not; you can always tell authors who are putting themselves in their plays. It is usually a character relatively younger than the author, and the action of the play grinds to a halt, somewhere in the third act, usually, as this character stands up and talks for fifteen minutes about the meaning of the play. And so I try to avoid that. Whenever I feel that urge coming on, I leave the typewriter.

Q: Some of our colleagues have mentioned that *Seascape* seems to be a little more affirmative than *Who's Afraid of Virginia Woolf?*

A: I'm not convinced that it is. In *Who's Afraid of Virginia Woolf?*, George and Martha end the play having exorcised some self-created demons and cut away through all nonsense to try to make a relationship based on absolute reality. Strikes me as being a fairly affirmative conclusion to apply. In *Seascape*, two absolutely innocent creatures have been corrupted to a sense of their own mortality. Is that more affirmative? I wonder. I'm not sure.

Q: Maybe there just wasn't as much tension in *Seascape* to begin with.

A: I imagine some people thought it was less tense but I know there's a fair amount of danger going on there because the human beings could have been wiped out in a second by the sea creatures, the lizards, any second.

Q: Let's try another student question: "Why do you show so much hatred or disappointment in the family?

A: As opposed to . . . ?

Q: We got this question over and over again . . .

A: Yes, as opposed to the families in Shakespeare's plays, like the Lears, the Macbeths? Like the families in Chekhov and Ibsen? The nature of drama is conflict and people not getting along terribly well, with the possible exception of *Oedipus Rex*, where everybody was getting along too well. Most plays are about people in conflict and not getting along and most plays are about people who know each other and most people know each other in some kind of relationship. And so, every playwright, every generation, keeps being asked the same question. I'm sure when they asked Ibsen, he had to make reference to the people who came before him.

Q: The frequency of this question might stem from the fact that in our cultural area, where the family hangs together, the students feel very strongly about this issue of family relationships.

A: There are several ways for families to hang together. One is to ask no questions, another is to ask all questions. When you ask no questions you hang together until you just disintegrate and aren't aware of why the disintegration is taking place and if you ask all questions you may possibly recreate a family structure but with firmer bonding.

Q: There was another question about the use of Virginia Woolf in the title of the play. What sorts of connections are there beyond the obvious nursery rhyme word punning?

A: There were none.

Q: You disappoint me. I found an entry in one of Woolf's journals that said if her father had not died, she would have had no life of her own and I thought, ah, that's Martha! She can't be a real person because of her father . . .

A: One of the dangers of scholarship.

Q: Do you think that would be a good place to end? " . . . the dangers of scholarship."

A: Somebody once spent three pages examining in that same play why the Western Union messenger was called Crazy Billy.

Q: I don't go quite that far.

A: They did, really, and they came up with some rather interesting reasons except for the same one: that it was a local, private joke. Why were Leslie and Sarah in *Seascape* called Leslie and Sarah? Because they were the names of the cats that I had at the time.

Q: Is that true?

A: Sure.

Q: Well, we are going to give you a chance to get some sunshine.

A: Some cloudburst.

Q: Thank you very much.

A: I've had fun, thank you.

The Writing Life: Avant-Garde Albee

Bob Woggon/1980

From *Writer's Digest*, 60 (October 1980), 18, 20. This interview was done at Northern Illinois University. Reprinted by permission.

Scene: The present. Interior. A bare theater stage. Reporters and theatrical hangers-on are clustered center-stage around a famed avant-garde playwright.

The playwright is Edward Albee, and the stage is in the O'Connell Theatre at Northern Illinois University. Albee has come to talk to theater and writing students after performances by the touring "Albee Directs Albee" road company, which has presented *The Zoo Story* and *The American Dream*, two of Albee's earliest plays.

Settled back into an upholstered chair, Albee smiles as he says that he is now old enough to refer to his own "earlier works." He's 52, but looks younger.

"When did you decide to switch from writing to directing?" someone asks him.

"I've never switched."

"You're still writing now?"

"Oh, sure. I write a play a year. Have for 20 years."

Albee explains that he writes for about four hours each morning, "before my brain gets tired," and might work for another hour or two later in the day. Albee's afternoons are reserved "for private things—the type of things everybody does. . . . I'm getting ready to write a long one-character, one-act play called *I Think Back Now on Andre Gide*, and then I have a play about Attila the Hun that's in my head and that should probably take me through, oh, middle of 1981."

The subjects of his plays are unusual, and the plays themselves take a bemused look at modern living. Albee describes one of his recent scripts, *The Lady From Dubuque*, as "a rather complex play about whether or not our existence is determined by other people's views of it. Another comedy, in other words."

155

These are not commercial plays, and Albee prefers them that way. "I tend to be more protective of those plays of mine that are least popular, and of those that are most experimental, that audiences have the most trouble understanding." His disdain for commercial entertainment is particularly evident when his discussion turns to television. "The stage is fundamentally an oral experience, film is fundamentally a visual experience, and on television, you can't see or hear."

"Commercial TV in this country is destroying the minds of young people, turning them into Cream of Wheat." Still, he acknowledges that he would at least consider accepting a commission to write a teleplay. But he quickly cautions: "The problem is that no network is going to commission a work that it doesn't have censorship control over. You get very spoiled in theater. Nobody tells you what to do. Lots of people *try* to tell you what to do, but they can't make you do it. But when you're writing for films, for television, there are people who have control over what you say."

Albee views the state of American arts—including the state of theater—as "not at all good. . . . We live very dangerously as a society," and seem perilously close to "semantic collapse."

He elaborates: "Humans are the only animals who consciously create art, who use metaphor to understand themselves." Americans are in danger of "losing the metaphor," and of becoming hopelessley mired in escapist entertainment, rather than in art that engages them. We are too fascinated by fantasy, and apathetic about reality, he says.

Albee confesses that this doesn't surprise him, because the arts in a free society are controlled by a mass taste that is "short-sighted, hedonistic, self-gratifying." He insists that he prefers the free marketplace, but fumes when he says, "Most people prefer what is inferior—that's taken for granted."

That's why Albee says he wants to get his message through to "the Philistines" who never hear from him, the 95% of the American public he estimates never attend theater performances.

Yet, Albee has had chances to get his work before mass audiences. Two of his plays—*A Delicate Balance* and *Who's Afraid of Virginia Woolf?*— have been made into feature films. He describes the Hollywood version of *Virginia Woolf* as "reasonably OK."

Albee seems as displeased with critics as he is with the tastes of the American public. Once, he made a list of 25 contemporary playwrights cited by various critics as having obvious influence on his plays. Albee was unfamiliar with at least five of the 25, and made a point of reading their work. "Indeed, I had been influenced by them, which means only that there are certain stylistic and thematic matters that are constant in work of any period, and we all take from the same sources. So that, indeed, one can be theoretically influenced by somebody one doesn't know. It also proved to me that critics are a little silly, as if I needed any proof of that."

And how does Edward Albee criticize the Albee opus? He admits that *Malcolm*—his 1966 adaptation of the James Purdy novel— "was pretty lousy. But most of the rest are ok . . . some probably a little better than ok. Actually, I'm always fondest of the newest one that I haven't been proved wrong about yet."

Living on the Precipice:
A Conversation with Edward Albee

Edited by Mark Anderson and Earl Ingersoll/1981

Speaking with Edward Albee were Stan Sanvel Rubin, the current director of the Forum; Adam Lazarre, the former Dean of Fine Arts; and Mark Anderson, who teaches Renaissance and contemporary drama.

Rubin: It has been said that the hallmarks of your drama are "cruel mocking wit, dramatic explosiveness, and poetic eloquence." Would you agree?

Albee: I like the sound of that. But I don't think about myself in those terms. I read these quotes about myself, and they're very nice for book jackets, but I don't think about myself in the third-person.

Anderson: In all of your works, though, you do seem to have a very great concern for words, for getting the words right, and for examining the process of human communication—people's attempts to make contact with each other and other people's failure to understand those attempts.

Albee: And other people's refusal to communicate with one another, which I sometimes think is probably much closer to the problem—not that people can't communicate with each other, but that they choose not to, because it's easier and safer not to. Not enough people are willing to live on the precipice. And if you're a writer, I guess you should concern yourself with precision of language.

Lazarre: You made a couple of points last night in your talk that struck me quite forcefully. You said that people's ability to govern

158

themselves is connected quite closely with their aesthetic response to art, and you went on to draw some parallels between Eastern European societies, particularly the Soviet Union, and our own. You said also that man is the only animal that produces art.

Albee: He is the only animal that *consciously* produces art.

Lazarre: That's right. You finished by saying that ability to produce art was important to our evolution. Could you expand on that point?

Albee: I don't know if I can. It never occurred to me until all of a sudden I heard myself saying it one night. And I thought, yes, it must be part of the evolutionary process, or why else would this human animal be doing it? If we assume that we are not a lunatic mutant, that there is some kind of internal logic to what happens as we evolve, the fact that our tails have fallen off and that we have developed metaphor strikes me as part of the evolutionary process. I haven't thought much about it beyond that, aside from the conclusion that participation in the arts is something natural to us, rather than something ephemeral or decorative, or, as many people feel, obscene.

Lazarre: What you've said suggests that in captive societies people have been known to go to the wall for their right to read or to express their ideas in art.

Albee: Unfortunately those people are in the minority. I don't know which conclusion I'm coming to. I used to think it was man's nature to live in a society where he can govern himself, but the more I think of it, the more pessimistic I become: it may well be man's nature to wish to live in a totalitarian society, to be governed. We may be at an evolutionary turning point. The role of the writer is to be, axiomatically, against any society he happens to be living in— or at least to be to one side of it—to examine it, to question its too-easily-held values. That's why, especially in totalitarian societies, it is the writers who find themselves silenced more quickly than anybody else because their governments realize the power of the creative mind. I worry in this country, too, whenever we have governments that feel the press has too much freedom of expression. It happened most recently, of course, under Nixon who was trying to get some laws passed to bridle the press, and who had a strong and often expressed anti-intellectualism and fear and loathing of the Northeastern intellectual establishment. I sense it under Reagan as well.

Lizarre: The anger and violence expressed by writers like Solzhenitsyn seem surprising to many Americans.

Albee: It's so interesting about Solzhenitsyn. While he was a dissenting writer in the Soviet Union, everyone in the United States thought he was wonderful. As soon as he was thrown out of the Soviet Union, came here, and started telling us that we had a couple of problems too, I noticed that a lot of people in this country lost some of their enthusiasm for him.

Anderson: Do you think it's the function of the artist to stir up controversy, to challenge people's assumptions?

Albee: Not merely to stir things up because you wake up in the morning and say, "Well, I'd better stir something up." If we lived in utopia everything is perfect, and the function of art is to correct. Since, however, we do not live in a utopian society, there is enough to worry about, to complain about, to wish to change, and it is the writer's function to educate, to inform, to hold a mirror up to people.

Anderson: To disturb them?

Albee: If you're going to hold a mirror up to people, you're going to disturb them.

Anderson: Should this be a conscious goal?

Albee: No, it's part of a writer's function—it comes with the territory.

Anderson: Do you get the feeling that the artist is a kind of superman, or that he is at least better than other men?

Albee: No, different—that's all.

Anderson: But he has an extremely important function in society, to articulate what the society is. Going back to what we were talking about earlier, aren't a writer's words a part of what it means to be human, a part of the evolutionary development of man?

Albee: It's a function he has that no one else can perform as effectively as he can, just as the writer cannot shoe a horse as well as someone whose job that is. Other than to write, about the only thing a writer can do as well as anyone else can—I tell you this from experience—is to deliver telegrams. I used to do that, and so did

Henry Miller, long before I did, although I didn't know it at the time. The writer has a unique usefulness. If writing and the other creative arts hadn't a useful function, they'd have absolutely no worth whatever.

Anderson: You're saying the writer is almost a Western Union man delivering messages to his audience. What kind of messages does the contemporary audience need? What are your concerns as an artist?

Albee: My concerns are the facts that we are too short-sighted, that we will not live on the precipice, that too many people prefer to go through this brief thing called life only half-alive, that too many people are going to end up with regret and bitterness at not having participated fully in their lives, that it's easier not to deal honorably with one another, that communication is a vitally important and dangerous matter. We are supposed to be a revolutionary society. The reason for our existence, however, was an economic revolution, rather than a revolution for freedom as we all like to pretend. It was caused by an upper-middle class trying to get richer—like many revolutions. We've had a continuing revolution from the first one on to the social revolution of 1932. If we've become static and stagnant, we may indeed have lost our value as a society.

Anderson: In regards to the "American dream" or the mythology we carry around with us, which you've dealt with directly in your play *American Dream* and indirectly in many of your other works, do you think there are fundamental American lies that need to be dispelled?

Albee: I don't know whether they're American lies or universal lies. Again, we're getting into an area that I'm not terribly good at articulating except in my work. What do my plays say? There lies the answer. [Laughter] We do live in a society where we are subject to different self-deceptions. Unlike other societies, we're permitted short-sighted and selfish decisions, cruel election jokes and things of that sort, that other societies which are controlled and whose people are not given the freedom of self-destruction don't have. These choices that we're permitted result in great danger and an extraordinary latitude for the right decision. Therefore, we have a responsibility, given the danger of freedom of expression and freedom of choice, to make informed decisions.

Anderson: Yesterday you mentioned the artistic revival and the great spirit of optimism in the 60s. But in your works of that period, instead of conveying the optimism you seem to be puncturing the lies. In *Who's Afraid of Virginia Woolf?* and your later plays, that seems a central concern: there are life-lies that are dangerous to human existence and prevent communication.

Albee: That period gave a writer, faced with an enthusiastic, participating audience, the opportunity to examine continuing problems with some freedom. *Who's Afraid of Virginia Woolf?* was the result of my examination of the 50s, as much as anything. Many of us suspected that even though we were terribly enthusiastic about the Thousand Days of Kennedy before terribly long it would be business as usual and things would slide back to the way they were. And, indeed, quickly enough they did.

Lazarre: One of the interesting paradoxes of theater in this country is that although here, and elsewhere in the world, it does have a revolutionary quality, it ends up being the province of the bourgeois, at least in capitalistic countries. How can writers reach the audience they want to reach?

Albee: But there are so many theaters in America. The commercial Broadway theater, indeed, is the possession of the middle class, which does not wish to be disturbed. But we also have experienced experimental theater as well as university theater, which is living up to its responsibility by producing brave and venturesome drama. We have regional theaters, which at their very best are doing the best of the new plays. There are a number of theaters. Unfortunately what happens on Broadway affects to a too large extent the public consciousness of what theater is all about. That's why some of us keep banging our heads against the wall and insist on having our plays done on Broadway, rather than in something safer and more comfortable like the regional theaters. Broadway should not be abandoned to the safe, the easy, the middle class, and the middlebrow.

Lazarre: Even in the regional theater there are many who in an attempt to attract larger audiences continue to use the same material over and over again. I mean, how many times can you do Feydeau? Not that there's anything wrong with Feydeau.

Albee: There's nothing wrong with Feydeau. The problem is that there are so many people who think they should be doing Neil Simon, rather than Feydeau. Feydeau is funnier than Neil Simon. Feydeau is a step toward Moliere, and Neil Simon is not.

Lazarre: You were talking about plays that disturb, that strike to the heart of our present human condition.

Albee: That can be done with comedy, as well as with the stark humor in tragedy. In fact, most useful teaching plays, the very best plays, have some humor to them.

Anderson: From the very beginning, the comedy in your plays has had a biting edge. Jokes and aggression in many of your works seem to go hand in hand.

Albee: I find pain and laughter very close, and I've always been attracted to those writers who seem to comprehend that. Are there many more sadly funny writers than Borges or Nabokov or Beckett, for example? They are the three giants, I think, of the last half of the twentiety century.

Anderson: Is expression or communication an outlet for aggression, an alternative to physical violence?

Albee: On my own part? [Laughter]

Anderson: No, in the works you envision. For example, in *Seascape* when the characters are having trouble communicating together they both go into a very aggressive or defensive posture, out of fear and lack of communication. There is a potential for violence there that is in a way mitigated by communication.

Albee: To paraphrase Auden, we must talk to one another or die. It used to be "We must love one another or die." Toward the end of his life, he changed it to "We must love one another *and* die."

Anderson: You've often dealt with death in your plays.

Albee: As somebody says in one of my plays, *All Over*, "It gets you where you live."

Anderson: You've said that *All Over* and *Seascape* were part of a life-death play.

Albee: They were supposed to be.

Anderson: Is there any significance in the order? Did you write one to be performed before the other?

Albee: I guess you do *Seascape*, the comedy, first; then *All Over*. I don't remember.

Anderson: Do you sense that your views about life or the way you perceive reality is changing? Are you getting more optimistic, for example?

Albee: Only to the extent, I suppose, that writing itself is an act of optimism. I don't seem to be stopping that, so obviously I've retained some optimism.

Rubin: I'd like to ask you about your adaptations, which, I suppose, reflect another kind of optimism in literature. You must have a kind of love for a work or an optimism to wish to adapt it for the stage. You've done three adaptations of fine novels—McCullers' *Ballad of the Sad Café*, Purdy's *Malcolm*, and now Nabokov's *Lolita*. You're quoted somewhere as saying, "Adaptation is a difficult experience. I had to be both Nobokov and myself. I tried to write the play Nobokov would have written had he been a playwright." Would you comment on that statement?

Albee: I think that statement says it pretty succinctly.

Rubin: But why these three?

Albee: I don't really know why. I guess it struck me that they could be translated to the stage without any loss of power or effectiveness, and that I wanted to do it.

Rubin: Did you know in first reading the novels that you wanted to turn them into plays?

Albee: I think so with both *Malcolm* and *Ballad of the Sad Café*. I first read *Lotita* so long before I was a playwright that it didn't occur to me to make a play of it.

Rubin: When did it occur to you?

Albee: When someone called me up and said, "I have the rights. Do you want to make a play of it?"

Rubin: Did you speak with Nabokov about what you were doing?

Albee: No, he was dead.

Anderson: Do you work on your adaptations in the same way you work on your other plays? In other words, do you carry them around with you in your head?

Albee: Yes, I think about them for a while, and then I put them down very quickly. With *Lolita* I read the book again several times, thought about the whole project for about a year, and wrote it in ten days. I usually don't write quite that quickly, but I had a lot of the words.

Anderson: To broach an unpleasant subject, the New York critics have attacked you on your adaptations *every* time you've done them. Why is that true?

Albee: That's not quite true. *Ballad of the Sad Café* got away pretty well. *Malcolm* they attacked rather viciously—despite any merits or demerits the play might have—because it came out immediately after *Tiny Alice* and after a rather annoyed press conference I gave in which I complained that the critics had seriously misunderstood *Tiny Alice* because they were telling audiences they would not be able to understand the play since it was so complex. I heard myself saying at this press conference that I was puzzled why critics would assume that anything that would puzzle them would necessarily puzzle an audience. [Laughter] As a result, when *Malcolm* opened, it got unanimously hideous reviews— far in *excess* of any faults the play may have had.

Anderson: It seems that even with *Lotita* people are waiting for your demise.

Albee: Oh, I dare say that there are a lot of critics who would be perfectly happy if they could accomplish that act. And I think as much as anything they're annoyed by the fact that I don't just lie down and die.

Anderson: You seem to have had more than your share of harsh or adverse criticism. There seem to be people out for your blood.

Albee: It's probably because I don't react the way they would like me to: I don't become sycophantic. I don't behave myself. I strike back.

Anderson: Do you think this is because of your position, because you appeared on the scene very much in a cloud of thunder and lightning?

Albee: If you get in any kind of exposed position, there are those people who feel they are the ones who should create celebrity or fame—there are some critics like that. And if you don't act as if you are their possession and their creation, they try to destroy you.

Anderson: Do you think they have a different conception of your career than you do?

Albee: I dare say. If I read them, I sometimes wonder who they are writing about.

Anderson: What do they want you to be and what do you want to be?

Albee: I don't know quite what they want me to be. Certainly not who I am. I don't know that I can get more specific about it than that. Some of them get very annoyed by the fact that I use language well. They complain about the fact that my plays are well written.

Anderson: They do focus a lot on language. And there is always the side issue of vulgarity or profanity involved in the plays, but that seems to be a red herring. Somehow your language is very affecting to both your audiences and your critics.

Albee: Audiences seem to like it, but it turns the critics into mouth-foaming beasts. I don't quite know why that is.

Anderson: Do you think it's because it's language in the context of the family? A lot of your plays focus on family or domestic situations, and they get rough. They're not used to seeing that.

Albee: That possibly. Also I think there are some critics who feel the theater is not a literary experience but a terribly simplified experience, and that language gets in the way of the proper function of the theater. These are people who prefer plays that are coarsely written.

Rubin: You have directed some of your plays. Would you speak of the experience of directing and why you choose to direct some plays and not others?

Albee: Well, sometimes I'm busier than other times. I enjoy directing, and I don't believe this theory that playwrights shouldn't direct their own work, because if they can learn the craft, then indeed they should. I lead a fairly busy life, and I can't end up directing everything. Also there are some actors who still believe that a playwright knows far too much about his play to be permitted to direct it.

Rubin: That changes the chemistry with the actors, undoubtedly, when you're directing your own work.

Albee: There are frictions. But certainly the revival of *Who's Afraid of Virginia Woolf?* that I directed in '76 was every bit as good as the original production in '62. And there was nothing wrong with my production of *Seascape*.

Rubin: You've had some experience with turning your work into film. Or, at least *Who's Afraid of Virginia Woolf?* was made into quite a successful film.

Albee: It was a commercially successful film. I didn't think much of it as a picture. I thought the film of *A Delicate Balance* was far better, and that's the one where I exercised a certain amount of control. I had no control over *Virginia Woolf*—casting or anything.

Rubin: It's interesting that the film is often cited as a landmark in terms of obscenity in cinema.

Albee: Oh, this obsession!

Rubin: And this obession follows you at a point in 1981 when in our daily life and in our artistic life language is very free. And yet this association with obscenity does stick to you, perhaps for some of the reasons you mentioned earlier.

Albee: Yes, and if we are to judge by some of the reviews in Boston, I have committed an obscenity on stage with Nabokov's highly moral novel *Lolita*. Very odd. I never understand that reaction from people to absolutely natural matters.

Rubin: You don't really think the audience shares that response, do you?

Albee: Well, there is one scene in *Lolita*, the initial seduction of Humbert Humbert by Lolita—that's one thing people forget about the extraordinary book: that it's not this dirty old man who seduces this innocent young girl but the other way around—and right at the moment of Lolita's turning her back on us and opening her robe to show Humbert Humbert the future, there is always a couple or two who huffily get up and leave the theater.

Anderson: But it seems so strange, because this has been going on for the last ten or fifteen years on Broadway. We've been through *Oh Calcutta* and the nude scene in *Equus*.

Albee: But there's a problem there. The nude scene in *Equus* is titillation—I don't think it was in the text originally but added by the director to keep the show running, and *Oh! Calcutta!* is a piece of trash, so that's perfectly acceptable.

Anderson: It's acceptable as long as the audience doesn't consider the action real. Do you think you can actually affect a change in the American audience? You're going to Broadway and mainline theater, instead of regional theaters and off-off-Broadway.

Albee: I don't see why I should be made a second-class citizen just because I write fairly serious plays.

Anderson: But have you noticed a change in Broadway over the past twenty years?

Albee: I don't think it's quite as healthy an environment to work in. I think it's worse. One or two plays of any serious pretension in a season are allowed to survive with the froth and the trash, but usually not more than that. And producers are becoming more cowardly with the economic chaos in the theater: the rising costs and therefore the rising ticket prices make cowards of the producers. And audiences expect not to be disturbed, but to be made happy when they spend all that money.

Rubin: Last night you said that audiences may no longer know the very basic things artists assume they know. In what specific areas would you like to see the audience improve?

Albee: I just wish audiences would come without having predetermined the boundaries of the theatrical experience they're willing to have.

Rubin: You mean that they don't want to be affected by the experience?

Albee: No, I don't want them to come to the theater determined that only this and not that kind of experience is tolerable. I want them to come to the theater as if they had never been to a play before in their lives. They must come with a kind of awe and innocence, leaving their preconceptions—moral, intellectual, emotional—out in the checkroom.

Rubin: Do you see a new audience there? Did the participation and the breaking down of the boundaries between spectator and performance in the 60s have impact on today's audience?

Albee: I don't know that it's affected the Broadway audience all that much, but certainly there's a healthier audience going to the off-off-Broadway plays and the regional theater. But you must remember that theater is such a minority participation in this country; no more than five percent of the people ever go to the theater, and I dare say that only five percent of that five percent care about serious theater.

Rubin: I sense in your remarks a desire to educate the audience.

Albee: Oh, I think the world would be a far better place, or at least this country would be, if everybody went to the serious theater all the time. Television is so terrible that it's driving people out of the house, and maybe some of them will end up in the theater, rather than the bowling alley or the movies.

Rubin: From your experience with having your work made into films, how do you feel about film as a medium?

Albee: The only way for a playwright to work in film properly is to be allowed to write and direct his own films.

Anderson: Is that possible here?

Albee: It's possible, but not very likely. I'm not holding my breath.

Anderson: Are you looking for that kind of experience, to reach a wide audience?

Albee: The commercial success of the film *Who's Afraid of Virginia Woolf?* means that it's probably been seen by more people than have ever seen all of my plays produced all around the world, or will for a hundred years. It's nice to reach a large audience, but that always reminds me of what kind of information is reaching an audience that large all the time. We are a film and television culture, not a theater culture. And film and television misinform.

Rubin: Do you have a sense of your audience as you write?

Albee: No, I'm always concerned with the reality of the piece that I'm doing.

Anderson: What about a sense of form or structure? Does it grow out of the content or characterization?

Albee: I am aware that I am creating structure as I write. Form and content co-determine each other.

Anderson: You have written very different kinds of plays. When we get to something like *Seascape*, you take some real theatrical chances—for example, putting animals on the stage.

Albee: All of my plays have been filled with animals! [Laughter]

Anderson: That's right. You started out with *Zoo Story*!

Albee: No, the people wandering around in most of my plays are animals. We *are* animals, are we not? Why not take chances? What fun is there if you don't?

Anderson: Are you trying to emphasize the bestial in man, the aggression, the thrust and parry, in human relationships?

Albee: I'm interested in the fact that so much of what I think is wrong with the world has to do with the fact that man's nature is so close to the bestial. And we had better be a little more aware of it.

Anderson: What can we do to be human then? Is it to throw away the lies? Some writers, O'Neill for example, maybe Ibsen, would say that the lie is important; it enables human beings to go on.

Albee: I know. I think I probably became a playwright as much as anything to refute that whole argument of O'Neill, expressed most forcefully in *The Iceman Cometh*. I do think people probably need self-deception and lies. The only distinction I would make is that I think people should have them but be aware that they are deceiving themselves.

Rubin: You've done a lot to encourage young American playwrights. What do you see as the state of play-writing right now?

Albee: We've probably got more interesting young playwrights than we had twenty years ago, but they find it harder to get their work in front of a large public.

Rubin: All of the government subsidy of the arts hasn't helped?

Albee: The government subsidy in this country—and we won't have to worry about it too much longer if Reagan has his way—has never given enough money as direct support to the individual creative artist. It's been far more concerned to make the public happy by supporting the symphony hall or the ballet group. Very little of the money goes directly to the creative artist; it's going to the interpretative artist and the place that houses the interpretative artist.

Anderson: Do you see any improvement in this situation? Obviously you're a champion of playwrights, but the theater is in the hands of managers and directors and actors.

Albee: You'll always have some first-rate playwrights in this country. The only question is, will anybody ever see their work? The theater is not going to stop. Serious play-writing is not going to go away. But the audiences may vanish completely. The economic situation may make it impossible for this work to be seen. But it will still be done.

Rubin: I'm interested in the writing process itself. To what extent do you recognize that your characters draw upon people you know?

Albee: Characters are, I guess, a combination of people one has seen or know, oneself, and this odd animal called "creativity," and it's probably best not to examine where each facet of the character comes from, but just be grateful it's an individual.

Rubin: Do you read your lines aloud, or do you try them out on someone you know?

Albee: No, I can hear the lines as I'm writing them down.

Anderson: Do you do much revision?

Albee: Not terribly much. Not as much as most people do. But I probably make a few more revisions than I admit to.

Anderson: Do you trust other people's judgments on your plays, or only your own judgment?

Albee: Ultimately my own. I don't look only for corroboration, of course; I'm willing to grumpily accept advice and criticism from time to time, and then I pretend it was my own idea anyway.

Rubin: How do you feel about seeing your work in book form?

Albee: I remember the first time I ever saw my play in book form; I was so excited. Or, even before that I remember seeing my poems in literary magazines at Choate: there was such a difference between the poem on the typed page and in print. I would touch the printed page and think it was really quite wonderful. But a play for me is complete, the experience is complete, as I write it down.

Rubin: Some dramatists feel that their work has to be realized on the stage, as a theatrical product. Does the performance complete the play?

Albee: No. If the play is any good, the performance is merely a confirmation. If the performance is an improvement, then the play has not been well written.

Rubin: Are you conscious of your style changing over the years?

Albee: Not really. I think it's always had its particular concern with precision of expression. In *The Zoo Story* Jerry speaks with as much precision as Agnes in *A Delicate Balance* or any of the later characters.

Rubin: Do you feel that you are working against your audience's expectation that a play will have more action?

Albee: It's true that most of the action in my plays is interior rather than exterior action. But I take my model there from Chekhov. I mean, what really happens on stage in *The Cherry Orchard?* Absolutely nothing! An estate is sold, and the selling is offstage. There is absolutely no physical action of any import in that extraordinary play.

Anderson: You have a very effective visual imagination: your plays are not just literary texts put on stage but also visualized beforehand. Don't you think that there is a danger if the dramatist worries too much about physical action?

Albee: If you're not going to have any physical action on the stage, you've got to have the illusion at least of visual psychological or philosophical action to compensate for it. Silence is as dramatic as sound. The answer a person does not give is as full as the answer a person does give. You must have to find the dramatic moment in evasion, in silence, as well as in engagement, in speech.

Anderson: Is there any easy answer for that? How do you make language active? How do you get involvement? Language can be just words that lie there.

Albee: I guess you do it, if you're a playwright. It comes with the territory.

Rubin: Did the kind of early success you had—*Virginia Woolf* was immediately canonized as a contemporary classic—change your relationship with your own work?

Albee: I suppose it's useful because it gives you a certain amount of liberty to make the kinds of experiments that you might have been too cowardly to make before. It has the disadvantage that everyone wants you to write it over again and again. You know, *The Son of Virginia Woolf* and *Virginia Woolf II.* They're not going to get it because I'm done with those characters.

The Playwright as Curator
ARTnews/1982

From *ARTnews* (May 1982), 17-18. © *ARTnews* 1982. Reprinted by permission.

For more than 20 years, playwright Edward Albee has been critically acknowledged—if not always uncritically acclaimed—as a towering presence in the American theater. It is perhaps less widely known that the author of *Zoo Story*, *Who's Afraid of Virginia Woolf?*, *Tiny Alice*, the Pulitzer Prize-winnning *A Delicate Balance*, *Seascape* and, recently, *The Lady from Dubuque*, among other plays, has long been a venturesome collector of art and, through a private foundation he established 15 years ago, a steadfast and knowledgeable supporter of younger painters and sculptors. Later this month, the Guild Hall Museum in East Hampton, Long Island, will present "Edward F. Albee Foundation Artists," featuring 16 of the artists who have worked at the foundation's Montauk facility, where up to nine painters, sculptors and writers are simultaneously in residence from June through September. Curated by Albee, this exhibition follows last winter's show at SoHo's Harm Bouckaert Gallery which presented five artists, also chosen by the playwright, who (as the announcement for the show put it) "for some dumb reason don't have New York galleries."

That contentious note is no accident. "I think it's important to support artists when they're young," says Albee. "That's when they need it. But more broadly I'm interested in those artists, whether young or not so young, who don't hop on the bandwagons, who have their own demons and their own goals to pursue. Such artists are their own people, while so many on the scene today are, in my opinion, basically con artists, whether with or without talent."

The Albee Foundation has two barns located on six acres in a wooded area of Montauk, on Long Island's eastern tip. The ocean is nearby as is the playwright's own country home (in New York, he lives in a large, richly appointed Tribeca-district loft). Albee himself does the initial screening of those applying to spend one month in the no-frills surroundings. "We get more applications than we can accept," Albee says. "Of course, everybody seems to want to come in August. We differ from the MacDowell Colony or Yaddo [two well-known retreats for writers and artists] in that we're more oriented toward people who have yet to make it in a big way. It's a fairly spartan, communal life. The participants share all the chores. While it's an opportunity to get away from the city for a bit and is hopefully not without its enjoyments, one thing is quite certain: people are at the foundation to work." The foundation's board, which advises Albee, includes painter Lee Krashner, poet Howard Moss, novelist Reynolds Price and producer Richard Barr.

In addition to the shows at the Guild Hall and Harm Bouckaert (another is planned there for next winter), Albee has also been a guest curator at Hartford's Wadsworth Atheneum, where in 1979 he presented paintings by Ellen Phelan, and at New York's Clocktower, which hosted his "Material Matters" exhibition of seven artists in spring 1980. He also has directed a show of painters David Craven and Jonathan Thomas at the Mallon Art Center in Wallingford, Connecticut. Albee himself has a substantial art collection, including works by Vuillard, Kandinsky, Arp, Walt Kuhn and Milton Avery ("one of my oldest enthusiasms") but emphasizing younger contemporary artists. He is also interested in primitive art, especially Pre-Columbian and pieces from New Guinea. But Albee says he doesn't think of himself as a collector in the true sense: "I'm not building a collection. I have no one advising me. If I see something that I like and can afford, I buy it. My response may be said to be intuitive, but I think it's an educated one. Of course, I've made some mistakes, at least in a monetary sense. But I usually can tell if I'm relating to what I see and thus if I want to spend more time with it. I don't believe in being doctrinaire about art or being the captive of trends. I'm so weary of all those wealthy homes with their obligatory Stellas, Rauschenbergs and Morris Louises. I'm dying to go somewhere and find, say, a Frederick Kiesler."

The forthcoming Guild Hall show will include work by four sculptors and 12 painters. "I think the show works as a coherent selection," Albee says. "I made the choices based on what would create an integrated show, and it's in no way a judgment of the quality of the other artists who've been at the foundation but who haven't been included. If one were to look at this work as expressive of my taste, I suppose you'd find some esthetic at work, some cohesiveness. But I'm damned if I know what it is."

Albee After the Plunge

David Richards/1982

From *The Washington Post*, 24 January 1982, sec. K, 1, 5. 1982 © by *The Washington Post*. Reprinted by permission.

If playwright Edward Albee depended on the kindness of critics these days, he would probably be lying in some dark alley, semi-comatose and caked with dried blood.

Although he has written 16 plays since commanding overnight attention with *The Zoo Story* in 1959, and has won the Pulitizer Prize twice, he remains in the eyes of many critics the man who asked the world *Who's Afraid of Virginia Woolf?* and never again came up with half so riveting a dramatic question.

It is a fairly common practice in criticism to put a playwright on a pedestal on the promise of a single play, only to send him toppling to the dust on the evidence of the next. In Albee's case, the rise and fall have been particularly exaggerated. In the early 1960s, he was hailed as a virtual savior of the American theater. Last year, when his most recent play, an adaptation of Nabokov's novel, *Lolita*, opened on Broadway, the *New York Times* felt compelled to note that not only had Albee abandoned his gifts, but he had "forsaken the humane impulse that is the minimal, rock bottom essential of art."

"I have been both overpraised and underpraised. I assume by the time I finish writing—and I plan to go on writing until I'm 90 or gaga—it will all equal itself out," comments Albee, who, at 53, still has some distance to cover. "You can't involve yourself with the vicissitudes of fashion or critical response. I'm fairly confident that my work is going to be around for a while. I am pleased and reassured by the fact that a lot of younger playwrights seem to pay me some attention and gain some nourishment from what I do."

This particular morning, Albee is dressed in faded jeans, a flannel shirt and work boots. His hair, not quite shoulder length, and his droopy gunslinger's mustache combine to give him the look of a slightly perverse denizen of Marlboro country. He converses mostly in a low-pitched mumble, a tone similar to that taken by excessively bashful adolescents and irritable chairmen of the board.

"Maybe I've got a survival mechanism built into me," he says, stretching out his legs and locking his hands behind his neck, thereby increasing the impression of lankiness. "I survive almost any onslaught with a shrug, which must appear as arrogance, but really isn't, because I'm not an arrogant person. When you write a play, you make a set of assumptions—that you have something to say, that you know how to say it, that it's worth saying, and that maybe someone will come along for the ride. That's all. And then you go about your business, assuming you'd be the first to know if your talent had collapsed.

"I don't think I've been a commercial playwright ever. By some curious mischance, a couple of my plays managed to hit an area where commercial success was feasible. But it's wrong to think I'm a commercial playwright who has somehow ceased his proper function. I have always been the same thing—which is *not* a commercial playwright. I'm not after the brass ring. I very seldom get it anyway, and then it's accidental when I do. . . . So I write those things that interest me."

Midstream, which is where he puts it, Albee's career is a paradox. Despite what he calls "the ritual slaughter of Albee" each time he unveils a new play, he remains one of the key reference points of the American theater. On the basis of such plays as *Tiny Alice* or *All Over*, he is judged to be dour and hermetic, and yet his work is, as he himself puts it, "funnier than it's not."

Virginia Woolf made him a wealthy man, and that "economic leeway," he points out, freed him "from having to go around writing *Son of Virginia Woolf*." With almost predictable regularity, however, everything he turns out these days, is measured against *Virginia Woolf* and, when it fails to conform, is found lacking. Albee's last commercially successful work on Broadway was *A Delicate Balance*, 15 years ago, and he complains that Broadway today simply can't tolerate plays of any complexity or depth—meaning, among others, his. But he also notes that "every play of mine I thought should be produced on Broadway has been produced on Broadway," adding "mostly because of Richard Barr."

Barr's loyalty goes back to the beginning. He produced *Zoo Story* off-Broadway and has since brought nearly all of Albee's major plays to Broadway. Understandably, if no less passionately, he defends his author against the rampant charges of burnout. "I think Edward's got his best play still in him," he says. "There's nothing the matter with his talent. As a matter of fact, he's more alive and interested in everything around him than he was when I first met him in 1959. He's focusing in a way I haven't seen in years. Literarily, socially, he's making himself a part of the world he's in. In 1959, he was Peck's Bad Boy, and I don't think there's a bit of that now. He's really a much wiser human being."

For Barr, it's merely a question of "the critics just not being as bright as Edward is. His reputation is still very big—in Europe, in regional theaters, everywhere but on Broadway. Without going into a long dissertation, Edward was the first playwright to say that people invent their own illusion to give themselves a reality. And his characters are *aware* of it. . . . A Blanche Dubois doesn't know she's living an illusion. But Edward's characters—certainly those in *Virginia Woolf* and *Tiny Alice*—are aware they're creating the illusion themselves. That's the giant step. The awareness was what was new."

In the best of all worlds, or at least the best of all of Albee's worlds, the playwright envisions a Broadway theater "filled with Aristophanes, Chekhov, Beckett, Shakespeare, Pirandello and Brecht, plus me now and again, and a lot of other people. But that isn't the way it works for a number of reasons, many of them economic. I hate to attack another playwright. It's tough enough for us all. But let's just say that I lament the fact that the middlebrow is now what passes for excellence in the theater. It's conceivable that in 10 years no straight play of any real worth will be done in the New York commerical theater. Since most people take their clues about the nature of American theater from Broadway, I worry about the misinformation that is passed along to our younger playwrights."

Undaunted, Albee continues to write a play a year. The actual writing takes him "about three months." The thinking takes longer. At any given time he may be carrying three or four plays around in his head. Along with Tennessee Williams and Lanford Wilson, he has been commissioned to write a drama for the New World Festival of Arts, to be held in Miami this June. His contribution will be a three-character work entitled *The Man Who Had Three Arms*. "It's about a man who had three arms," he offers by way of explanation. Given the troubles he had finding the right nymphet for *Lolita*, he is asked if this won't pose even greater difficulties.

"Well, as I said, he *used* to have three arms."

So maybe he has only two arms when the curtain goes up?

"Unless someone comes into the casting call who fills the bill perfectly," he says, lapsing into a silence.

Albee never begins the actual writing until he is convinced that each of his characters has developed a vital identity and a voice of his own. One of his methods of testing them is to go for long walks on the beach at Montauk, Long Island, where he maintains a sleek summer home. "I take some of the characters I plan to have in the play along with me. Then I think up a situation that isn't in the play. If I can improvise on-the-spur dialogue for the characters in this new situation, then I feel that I know them well enough to go ahead and put them down on paper.

"It is very dangerous, whenever you sit down to write a new play, to think about how it is going to relate to what you have already done. So I try very hard not to dwell on continuity, progression. Oh, I reread my plays. Not a lot, though. I look at them with a kind of . . . mild . . . curiosity. I possess them, but they no longer possess me."

If Broadway has proved increasingly inhospitable to Albee's talents, he is still a familiar presence in the country's regional theaters and, to an even greater degree, on college and university campuses. Ironically, his earliest plays, *Zoo Story* and *The American Dream* are the most frequently done, but *Virginia Woolf?* is regularly revived, as is *A Delicate Balance*, which won him his first Pulitzer.

The latter will be getting a major revival at Arena Stage, opening Thursday, with Robert Prosky and Myra Carter in the roles originally created by Hume Cronyn and Jessica Tandy. It is Albee's study of Agnes and Tobias, well-bred, prosperous New Englanders, who find the tenuous truces and the fragile relationships of a lifetime jeopardized when their neighbors show up on the doorstep, fleeing an unnamed terror and demanding sanctuary.

For Zelda Fichandler, who is directing the production, it is "my favorite of all of Albee's plays, more complex than *Virginia Woolf* and maybe less accessible, but the one that moves me the most." It is what she calls "an autumn play," about older characters who have side stepped truth and their real passions and settled for a web of interlocking dependencies.

And for Albee? He reflects. "At the time, I was interested by the amount of misunderstanding it provoked. Of course, I'm often misunderstood, which always surprises me because I don't think I have a terribly complicated mind. What I write is perfectly clear to anybody who is willing to perceive it. I've always believed the difficulty most people have in perceiving things lies not in the complexity of those things, but in people's unwillingness to participate. Most misunderstanding is intentional.

"Originally, much of the critical high school—I was going to say the critical college—viewed *A Delicate Balance* as a play about the demands and responsibilities of friendship. I certainly didn't. I thought it was basically about the fact that we became rigid through disuse and that the oppportunity for making choices vanishes ultimately. What Agnes says in the third act. Of course, plays are about more than one thing, and that's a simplification. But it does seem to be about how we compromise our abilities away."

He pauses, smiles, taking pleasure from the past. "I do remember I had a good time writing *A Delicate Balance*." The smile is engaging, but just as quickly as it can light up his face, it can also vanish without a trace.

About five years ago, Albee gave up his Fifth Avenue address— and the posh East Side of Manhattan he called Fancyville—to move into a former cheese warehouse within shouting distance of the World Trade Center. The nondescript building is tucked between a couple of food coops. The entrance is from the loading dock, and a handlettered sign above the battered metal door asks the neighbors kindly to keep their garbage off the premises.

The creaky freight elevator that jerks its way up through a drafty shaft gives no indication of what lies on the top two floors; polished oak floors, lined with cork, running 75 feet from front to back; solid brick walls two-feet thick; nearly 6,000 square feet of living space.

Loft hardly seems the right word for Albee's domain. It looks more like a museum lobby, furnished with a kind of cool, elegant formalism that also characterizes such plays of his as *Listening* and *Counting the Ways*. Tuxedo couches stand at either end of the teak Korean bed, which has been converted into a gigantic coffee table. An oak banquet table defines the dining area. The walls bear witness to Albee's collector instincts—paintings by Kandinsky, Milton Avery, Vuillard—as do the liberal spotting of abstract sculpture, a pair of ceremonial drums, and even a wooden doorjamb from a pygmy's hut in New Guinea.

"Edward is a man of tremendous civilization," says actress Irene Worth, who created the enigmatic title characters of both *Tiny Alice* and *The Lady From Dubuque*. "He has a profound taste for works of art. He's a fantastic cook and has a great knowledge of fine wines. And he's a very giving person. I think we share a common attitude toward life and the arts, although I've never discussed it with him and never would. Words spoil things."

"I just surround myself with things I like," Albee says simply. "Some of them are very good. Some, I suppose, are mistakes. Most of them tend to be abstract and have something to do with geometry, which may tie in with my interest in contrapuntal music. I wanted to be a composer when I was 11 or 12. When I discovered Mozart. Whenever that was. But I was too lazy. I always think I'm writing a string quartet when I'm writing a play. It's the same aural experience, and you have to be as precise in your notation."

There is a lavishly appointed office on the premises, with 20-foot book shelves and a skylight to let in the milky Manhattan light, and a handsome 19th-century French desk, given to the playwright by his mother. Most of the time, Albee admits with a touch of embarrassment, he composes his plays on a typewriter on the kitchen table.

"I write only when I think I have something to say. Judging from the plays that are successful these days, maybe I should write only when I have nothing to say."

The writing is complemented professionally by a fairly active lecture schedule on the college circuit, where Albee tells "a few jokes, a few lies and a lot of truth." One of his recurrent themes is the mutual responsibility of the people who make art and the people who receive it. He also has his "official" duties, as a member of the New York State Council on the Arts, the Dramatists Guild, and the six-man directorate of Lincoln Center, although that last position seems to have been put on hold, while the Vivan Beaumont Theater undergoes remodeling.

An inveterate New Yorker, Albee rises early. "I like to go to museums, art galleries. Wander about the city," he admits. "I have a number of close friends. And a lot of acquaintances. But I like to be alone a lot, too. I have to have some time for myself every day, some long uninterrupted periods, where I don't have to deal with people at all. I'm gregarious . . . and I'm not."

No one would say that Albee has completely mended his peremptory manner. He found Donald Sutherland's behavior reprehensible during the brief run of *Lolita* and was so vocal about it that he has since been cautioned by Sutherland's lawyer not to discuss the actor in public at been all. When Barr and his six co-producers closed *The Lady From Dubuque* after 12 performances in 1980, Albee, in a fit of pique, referred to them as "the seven dwarfs."

But he can also turn the barbs on himself. Recollecting his work on the ill-fated musical version of *Breakfast at Tiffany's*, Albee says, "Oh, yeah, that was fun. I took a show that would have been a mild failure with an eight-month run on Broadway and turned it into an outright commercial disaster." (It closed in previews).

He likes to joke about his "very interesting relationship with Hollywood," which consists of Hollywood occasionally paying him large sums of money for a screenplay, which never gets produced. "There is one simplification I would like to bring to this relationship, however. They should commission me to write a movie and pay me a great deal of money. But I would not have to write it, since they have no intention of producing it anyway. . . . Of course, I'd *like* to reach a lot of people with a movie, but the writer doesn't have the final say in films as he does on the stage. Legitimate actors can't go around changing my text all that much . . . unless they're Donald Sutherland."

Albee gulps in mock surprise—"I didn't say that, did I?"— chuckles softly, then looks up to see if the joke is shared. He has not entirely divested himself of the protective spines of the past, perhaps, but he's more relaxed, more ingratiating, more openly hospitable than he's been in the decade.

"Many are surprised to find I'm still alive," he says. "I've only been writing plays for 22 years. But people keep saying to me, especially ladies on the lecture circuit, 'Gee, I thought you'd be a much older man.' I tell them that if I keep hearing that, I will be.

"I used to treat myself far worse than I do now. I used to drink a lot, smoke, and not take care of myself. Now I don't drink, I don't smoke, and I lift weights." The boy wonder of the American theater—middle-aged, but not so badly off for that—smiles another of his enigmatic smiles.

"Getting younger all the time," he boasts.

Albee at Notre Dame

Kathy Sullivan/1984

This transcript was prepared by Kathy Sullivan of her interview of Albee on 3 December 1984 while he was lecturing at the University of Notre Dame. © Kathy Sullivan. Used with permission.

On the evening of December 2, 1984, Edward Albee arrived at the University of Notre Dame to address the student body and to conduct a writing and directing workshop the following day. That night Albee performed in Washington Hall, the just remodeled auditorium that lacked a finished heating system. Though temperatures dipped into the low 40's, Albee's captivating readings tempered the chill as the audience partook of the worlds of Jerry and Peter and He and She. The next day I interviewed Edward Albee, asking him questions that had surfaced from my work on my dissertation.

Sullivan: Storytelling is a central activity for the characters in your plays. How do you see the story functioning in your plays?

Albee: What stories usually seem to be (I don't put them in for this reason) end up being a microcosm of the play. Take the cat story in *A Delicate Balance*, for example; that is really what the play is about. I suppose the dog story in *The Zoo Story*, to a certain extent, is a microcosm of the play by the fact that people are not communicating, ultimately failing and trying and failing. I suppose that's what they're there for, and I don't like them there as symbols or signposts. But I think they are microcosms, and they occur so frequently in the play as in *The American Dream*, the young man telling Grandma about what happened to his identical twin. But various times they do occur in the course of the plays. Even subtly, in the *The Lady from Dubuque*, for example, in one of my more recent plays, there is a story about a dream about the end of the world. They're there for a reason, but I discover it afterwards.

Sullivan: Along with storytelling, the playing of games frequently occurs in your plays. I've noticed, however, that critics largely restrict

184

their discussion of game playing to three plays—*The Zoo Story*, *Who's Afraid of Virginia Woolf?*, and *Tiny Alice*.

Albee: Well, they shouldn't of course. There are games running all through the others too.

Sullivan: Do you use games as a metaphor for life?

Albee: I don't think so. I think it's simply that people play games. Subtle and intelligent people play subtle and intelligent games. Everybody plays games. People play games with truth; they play games with reality, with illusion and since everybody does, I don't see why they're so surprised to see it turning up in the play. There it is. I mean, look at the games families play with each other: power games, guilt games. I suppose it's a good method, a good technique. But I don't employ it for the sake of technique. I'm probably aware that it has a kind of effectiveness while I'm doing it.

Sullivan: What about your use of games compared with people like Beckett and Pinter? Is it similar? Different?

Albee: I don't know. I never think in those terms. I really don't. I don't think about them. Does Harold use games? I suppose he does, of course. So does Beckett. Well, we're all children of Beckett so, well, why shouldn't we.

Sullivan: Do you ever play games with your characters or with your audience?

Albee: Well, it's nice to keep people off balance. I try to do that. That's part of dramatic intensity—keep people off balance. I don't play games in any pejorative sense. I try not to.

Sullivan: I'd like to ask you a broad question. What changes have your characters, your language, your overall perspective on playwriting undergone since you wrote your first play?

Albee: I'm going to answer a slightly different question because I don't know the answer to the question you're asking. Because I don't think of myself as a third person, and I don't examine the 25 plays or however many there are and try to come to conclusions about them. Each play is a different experience; the reality is different, the style is different, the content is different, the nature of the character is different, the nature of the writing is different, the nature of the whole experience is different. So there's where the difference comes to my mind, the only difference that I can understand. I'm not the one to examine trends.

Sullivan: In your talk last night, you said that your craft has improved since your early plays.

Albee: Well, I know I've got it more under control. Yes.

Sullivan: In what way?

Albee: I can probably do things more quickly and more effectively than I used to be able to do. I know how to use one word when I used to have to use ten, for example. I'm also more aware and this naturally happens when you write. I'm more aware of the limit of the stage.

Sullivan: Do you think your more recent plays are more preoccupied with language than your earlier works?

Albee: Some critics complain that my language is getting too baroque; some say it's too stylized, too precise, too concerned with language. I've been accused of being overly concerned with language which is an odd comment to make about someone who's a writer. Some people like very simple straightforward prose. Sometimes I don't write it—if my characters don't speak it.

Sullivan: Your characters in *The Lady from Dubuque* don't speak with the cleverness of a George and Martha. But your point is that they are not George and Martha.

Albee: True. That's true.

Sullivan: You use abundant profanity in that play, something that I didn't detect in your other plays.

Albee: Of course. That's because these are different people.

Sullivan: *Who's Afraid of Virginia Woolf?* as well as your other plays is particularly effective in its depiction of betrayals and violence. Could you discuss these elements in your plays?

Albee: Playwrights should learn early enough that the mistake is to have two characters who know each other terribly well, telling things about each other for expositional reasons. And I don't know how to talk about the violence. There are two kinds of violence— physical and psychological. Both occur in my plays, and I suppose in *The American Dream* you have symbolic violence which is both physical and psychological. I don't know how to talk about the violence in my plays. You have to have action in the plays. Action concerns change, concerns conflict. So there is conflict and change produced by a clash, and the clash can come from swords or it can come from arguments and ideas and betrayals.

Sullivan: You're quite good with producing the clash, the argument.

Albee: It seems to be a natural way of doing things. It's nice to write about fairly articulate people.

Sullivan: I assume that if you didn't think it were possible to love, to understand, to sacrifice, to commit, to trust, you'd give up trying to reveal our failures to make contact.

Albee: Yes, of course.

Sullivan: Yet in your plays, we have very few examples of characters who work through their betrayals.

Albee: Well, George and Martha do in *Virginia Woolf*. I think they do ultimately. I think they love each other very much. It's not an "S and M" relationship. I mean there's some problems there. They've had a lot of battles, but they enjoy each other's ability to battle. I think once they've brought their marriage down to level ground again and gotten rid of the illusion, they might be able to build a sensible relationship. You can write a play I suppose in theory about two people who are getting along perfectly well without any problems whatever, but I don't know where your dramatic action will come.

Sullivan: Why not write plays where characters experience ruptured relationships but emerge wiser and more compassionate? Take O'Neill's *Long Day's Journey into Night*. Now that's not a play where people are getting along and where everything is fine. It's a play with phenomenal confrontation, phenomenal pain. But in the end there has been some advancement.

Albee: Yes, there are in *Virginia Woolf?*, too. Even in *The Zoo Story*, Peter is a changed person; Jerry is carried through his crucifixion that the world has taught. Peter is not going to be able to be the same person again. With the exception of *The American Dream*, which is not intended to have any hope in it at all, except that poor Grandma gets out, most of the characters have something to be said for them. I could really never write about anybody that I couldn't relate to or empathize with at all. I've never written about somebody I despise totally.

Sullivan: I'd like to ask you some specific questions about *The Lady from Dubuque* and *Tiny Alice*. I have difficulty feeling sympathetic for Jo's condition. You do want the audience to feel sympathy for her, don't you?

Albee: Yes. I had to balance my sympathies. I want them sympathetic for Sam—what he is going through, but to understand her impatience, her retreat into another reality. I'm convinced also that you cannot, without getting sloppy and sentimental, feel sympathetic reactions toward somebody who'd be doing something like dying, which produces effects in you of distasteful emotions.

Sullivan: You can't feel sympathy?

Albee: No, you can feel pity, but no sympathy.

Sullivan: It seems to me, however, that you have excluded Sam's needs.

Albee: But Sam's reality is less important than Jo's needs. He's surviving while she's dying.

Sullivan: I have difficulty relating to Jo since she's so cruel, such a nasty person.

Albee: She doesn't put up with any shit, as we say. She hones right in on the truths and doesn't want any wasted time. Pain turns people mean. Of course, Jo and Sam have a lovely time at the end of Act One. She can be cheerful, but she doesn't want to hear all the chatter and everything while she's spending the last moments of her life surrounded by these friends, these people. Of course, she's nasty to them.

Sullivan: I do have problems with the realism of the woman who is supposed to be Jo's mother. I can appreciate the woman on a symbolic level but not on a realistic level.

Albee: Well, what I was trying to do is one of these things that some people told me doesn't work—making the real and symbolic moment identical.

Sullivan: Do you think this concept works in *The Lady from Dubuque*?

Albee: Well, I know questions have been raised about whether it works. I've seen a production where it works. I've seen a production where it doesn't work. It's a tough play to perform, but most of my plays are tough to do properly. You see so many bad productions and you end up misunderstanding.

Sullivan: Perhaps of all your plays, *Tiny Alice* has generated the greatest controversy and probably the greatest misunderstanding. It seems to me a key to understanding the play revolves around the Butler's comment to Brother Julian about waiting in the locked closet for someone to open the door. Julian agrees with the Butler that he wouldn't care who comes, just so long as someone would come.

Albee: That of course is a metaphor for the whole concept of the creation of God in man's image. I don't care who you worship as long as there is someone to worship.

Sullivan: No matter what the being be.

Albee: That's right. Benign, malignant, whatever. Julian's death is a final betrayal of why he became a lay brother to begin with. He says he became a lay brother because of his unhappiness with the misuse people put religion through—creating God in their own image. And then in the very end, he does it.

Sullivan: Is there any facet of your drama that critics have left unexplored?

Albee: The relationship between my dramatic structure and musical form. Along with Beckett and Pinter, we are the three playwrights who write, I think, with closest understanding of the relationship between the two structures. And some interesting experiments could be done there. One should go so far as to listen to the works, examine the sound in relation to the silences, the specific rhythms, the speed of speeches, the fast and the slow and the cyclic returning of themes. And you'll find, I know in my work, you'll find a very profound relationship between dramatic structure and musical form. One must include Chekhov, too.

Sullivan: One hundred years from now what do you hope people will be saying about your plays?

Albee: Same things as they're saying now perhaps. As long as they're saying something, it will be okay with me.

Well-known Playwright Directs University of Houston Students

Jane Holt/1985

From *The Daily Cougar* [University of Houston—University Park],
11 April 1985, 6, 14. Reprinted by permission of the *Daily Cougar*.

Sand, a collection of three plays written and directed by Edward Albee, opens Friday, April 12 at 8 p.m. in Wortham Theater. Performances continue Saturday, April 13, and the following weekend, April 19 and 20, also at 8 p.m.

Albee has been in residence at University Park for the past month working with drama students on *Sand*, which includes his plays *The Sandbox*, *Box*, and *Finding the Sun*.

Finding the Sun is unpublished. This is only the fourth time it has been performed.

The Sandbox and *Box* are each only about 15 minutes long, Albee said in an interview Wednesday. The first two plays will be performed without intermission. After the intermission, *Finding the Sun*, which runs about an hour and five minutes, will be performed. "It should be a full experience," Albee said.

Albee visited the drama department in late February to view the talent available on campus before deciding on a production. "All three of these [plays] have the same set—a sand dune," he said. "I think they make a good evening together."

Albee, 57, said he finds it funny that he works with universities and has several honorary doctorate degrees considering his sparse and unconventional education. "I kept getting thrown out of prep schools for not going to classes," he said. "Maybe I wanted to be home, maybe I didn't want to be away, and maybe I was in rebellion against everything for the sake of being in rebellion against it.

"I even got thrown out of college in the middle of my sophomore year [Trinity University in Hartford, Conn.] for majoring in

190

"I think I probably learned how to educate myself," Albee said. "If you have a few good teachers who point you in the right direction, once you leave your formal education you do a lot of reading, looking, listening. I wasn't illiterate or anything; I just didn't like most of the courses I was being given.

"There are a lot of people hanging around colleges that don't need to be there unless they need a degree specifically to get a job," he said. "Once they've learned the process of educating themselves, how to do it, why stick around?" After leaving college at 20, Albee moved to Greenwich Village where he lived for 10 years before the publication of his first play, *The Zoo Story*. As lean as these years were, Albee did not consider them hard times.

"I decided when I was very young that I wouldn't settle down to a nine-to-five job. I never wanted to have a boss. I never wanted to be an employee. I moved to New York City. I spent this 10-year period absorbing everything I possibly could, taking odd jobs, never taking a job that could become a career. I lived almost on the periphery of society. I saw every gallery, every play, and every concert I could sneak into for free, trying to learn what living was about, what consciousness was about, what I was about and not settling in too quickly on a life goal.

"When you get out of college at 21 or 22," he said, "how the hell are you supposed to know what you want to do for the next 50 years of your life? It's absurd to be expected to know that. I think everyone should take off five years at least. Bang around."

He conceded that it isn't always easy to do. "It goes against what's expected of people and if they're after security and wealth, it's not right. Those are our goals in society, the great legacy of the Reagan administration; vanish into society, make a lot of money, then you'll be happy. If that's the goal, super, but a lot of people are going to wake up 20 or 30 years from now and realize they've wasted their lives."

Albee's childlike love of life is a stark contrast to the violent and depressing themes of his plays such as *Who's Afraid of Virginia Woolf?*

"All worthwhile plays deal with people in conflict with others and themselves," he said. "The essence of drama, as you know, is conflict, so you have to do it. There aren't too many other things to

"All worthwhile plays deal with people in conflict with others and themselves," he said. "The essence of drama, as you know, is conflict, so you have to do it. There aren't too many other things to write about but life, death, people and other animals. So I write about life, death, people and other animals." He does not fit the stereotype of the suffering artist. "I don't suffer," he said. "My characters suffer. I don't. Many writers are alcoholics because they don't get it out of their system in their work. I'm not an alcoholic. I don't take drugs and I'm not falling apart. I either don't have personal problems others have, or I get them out of my system in my work. I'm not sure which. My characters are unhappy, not me."

He admits that he is not in a state of bliss, and far from content. "I don't like the way the world is being run. I don't like the way people waste their lives, cruelty, evasions . . . people don't deal with each other as well as they should. That doesn't make me content, that makes me discontent, which is one of the reasons I write. I try to get people to stop doing the things they do, but I don't let it get me down. I write about it. Maybe if I didn't write I would be lying on the floor somewhere."

Despite the fact that many of his plays deal with families and their mishandling of each other, Albee said he has nothing against the institution of the family. "It seems to be the basic structure," he said, "not only in humans, but in the animal kingdom as well. I think it's fine. I do think, however, we have imposed from time to time, arbitrary, moral and philosophical values on what is an instinctual animal instinct. We have imposed what we call civilized values on it. The trouble the family gets into is when these imposed values don't work anymore. It's not the family unit that's at fault, it's what we've turned it into."

In the past, critics have accused Albee's plays of being anti-female, but he vehemently denies it. "I'm not anti-anybody," he said. "The only people who think that way are men; women don't think that. Men don't like the way I write about them, because I puncture the male fantasy of what they think they ought to be. I show them as they really are and this upsets a lot of them. Women think I'm right on target."

Albee has said that entertainment and advertising do not encourage excellence, but he does not feel he could write for employee. Nobody tells you what to do. You write for TV or movies and you're a fieldhand, so why do it?"

Albee said he writes plays "because I'm a playwright. It's that simple. I've written poems, short stories and essays. I was terrible at them all." W. H. Auden suggested to Albee that he write pornographic verse. "Perhaps to make my poetry more interesting," said Albee, "and make people want to read it."

Many people consider Albee a private person, but Albee said, "I get a lot of publicity for being a playwrite and have for the past 25 years. I don't go around acting scandalously—that may be why my private life may seem dull and uneventful to most people. There's a certain objectivity to privacy."

He takes exception to those who feel that a writer's life is a key to understanding or appreciating his work. "I think there is a danger in, and people get into a lot of trouble by, trying to find sources of the author's life in what he writes about. It's a kind of voyeurism which is less valuable than the biographers think it is, but they've got to make a buck too, you know."

Albee wants those who come and watch *Sand* to get a "complete experience," and come without any preconceptions of what a play is meant to be like. "Be willing to experience each play as it happens," he said. "It's all you can expect or ask any audience to do."

Edward Albee in Conversation with Terrence McNally

Terrence McNally/1985

From *Dramatists Guild Quarterly*, 22 (Summer 1985), 12-23. Reprinted by permission of the Dramatists Guild, Inc., copyright 1985.

The following "Conversation With" session with Edward Albee, conducted by Vice President Terrence McNally and arranged by the Dramatists Guild Projects Committee, Gretchen Cryer chairman, took place on the West Coast. This transcript was edited with the approval of the participants.

Terrence McNally: Do you remember the first play you saw?

Edward Albee: *Jumbo*. I was tiny. I remember the elephants, and I remember Jimmy Durante, and that's it.

My grandfather had a whole vaudeville chain, the Keith-Albee circuit. Out of some lack of wisdom, he sold it in the depths of the beginning of the Depression, so I didn't really have much contact with the theater when I was growing up—though I do remember that Ed Wynn and Sophie Tucker and other strange people who used to be in vaudeville would come by the house from time to time. I don't know whether this generated my interest in the theater or not.

My grandfather used to send me to see plays. Some of them had a powerful impact on me. Whether they were any good I don't know. I remember seeing *The Iceman Cometh* when it was first done. And I remember being enormously moved by one of Tennessee Williams's plays, *Suddenly Last Summer*. That was an extraordinary theatrical experience for me.

McNally: You were much older when you saw that.

Albee: Yes.

McNally: But you were not a child who went to the theater a lot?

Albee: We didn't have regional theater in Larchmont.

194

McNally: I thought you grew up in the city.

Albee: No. We lived in Larchmont, which is about twenty miles outside of New York City. After I left—indeed, got thrown out of—college, I moved to New York. I lived in the Village then, of course. I started going to the theater twice a day. This was back in the middle 1950's, in the beginning of off Broadway, when you could see things like *The Dog Beneath the Skin* or *Who Was Francis?* and Picasso's *Desire Trapped by the Tail*. I was exposed to Beckett, Ionesco, Genet and Williams and a number of other provocative playwrights. What I didn't see, I read. So I knew what a play looked like, basically, but I didn't know what the experience of writing one would be like until *The Zoo Story*. But I'm trying to think of the first play that was not a musical that had a profound effect on me. It was probably the O'Neill play. Either that or my first experience with Chekhov, down in lower Manhattan at the Folksbiene Playhouse, which was probably in 1950 or 51.

McNally: Did you participate in theater when you went to Choate? Did you ever act?

Albee: At that point, they only did Gilbert and Sullivan and minor Shaw. I think I played something not very interesting in *Androcles and the Lion* once. I concluded my acting career just before I got thrown out of Trinity College (not for my acting, though that might have had something to do with it). I played the Emperor Franz Joseph of Austria in Maxwell Anderson's awful, awful verse play *The Masque of Kings*.

McNally: When did you start writing plays? One of the myths about you is that *The Zoo Story* was your very first play.

Albee: Let's perpetuate that.

McNally: I know you would like to, but I don't think it inspires people. I think they find it depressing to think that it's your very first play.

Albee: Well, it isn't. I wrote a very brief three-act play when I was 12. Then, having lost my mind when I was 19, I wrote a very foolish play called *The Making of a Saint* which I sent to Virgil Thompson asking him if he would like to make it into an opera. Virgil generously declined. He said, "I have already done my 'Saint' opera."

If we are to believe a scholarly paper that has been written by Andy Harris at Columbia University, I made several false starts on other plays. There are fragments of plays. There's even a rumor that he has a complete play by me. I deny it, but he has it.

It wasn't until I wrote *The Zoo Story* that it all clicked into place. I was 29, and maybe I had gotten my head together just a little bit. That was the first time in my entire life I felt that I had written something that was at least half-way worthwhile.

McNally: When did the notion of being a playwright occur to you, as opposed to being a poet or a novelist?

Albee: After I wrote *The Zoo Story*.

McNally: But when you wrote *The Zoo Story* you weren't a playwright.

Albee: No. Well, I mean, I was, but I didn't know it. Once I wrote it, it all fell into place. I said, "Ah ha, you silly person, you've been a playwright all these years! Why haven't you been writing a lot of plays?" I had started writing poems when I was very, very young—6 or something like that. I wrote thousands of poems, and I wasn't a very good poet. I wrote two novels in my teens—enormously long and enormously bad novels. And I wrote essays and short stories. Anything except plays. And then, finally, when I was 29, I wrote a play.

McNally: With *The Zoo Story*, you had what seemed to be an overnight, meteoric triumph.

Albee: I have never anticipated anything in my life. I am astonished by many things, but I have never been surprised by anything, if you understand the distinction. I didn't know what it was like to be a playwright until I wrote *The Zoo Story*. I had absolutely no expectation of whether the play would be well or badly received. Does it sound immodest if I say that, since it was received the way it was, that suggested to me that it was a rather good play? I had not yet come to understand I equated the two. But remember one other thing: There were very few younger American playwrights functioning at the time. There was Jack Gelber who had done *The Connection* the year before. Then I did *The Zoo Story*, and then Jack Richardson did *The Prodigal*, and a year or so later Arthur Kopit did *Oh Dad, Poor Dad*. There was just a handful of us. Lanford Wilson hadn't even begun yet, I don't think. People were sort of waiting for this new generation of American theater, so it was an ideal time for us to come along. We probably got pushed at least as much as we deserved, certainly no less.

McNally: Pushed?

Albee: By critics, by the popular press which said how wonderful it was to have a whole new generation of American playwrights.

McNally: There really wasn't an off Broadway until almost precisely that time.

Albee: Oh, in the middle 1950s there were maybe eight or ten productions a year in small experimental theaters. Then, by 1964, there were three hundred. The whole thing exploded.

McNally: An incredible explosion of new plays and playwrights.

Albee: Nothing compared to the quality and quantity of new playwrights we have now.

McNally: *The Zoo Story* was done first in Germany.

Albee: Yes. The point is, I didn't know what you did with plays when you wrote them. I knew no theater people when I started, but I did know some composers. I knew Aaron Copland, so I sent the play to Aaron. Aaron sent it to William Inge, who wrote me a very nice letter saying, "This is a very interesting play." He didn't do anything else, but you know that was nice. David Diamond was living in Italy at the time he read *The Zoo Story*, and he gave it to a Swiss-German actor friend of his. This actor made a translation of it and recorded it into German, playing both roles. He sent it to a friend who ran the S. Fischer Publishing House in Frankfurt and who arranged for its production in West Berlin in German. It had its world premiere in 1959.

At the same time that was happening, the play was floating around New York. I believe it even had a reading at the Actors Studio. I think it was picked up by Richard Barr, who decided to produce it off Broadway with the same play it had been produced with in Berlin—Beckett's *Krapp's Last Tape*. So the New York production wasn't the result of the Berlin production. While I was in Berlin in September 1959, Dick Barr acquired the world-wide rights from my agent. I came back to discover that I had a New York production planned for January.

McNally: How did it go in Berlin?

Albee: Well, that was rather exciting. I had never seen a play of mine, of course, and I didn't know how it was supposed to be. And, of course, it was being played in German. I knew the play fairly well, not as well as I know it now, since I have directed it so often since, but I could sort of follow it. I didn't know, though, quite how an audience was supposed to respond. I remember watching the audience during the premiere performance, being fascinated by the way it was responding to something I had written. It was my first experience of seeing and sensing and smelling an audience's response to something I had done.

The end of the play came. Jerry was dying on the bench, and Peter said, "Oh, my God!" offstage. The lights went down, and then there was absolute silence in the theater for what struck me as being minutes. It was probably only eight seconds. However long it was, I was a bit put off by the silence. And then thunderous applause started. That was a very exciting moment.

As I think back on it and some of the productions I have seen since—it was pretty good. It was a damn good production. Much better than the production of *The American Dream* that was done the next year in Berlin. It's supposed to play about 52 minutes, and that version ran just under two hours. It's true that things *do* take a little longer in German, but. . . .

McNally: Milton Katselas directed *The Zoo Story* in New York, didn't he?

Albee: He directed the first three weeks.

McNally: Alan Schneider directed *Krapp's Last Tape*, the other part of the bill. Did he have any involvement with *The Zoo Story*?

Albee: Not to my knowledge. But that's when I met Alan. I guess I had seen some of his work before.

McNally: I'd like to ask you a little bit about working with Alan. Certainly anyone who writes was very saddened by his death.

Albee: Within a short time, I had a double family loss—Alan getting killed in London and then William Ritman dying. Alan directed thirteen or fourteen of my plays, and Bill designed the sets for certainly an equal number. To lose both of them in such a short period of time was awful.

Alan was an extraordinary director. He set a kind of standard for respect of text. He only directed plays he had some respect for.

Since he did respect them, his interest was getting the author's
intention, whatever it was, whether it was right or wrong. He would
try to help the author a little bit here and there. Not to impose, but
to get the author's intention onstage as accurately and as clearly as
possible. Some people found him difficult to work with, but he and I
never had a serious problem. He was the kind of director who
would want to have conversations six months before rehearsals
began. He would keep coming with lists of twenty, thirty, forty
questions to ask me about the play. Rather nice to work that way,
rather than how you sometimes do—walking into rehearsal the first
day and meeting your director for the first time and discovering he's
planning to direct a play somewhat other than the one you think
you wrote. Alan was an intelligent and dedicated man.

    McNally: You told me you thought this would be a good
opportunity to set the record straight on *Who's Afraid of Virginia
Woolf?*. What sort of things would you like to set straight?

    Albee: Well, I remember when I read the transcript of the
Dramatists Guild session on *Who's Afraid of Virginia Woolf?* I had a
couple of quarrels with people's memories. Everybody remembers
what they want. Everybody corrects fact, you know. But facts aren't
interesting. Truth is.

    One thing I did want to get said was that Uta Hagen was not the
first person who was asked to play the role of Martha. I am damn
glad she *did* play it, because she played it extraordinarily well. But I
asked Gerry Page to play Martha first. She read the play, liked it a
lot and said that she had to ask Lee Strasberg. Why she had to ask
Lee is her own business. I got a message back saying that Gerry
would be very happy to do the play, but Lee had to be at all the
rehearsals as a kind supervising eminence. That indeed was the
situation. She wanted Lee to be there. Alan was already set to
direct it, and it didn't strike us that you could have two directors.
Besides, I had seen Strasberg's work as a director, and I wasn't
terribly happy with it. I had also seen his work as a supervising
eminence on a Chekhov production, and that made me even
unhappier. So Gerry Page did not play Martha and Uta Hagen did,
and wasn't that wonderful?

    Around that time, though, we did try to start a playwrights theater
at the Actors Studio: Geraldine Page, Arthur Penn, Rip Torn, Jack

Richardson and I—and I think Paul Newman was involved. There was a playwrights unit at the Actors Studio at that time, so we all got together and thought, "How wonderful. We have got a marvelous pool of acting talent, some wonderful directors, all these writers. . . . " But it didn't work out.

McNally: But you and Dick Barr and Clinton Wilder started the Playwrights Unit at the Cherry Lane Theater.

Albee: Well, you know, we were making an awful lot of money on *Virginia Woolf*, and it was going to go to taxes if we didn't figure out something else, so we put it into doing this experimental theater. Over a period of—what?—ten or eleven years, I guess we did a hundred and twenty workshop productions of almost everybody's first play. Sam Shepard, Lanford Wilson, John Guare and just about everybody had their first done there. And you, too.

McNally: A lot of famous plays were first done at the Playwrights Unit—*The Boys in the Band* . . .

Albee: That was one play I didn't want done. I thought it was a lousy play. Dick wanted me to coproduce it when he transferred it to off Broadway. I put principle above principal, I guess. Anyhow, too bad.

But we did an awful lot of interesting work at the Playwrights Unit. That was a nice time to be working off Broadway, off off Broadway. Everybody worked terribly hard and for nothing. The audiences were interested and enthusiastic. It hadn't become riddled with commerce the way the off-Broadway theater has now.

McNally: The Playwrights Unit was really the founding spirit for so many other organizations.

Albee: The Living Theater had begun it all, of course. They were doing Paul Goodman and Jack Gelber. And the Judson Poets Theater was doing some good work.

McNally: But, because of your name and, I think, Alan's involvement, the Playwrights Unit had a promise of new American plays in a way the others didn't. The new dramatists always seemed more traditionally Broadway-oriented. The Actors Studio, for all the good work that was done there, was always Lee's building somehow. Even though there was a playwrights unit there, you felt that you were talking about acting as much as the play. It was so hard to escape Lee's presence. It was your Playwrights Unit that really was so important.

Albee: We had a good time doing it. Then other people started doing similar things, and the other people seemed to be able to get the foundation grants and government support. At the same time, it began to be enormously expensive for us, so we had to stop.

McNally: At that time, after *Virginia Woolf*, when everyone was saying. "What's he going to do next?", you did your first adaptation.

Albee: Carson McCullers' *The Ballad of the Sad Café*, I seem to lose my mind about every fifth play and do an adaptation. I was quite happy with *Ballad*, and so was Carson. It didn't run more than eight months. I got a very nice compliment from one of the critics on it. He said, "Albee didn't do very much with this adaptation. All he did was take the dialogue from the book and put in on the stage." That's one of the nicest reviews I ever got because there is not one line of dialogue in Carson McCullers' book.

I have done four adaptations, and none of them has contributed very much to the luster of my career. My adaptation of James Purdy's *Malcolm* sank the Lusitania. *Everything in the Garden*, which I adapted from the play by Giles Cooper, had a respectable run, but nothing great. And my adaptation of Nabokov's *Lolita*, of course, was never done on Broadway. Something called *Lolita* with my name attached to it was produced on Broadway, but it was not my adaptation of Nabokov's *Lolita*. The one really truly ugly theater experience I have had in a long and reasonably happy career was the experience of losing control of the production of that play. It never happened to me before and I will never let it happen again. The script has been published by Dramatists Play Service, so maybe it will be done somewhere as written.

McNally: Did you think of closing the play, of saying, "I am a member of the Dramatists Guild, and you can't change the script without my approval?"

Albee: I kept wanting to do it. I should have had the wisdom to pull out and make them close it. But you know, you get involved in something like a losing musical, and you keep thinking that if you go on with it, maybe it will turn out right in the end—and you get deeper and deeper into the quicksand. So the damn thing opened finally, not my text, not acted or directed or produced the way I wanted—and guess who got the bad reviews?

The Dramatists Guild does protect its members by a contract which permits no tampering with the text and gives the author certain controls over casting and choice of director. What often happens is, our beginning authors, out of—what?—insecurity, or, occasionally, greed, give up all their protections. They tell themselves somebody else knows better, so they rewrite that marvelous role written for a 26-year-old man because a 35-year-old star is available. If a writer gives into that situation, there's nothing we at the Guild can do to protect him. You really have to be on your guard at all times and as tough as you can possibly be. I'm still puzzled as to how all this happened with *Lolita*. If anybody is supposed to know better than to allow this sort of thing to happen, it is me.

McNally: You wrote the libretto for *Breakfast at Tiffany's*, and it closed in previews. As you can see, I am trying to bring up your famous flops.

Albee: I was sitting at home one day, minding my own business, when I got a telephone call from David Merrick, who, until that moment, I did not know had a sense of humor. David said, in effect, "Edward, I have a musical in trouble in Boston." I said, "That's nice, David." And he said, "I would like you to go up and take a look at it and maybe take over the writing of the book."

This struck me as such a bizarre idea that, well, I went to Boston and saw this musical which, at that time, was entitled *Holly Golightly*. A very creative move—to change the title from *Breakfast at Tiffany's* to *Holly Golightly*. But it wasn't bad. Abe Burrows had done a perfectly workmanlike job of translating it into a musical. It wasn't much like the original book. Truman Capote had written a rather tough little book, and the movie that they made out of it with Audrey Hepburn turned out to be about a hooker who was also a virgin. But that was what was on the stage in Boston—a musical of the movie, and it was all right. It probably would have limped along for about six months on Broadway. It had a couple of youngish people in it whose careers have not suffered too terribly by being involved with it, Richard Chamberlain and Mary Tyler Moore.

But I looked at it and I said, "Gee, maybe it would be interesting to take this over and bring it back to Truman's book, make it a real tough musical." I guess I thought I was going to be Brecht and Weill all over again, so I signed on. Never having done a musical, I thought it was nice to earn while I learned. So I rewrote it, taking out all the dancing boys and girls, reducing the size of the cast, taking out almost all of the songs that were in and putting back in all the songs that had been taken out because I thought they were a lot better.

The only trouble working on a musical is that you, the book writer, have to work with the lyricist, the composer, the director, the choreographer, the producer and the various stars. Trying to get everybody together for a meeting to make intelligent decisions was impossible because we couldn't coordinate. Anyway, I did indeed take the show over and managed, in only two weeks, to turn something which would have been a six-month mediocrity into an instant disaster.

McNally: You wrote the book in two weeks. And how many previews did you give in New York?

Albee: Five.

McNally: So you only saw your version performed those five times?

Albee: Well, we put a few of my scenes in during the last week in Boston. That was very interesting. The show would be going along on its own merry way, and all of a sudden one of my scenes—having nothing to do with anything else in the show— would appear, and then it would be over, and then it would go right back to doing what it had done before.

My version played in New York. I remember, during the previews at the Broadhurst Theater, after we had put in some of my changes, people were milling around the lobby at intermission looking for David Merrick: "Where is Merrick? How dare he do this to us?" I think, had we had another two or three weeks, we could have pulled it off. I think it could have been a tough and interesting musical.

McNally: Counting that script, then, you have done five adaptations. Do you think you're going to lose your mind again and do another one?

Albee: I always announce that I'm never going to do another one again. I wonder when the next one will occur.

McNally: Your last few plays have not been treated kindly by the critics. You don't let it stop you.

Albee: No, I don't stop. I go right on. *The Man Who Had Three Arms*, was commissioned by the Miami Arts Festival, where it opened and did rather nicely. It was picked up by the Goodman Theater in Chicago, where it ran for six filled weeks to very good press. Robert Drivas starred in it and did an extraordinary job. So it occurred to some people, since the play was receiving some very good audience response and good critical response, perhaps it could survive on Broadway. So we brought it into New York, where it opened, after playing, I think, ten previews to an enormously enthusiastic and friendly audience. It opened to an almost unanimously hostile press, an extraordinarily hostile reaction. Well, of course, given the fact that the play was, in part, about critics and about the bitch goddess success, and about a number of other misinformations that the public receives about itself through our press, I am not terribly surprised.

But what interested me most was that this play, of all my plays, is the one for which I received the most enthusiastic and favorable response from people in the arts—my peers. Writers, composers, painters, sculptors, poets—they seemed to like this play more than any other I have written. Isn't it interesting that the critical response was so hostile and negative?

McNally: In New York. This was not true in Chicago.

Albee: Only in New York. Very interesting.

McNally: What do you think accounts for the difference?

Albee: I don't know quite how to explain it. I am puzzled and interested by the fact that the New York critics did not review the play that I wrote but the play they wished I had written.

McNally: Do you feel you are a little provocative in that play?

Albee: Whatever do you mean, Terrence?

McNally: Well, the character kept referring to a lady of the press in the audience very unflatteringly. Surely, people must have said to you, "Edward, the critics are going to perceive this as an attack on them."

Albee: If they were bright enough to figure out it was an attack on them . . . you take your chances. This play was about an advertising man, somebody with absolutely no talent whatsoever, who grew a third arm. A literal third arm. Not a metaphorical third arm, as a number of people decided, but a literal and real third arm, through no fault of his own. And so then, all of a sudden, the arm starts going away. Now he has only two arms, and he's reduced to being on the lecture circuit talking about what it was like when he had his famous third arm.

What bothered me about the critical response to the play was that the press said that this play was a metaphor for my own career. They said, "Isn't it a pity that he doesn't write as brilliantly as he used to." But the play was very carefully contrived to be about somebody who never had any talent to begin with. If I was going to write an autobiographical play, I would have written it about someone who had at least *some* talent.

McNally: When I read the script, I thought it was a brilliant play. But I remember saying to you that I thought there was a danger that the play might be perceived that way. I thought you were terribly exposed in the play. The critics went for the most vulnerable spots.

Albee: But, you know, you shrug and go about your business.

McNally: What do you say to people who come up and say, "If you had done that play off Broadway, it would still be running"? Do you think that's true?

Albee: It's possible that the critical response might have been mitigated if the critics thought that the play would not reach a large audience by its being done in a small theater. That's quite possible, yes, because, after all, the safety and middle-browism of Broadway should not be tampered with.

McNally: And equally, I have heard people say that if the play had been done by a Dustin Hoffman or an Al Pacino, they wouldn't have dared. . . . A star makes the playwright less vulnerable.

Albee: That's quite possible. But I can't imagine anyone doing a better job with that role than Bobby Drivas did. There was a producer who wanted to do the play on Broadway who did ask me to do that, to take him out of the play and offer it to a star . . .

McNally: After he had done it out of town?

Albee: Yes, and I wouldn't do it.

McNally: You directed that play.

Albee: I've directed quite a few of my plays. I am one of those playwrites who, I think, can be sufficiently objective about his own works to be trusted with them.

McNally: How did you learn to direct?

Albee: I learned an awful lot from observing Alan direct, and I started observing other directors direct my work around the world—Zeffirelli, Ingmar Bergman, Jean-Louis Barrault, Peter Hall—people like that.

McNally: Do you feel confident directing your own work now?

Albee: Yes, I do. Every once in a while I run into an actor who will not permit me to direct my own work. If I want that actor . . . I'm thinking about *The Lady From Dubuque*. Irene Worth did not wish me to direct her, and I couldn't imagine a better actress for the role, so Alan directed it, and he did a very good job. But I like directing my own work. I do have kind of an access into what I intended, and I think, since I know the craft of directing reasonably well, I can probably give people as accurate a picture of what I had in my mind when I wrote the play as anybody can.

McNally: But directing a new play requires a lot of concentration. How would it be possible for you to do that and to handle extensive revisions, should you be in that situation?

Albee: I usually think about plays for quite a while before I write them down. I have kept some plays in my head—in one fashion or another—for several years. I have never written a play that I haven't thought about for at least six months. So I probably do less revision than most people do. I tend to do the revision in my head while I am thinking about the play.

McNally: Would you like to direct somebody else's play?

Albee: I would love to direct other people's work. There's only one problem—I would have to direct work that I respected without reservation. I have a fairly strong author's personality and, while I will not permit another director to mess with my work, I am terribly afraid that if I came upon a play I thought needed some work, I probably would want to do to it that which I as an author would not allow.

Sometimes, you know, I get better reviews as a director than I do an as author. One critic—John Simon, a provocative mind, sick with spleen—wrote in his review of *Seascape* on Broadway that my direction was so clear, so precise, so splendid, so right on the mark that one could see, without any quarrel, how terrible the play was. Something seems to happen to Simon's mind in the middle of sentences. How could he be so right in the first part of that sentence and so wrong in the second? This leads one to the conclusion that one should read only the first half of John Simon's sentences.

I was, in fact, invited to direct a revival of Tennessee Williams's *Sweet Bird of Youth*. Later I was uninvited, but while I was still invited, I said, "I think I have got to reread the play. I remember something I have a problem with." And so I went and read it again and remembered what the problem was. Tennessee wrote two plays there. He wrote a wonderful two-character play set in the bedroom, and then he added this whole second act with lots of other characters which didn't strike me as being anywhere near as interesting. I realized I couldn't direct that second act. I was going to have to go to Tennessee and say, "Look, what are we going to do about this?" Well, you couldn't go to a man who was the dean of American playwrights and tell him to do something about his second act.

I like working with young playwrights, who have works-in-progress and are interested in a few suggestions—but I don't believe in this business of "developing works." I don't think any play should go into rehearsal unless it is ready to be performed. I hate this notion of working through a play with the aid of actors and directors and audiences and critics. I think that's nonsense.

There are a number of classics I would like to get my hands on. There are a couple of things to be said about *Uncle Vanya* that are not said very often, and I'd like to do *Edward II*. But nothing fascinates me as much as writing. I don't get the sense of exhilaration from directing that I do from writing.

McNally: One of the questions writers are often asked is how much their characters are taken from life.

Albee: I have never written a character that is either autobiographical or biographical. I have never written about myself consciously, and I have never limited a character to a real individual. I find if you do that, you are limited. At the same time, every character I have written has doubtless been shaped by the limits of my own perception, by that which I have experienced. But a good deal of it is simply made up. It was interesting to me, of course, that within the first five or six years after I wrote *Virginia Woolf*, whenever I appeared at a university to lecture, almost invariably someone would come up and say, "You have obviously been here before. You must have known Dr. So-and-so." A simple matter of life imitating art, as it is supposed to do.

McNally: What about writing for a specific actor?

Albee: I think that would be very dangerous, because then you would be writing for the personality of a performer rather than the personality of the character. And what if the actor you've written for decides not to do the role?

McNally: When you wrote *Virginia Woolf*, who did you hear in your head as Martha?

Albee: Martha. I will grant that when I am three-quarters of the way through writing a play, and I know pretty much how it's going to go and that I won't be influenced by hearing other voices, I will permit myself to start hearing the voice of this actor or that actress as I am writing, but never when I am at the beginning of a play.

McNally: When you see *Virginia Woolf* now, do you sometimes hear the original cast still?

Albee: I hear Uta Hagen and Arthur Hill, but I was deeply involved with the second production on Broadway with Colleen Dewhurst and Ben Gazzara, so I hear them just as much. I don't hear Burton and Taylor as much.

McNally: It is true, as I heard somewhere, that there was once a third act of *Seascape*?

Albee: *Seascape* was originally a three-act play longer than *Parsifal*. There was a second act which took place at the bottom of the sea which presented a number of design problems, among others. When I had the first reading of the play in New York, I realized that I had written my own *Don Juan in Hell* and that second act was extraneous. At the end of rehearsal I said, "I'll see you guys tomorrow," and I went home and removed it. The first day of rehearsal it was a three-act play, the second day it was a two-act play. The fact that I could take out an entire act of the play so quickly and without any great loss does suggest that perhaps it was not absolutely necessary. When it was done in Holland, however, by mischance they got hold of the three-act version and had it translated. I tried to get them to do the two-act version, but no, they liked the three-act version, and so the second act was performed there.

McNally: Which of your plays would you most like to see revived?

Albee: I dislike the term "revival" so much. It suggests bringing back from the dead. I tend to have a protective affection for those which have been most profoundly misunderstood, and those are the ones I think should be done. *Who's Afraid of Virginia Woolf?* and *A Delicate Balance* can take care of themselves. But there are some plays which may be a bit better, a bit more provocative, that didn't do particularly well, that I think might be nice to have back again.

Outrageous Edward Albee

Joe Pollack/1986

From the *St. Louis-Post Dispatch*, 2 May 1986, 1G. Copyright, 1986, *St. Louis Post Dispatch*, reprinted by permission.

There are outrageous moments in many of Edward Albee's plays—outrageous in terms of the thinking of many people, if not the author.

The visitors in *A Delicate Balance* outrage their hosts, at least on one level, and the actions of the Memphis hospital staff in *The Death of Bessie Smith* are even more culpable. *Who's Afraid of Virginia Woolf?* is full of pain and disaffection of the sort that cause outrage.

Albee's personal style is equally outrageous, from another perspective; he loves to make the off-the-wall statement, the odd comment that will make a questioner think or shift gears or just stop an interview in full flight. "I think playwrights should be theater critics," he said during a conversation early this week. (Albee was in St. Louis to examine the state of the American theater in a lecture entitled "An Evening With Edward Albee" at Webster University.)

"I don't know why newspapers bother reviewing Broadway," he added. "If everyone left it alone, maybe it would go away."

That's the Albee style, I'm convinced. Speaking as one who finds the technique not only friendly but admirable, I loved every minute of it.

Besides, the sardonic smile under the scraggly mustache was a dead giveaway.

There was something warmly iconoclastic about the visiting playwright, winner of 2½ Pulitzer Prizes for drama. He isn't interested in the commercial pap of much of popular drama and is happier out of the mainstream, as long as there are colleges and regional theaters and other less stultifying areas in which he can work.

Albee, now 58, was an *enfant terrible* of the American theater in the 1960s, but he apparently outgrew it without permanent harm.

210

He owns Pulitzer prizes for *A Delicate Balance* (1967) and *Seascape* (1975). The half prize belongs to *Virginia Woolf*, which was recommended in 1963 (the year it won a Tony and a New York Drama Critics' Award), but turned down by the administrative board because of its language.

The controversy was strong enough that John Mason Brown and John Gassner, the board's two theater advisers, resigned in protest. And as far as the language is concerned, well, when the play was revived in 1975, harsher language was added to make it more realistic.

Albee wore a blue golf shirt and khaki pants during his visit here, the shirt emphasizing his gleaming, mischievous, light blue eyes. The salt-and-pepper mustache drooped at the ends; his graying hair hung in a post-tennis mode, rather dankly, to his collar. A Prince tennis racket stood at attention in a corner of his hotel room.

His smile can be extremely toothy or very tight.

Albee is quite optimistic about the future of American theater, if not of Broadway, which he tends almost to dismiss.

"It's simple," he said. "The Shuberts and the Nederlanders (owners of most of the Broadway houses and producers of many plays) are interested in making money. They don't want to do the 'useful' thing in terms of theater, which involves teaching people about themselves, or the art form, or the world.

"There are lots of people—the Broadway expense-account crowd—who just want to see the same plays over and over again anyway, so that's what the Shuberts and the Nederlanders give them."

At the same time, he pointed out that there are lots of outstanding playwrights who succeed without Broadway ever being a factor.

"Look at Sam Shepard," he said. "He's written hundreds of plays, and not one has ever been produced on Broadway. Of course, he seems to get a lot of work as an actor, but his plays are produced all over the country."

Shepard, along with Shakespeare and South Africa's Athol Fugard, were the three playwrights whose works were most produced by American theater companies during the 1985-86 season.

Unlike many playwrights, Albee is not a great fan of the collaborative process or the rewrite process.

"I spend a lot of time thinking about what I'm writing," he explained. "By the time I put it on paper, I'm usually pretty sure of where I want it to go. Then I usually do one rewrite, and it should be ready.

"Of course, then I like to direct my own plays, so that they go the way I want them to, and not the way someone else takes them.

"But if you go into rehearsal prepared to do a lot of rewriting, you're just not ready to go into rehearsal.

"Rehearsal is where you prove the play, not improve it."

Albee directs the plays of other authors, however. He has worked in Europe on and off over the last few years, and last fall directed the works of Lanford Wilson, Shepard and David Mamet in the English-language theater in Vienna.

And like most authors, he likes European audiences; they are more theater-oriented, he thinks, and more literature-oriented. They bring more understanding to the theater.

"I think it's because they're not as exposed to television," he noted. "They're willing to think more and are not so eager for the quick fix."

Albee's dual role as writer and director doesn't make him rigid where change or rewrite is concerned, but it does make him difficult.

"Oh, if a line can't be spoken, I'll take it out," he said, and the smile was tight. "But I'll rewrite it, and I'll take the credit for it."

He is less doctrinaire when it comes to technical assistance, but like most authors, he insists on a certain amount of control.

"I don't always know exactly what I want," he said softly, "but I seem to know exactly what I don't want. When someone shows me a drawing of a set, or a costume, I can tell immediately if it's right for the characters I've written. I think one just knows that."

He grinned happily, continued, "For example, I know that my characters would never wear 100 percent polyester."

The grin got wider and he went on, "Maybe 70 percent cotton and 30 percent polyester, but never 100 percent."

He paused once more, reflected a moment, continued, "I was in San Diego last fall, and as an exercise in a design class, some 20 students were asked to plan a set for *A Delicate Balance*. I was amazed at what came out; I'm certain that some of the students had never read the play, and some of the designs were quite good, but in between was some real strangeness. There was furniture that Agnes never would have bought."

Albee's "writers and critics" line is an old one; he's used it for years. His thinking has some logic, in that playwrights will tend to nurture the fragile egos of other playwrights more than newspaper types do. Of all the writers' egos I know, playwrights' are the most fragile.

"Actually," the author went on, "people just have to learn to read critics as those who are expressing their opinions and not necessarily fact."

On that one, there's complete agreement.

"One of the difficulties," he went on," is that too often the critics go overboard on a writer in their praise, and then go the other way when a next play comes out.

"It's almost as if—for whatever reason—they're setting up the playwright to fail."

As an example, he spoke of Beth Henley, whose first play, *Crimes of the Heart*, was enthusiastically received and won a Pulitzer Prize. Her next offering, *The Wake of Jamey Foster*, was roundly criticized.

"From my own point of view," the author said, "I didn't think *Crimes* was as good as everyone said, and I didn't think the second one was as bad as they said. I think *Crimes* should have been directed with more sensitivity and less broad comedy, but that's just a personal opinion."

("For another personal opinion, *Crimes* was more delicate when it was done at the Rep, shortly after its premiere at the Actors Theatre of Louisville. By the time it got to New York, and I saw it there, too, there had been plenty of rewrite, a character was gone and the humor was much broader. Some of the charm had gone. *Jamey Foster* was weaker, but not so weak as to have vanished from the repertory after a couple of weeks in the big city.")

Even though Albee is one of this country's most noted playwrights and has been for two decades, he needs the added income of

"John Guare told me," he pointed out, "that as generally successful as he had been, it wasn't until he wrote the screenplay for the movie *Atlantic City* that he got out from under."

The grin flicked out from under the mustache again as he continued, "Of course, I've always believed in living just beyond my means—kind of keeps you on your toes."

Albee continues writing; he is finishing a new play that is scheduled to open in the fall, a two-person drama about a couple that is trying to get a divorce but just cannot seem to.

"And after that," he went on, "I have a commission from the Alley Theatre in Houston to write another for the fall of 1987.

"I try to write one a year."

In addition, many of his earlier plays will be mounted during the 1986-87 season by regional and commercial theaters.

Thinking about the forthcoming two-character play, I asked Albee if he had anyone in mind for the roles.

"I can't do it that way," he said quickly. "Once you start to think about actors, you're writing roles, not characters, and I think that's wrong.

"In fact, when I'm writing, and I begin to see, or hear, real actors, I put the play down for a few hours until the real people go away and I can go back inside myself. When the play is finished is the time to cast, and not before."

Albee's Hollywood experiences have not been altogether pleasant, but he approaches the movie medium with a resigned if wry expression.

"I can't say I was totally displeased with *Virginia Woolf*," he said, "though I had been promised James Mason and Bette Davis instead of Richard Burton and Elizabeth Taylor.

"I was told that Ernest Lehman had written a screenplay, but there were enough problems that somehow they went back to much of my text."

The screen version of *A Delicate Balance* is Albee's favorite adaptation of his work, though he spoke rather ruefully of the unproduced screenplay he wrote for *The Death of Bessie Smith*.

"I was very pleased with the way it turned out, and I thought it might make a very good motion picture," he said, "but no one ever did it. Perhaps the criticisms of the racism and the display of the negligent attitudes among those who took care of her after the automobile accident were a little too strong for some people."

And then there's television . . .

"Someone asked me to write a play for television once," he said, obviously relishing the chance to tell the story.

" 'Write anything you want,' they told me, 'you're one of America's great playwrights.'

"And then the conversations began—they told me how their studies showed that audiences liked their male heroes in their mid-30s, their female heroes a little younger, and both attractive.

"And then someone said, 'We know you have this reputation of being a rather gloomy writer; don't you think you can add a little humor to whatever problems your characters have?' "

The grin got quite wide.

"And that," he said with happy finality, "was that."

After his St. Louis visit, Albee was on his way to Johns Hopkins and other universities, where he sees a lot of the theatrical future.

"The young people are willing to look about them," he said, "and to ask questions." I like the questions; I don't expect everyone to see my plays just the way I do. That would be silly.

"But I resent it when people refuse to think, refuse to understand—or worse—intentionally misunderstand what I write."

Index